The Philosophy of Socrates

History of Ancient and Medieval Philosophy

ALAN D. CODE AND CALVIN G. NORMORE, SERIES EDITORS

The Philosophy of Socrates,
Thomas C. Brickhouse and Nicholas D. Smith

FORTHCOMING

Aristotle, Alan D. Code

Maimonides and Medieval Jewish Philosophy, Daniel Frank

Late Medieval Philosophy, Calvin G. Normore

The Philosophy of Late Antiquity, John Bussanich

Plato, Richard Kraut

The Beginnings of Greek Philosophy,
Allan J. Silverman and Mark Griffith

THE PHILOSOPHY OF SOCRATES

THOMAS C. BRICKHOUSE

Lynchburg College

NICHOLAS D. SMITH

Lewis and Clark College

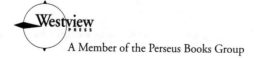

Westview
PRESS

A Member of the Perseus Books Group

History of Ancient and Medieval Philosophy

Copyright © 2000 by Westview Press, A Member of the Perseus Books Group

Published in 2000 in the United States of America by Westview Press, 5500 Central Avenue, Boulder, Colorado 80301-2877, and in the United Kingdom by Westview Press, 12 Hid's Copse Road, Cumnor Hill, Oxford OX2 9JJ

Find us on the World Wide Web at www.westviewpress.com.

Library of Congress Cataloging-in-Publication Data
Brickhouse, Thomas C., 1947–
    The philosophy of Socrates / Thomas C. Brickhouse, Nicholas D. Smith.
        p. cm.—(History of ancient and medieval philosophy)
    Includes bibliographical references and indices.
    ISBN 0-8133-2084-4 (hc.)—ISBN 0-8133-2085-2 (pbk.)
    1. Socrates. I. Smith, Nicholas D. II. Title. III. Series.
B317.P68 1999
183'.2—dc21
99-36572
CIP

The paper used in this publication meets the requirements of the American National Standard for Permanence of Paper for Printed Library Materials Z39.48-1984.

10   9   8   7   6   5   4   3   2   1

Contents

Preface

Just as he was about to engage in the most searching criticism of another scholar's views, the late Gregory Vlastos set the tone of his criticism with these words: "[O]nly those who are strangers to the ethos of scholarly controversy will see anything but high esteem in my critique" (Vlastos [1991], 39 n.2). In this book—and indeed in all of our scholarly work—we share this "ethos of scholarly controversy" by engaging in disagreement, criticism, revision, further development, and sometimes the simple endorsement of our friends' and colleagues' views. Those who criticize our work show in their efforts the "high esteem" of treating our work as worthy of all the effort and thought it takes to consider and evaluate our arguments. In this book, our highest esteem for many of our colleagues should, therefore, be evident in each of our critical efforts. Less obvious, but equally important, is our awareness that it was almost always our own engagement with the views of others that made it even possible for us to *have* a view of our own to formulate. Most scholarly work is done in response to what other scholars say or write on a problem they have identified—or have had identified for them by yet other scholars. We read our colleagues' work, mull it over, worry about it, and finally something occurs to us as a *better* way of understanding a text or solving the problem— and then we write our own interpretation, which is then usually critiqued by others and eventually improved upon by those with still clearer ideas or more clever or compelling solutions. Scholars rarely find themselves giving "the final word" on a text or a problem, and almost always, our colleagues will learn more from the process of exposing our errors than they will learn from accepting our interpretations.

Accordingly, even though our "high esteem" for those from whom we have learned so much will be evident in every citation we make of others' works, we wish to begin by acknowledging even more directly the assistance and education we have derived from discussions, debates, and critical exchanges with others who have taken the subject of Socrates as seriously as we have. The work of Gregory Vlastos has plainly kept us busy for many years now. The same can be said for all the time we have spent studying and discussing the arguments and interpretations of (in alphabetical order) Hugh Benson, Daniel Devereux, Michael Ferejohn, Richard Kraut, Mark McPherran, Terence Penner, George Rudebusch, and Paul

Woodruff. Often, we have been honored and challenged by their searching critical attention to our work. Each of these nine scholars has forced us to reevaluate—and sometimes, simply abandon—positions we have argued in the past. We count every one of them as friends. Every scholar whose name appears in this book and in the bibliography, moreover, may be counted as one of our teachers—as someone whose work has seemed to us to merit our attention and serious consideration. We single out the above nine scholars only as ones to whom we have found ourselves in debt repeatedly, over many years. We dedicate this book to them, with deep gratitude and in friendship.

Thomas C. Brickhouse
Nicholas D. Smith

The Philosophy of Socrates

Introduction

I.1 Our Purpose

This book is intended to be a general introduction to the philosophy of Socrates. We hope it will be of benefit to anyone who wishes to know about, or to know more about, who Socrates was and what his philosophical convictions were. Although we have sought to have our discussions informed by the most current scholarship on the philosophy of Socrates, the book is written for individuals who may have little or no familiarity with ancient Greek philosophy in general or Socrates in particular.

We undertook to write a book of this sort principally for two reasons: First, Socrates himself wrote nothing, at least nothing of any significance about himself or about what he believed. We must look, then, to other credible sources if we are to have any hope of learning who he was and what he stood for and why. Although there were a number of people who actually knew and wrote about Socrates, only one—Plato, a man who became a great philosopher in his own right and on whom Socrates exercised an enormous influence—provides us with a reliable portrait of Socrates the philosopher. But for reasons we explain in Chapter 1, not all of Plato's writings are about Socrates. Only in his early writings, the so-called early dialogues, do we find Plato revealing what he at least understood Socrates to have been about. Plato's early dialogues can be puzzling, however, and it is understandable that many readers become frustrated with them without at least some initial ideas of what Plato is trying to tell us about the man who had such a great influence on him. Thus, we think it is helpful for anyone who is coming to Plato's early dialogues for the first time, or at least without much experience with them, to have a fairly clear idea of how the issues discussed therein can be understood.

Second, even though there are a number of books that provided excellent introductions to the philosophy of Socrates at the time they were written, there is no introduction to the philosophy of Socrates, to our knowledge, that reflects the many significant advances in our understanding that have come about in the latter half of the twentieth century. What has been written about Socratic philosophy, especially since World

War II, has been written primarily by specialists for specialists. Those who are first approaching the study of Socratic philosophy are likely to derive little from reading these works. In undertaking to write this book, then, we are trying to provide a comprehensive discussion of Socratic philosophy that reflects the current state of Socratic scholarship in a way that will be helpful to someone who is confronting Socrates seriously, perhaps for the first time. In doing so, we are not trying to "water down" anything. On the contrary, we want our readers to get a good sense of just how deeply Socrates' thought penetrated the host of philosophical issues with which he concerned himself.

As we shall see, the study of Socratic philosophy is, in a sense, the study of a variety of fascinating puzzles. For one thing, Socrates himself, at least as he is characterized in the early dialogues, quite intentionally tried to show people just how puzzling some of the moral notions we take for granted can be. But in writing about Socrates, Plato sometimes created puzzles of his own, perhaps because he was trying to capture the spirit of his friend Socrates, perhaps because he was trying to create a state of perplexity and wonderment in the reader, perhaps because he himself was not sure what to say about the topic at hand, or perhaps because of all of these things. In any case, to understand Socratic philosophy, we need to resolve a host of problem areas. During the course of this book, we offer our own solutions to these problems, solutions that we hope will also give our readers some substantial assistance in understanding aspects of Socratic philosophy that might seem very obscure. Our focus is on helping the reader identify what the problem areas are and on explaining what the interpretive options are for dealing with them. Our goal in this respect is to assist our readers in finding their way through what would otherwise seem like a bewildering variety of conflicting interpretations that different scholars have proposed. No doubt, sometimes our readers will come to the conclusion that the various solutions offered by scholars are the result of a misunderstanding of the text under consideration. But if the readers' experience is like ours, they will see that carefully wrought scholarly interpretations and arguments can sometimes be mistaken in ways that shed important new light on what issues are at stake, on how certain assumptions lead one into interpretive and philosophical errors.

Perhaps the most important result that comes from seriously considering different interpretations is that they so often help the student of Socratic philosophy better appreciate both the complexity of the philosophical problems that Socrates addressed and the subtlety and philosophical sophistication of his responses. Of course, we often disagree with other scholars' interpretations of Socratic philosophy. But we have more often found that in considering the views of others, we have learned something important about Socratic philosophy and have been obliged to go back and revise our own thinking as a result. As we shall see, this disposition to revise one's own views in the light of opposing and better reasons for an alternative is at the heart of Socrates' own approach to philosophy.

I.2 Interpretive Principles

As we noted above, an understanding of Socratic philosophy requires working through the interpretations of writings about Socrates that have come down to us from antiquity. They are all writings that are *about* a character called Socrates. The evidence we have to work with, even the evidence provided by a single source such as Plato, is often seemingly conflicting and confusing. In trying to reach a sound interpretation, we must attend to different sorts of concerns and must often make judgments about which criteria and principles of scholarly adequacy must be applied. There are no "mechanical" or automatic formulas for us to apply. This does not mean, however, that formulating the interpretation is purely "creative" or "just a matter of opinion"—a kind of intellectual "free-for-all" in which any interpretation is as good as any other interpretation. After all, our goal as readers of these texts is to understand Socrates better and what he believed and why. Unless we think that everyone understands a text equally well, which is absurd, we must say that some interpretations are better than others.

This consideration leads to what might be regarded as an obvious criterion of interpretive adequacy, which we might call the *Principle of Interpretive Cogency:*

Principle of Interpretive Cogency: *No interpretation that is itself too difficult to understand or to interpret can be adequate.*

There may be some differences of opinion over what will count as "too difficult to understand or to interpret," but it is safe to say that any degree of difficulty in the cogency or comprehensibility of an interpretation counts against its success.

But let us not forget, either, that interpretations are supposed to be interpretations *of something,* and if the connection of the interpretation to the original text is not clear, even if the interpretation is itself clear enough, then the interpretation cannot be counted as a success. We might call this the *Principle of Interpretive Plausibility.*

Principle of Interpretive Plausibility: *An adequate interpretation must unproblematically and plausibly account for the text(s) it proposes to interpret.*

Interpretations can fail, moreover, not just by failing to provide plausible readings but—what is perhaps worse—by finding themselves actually *in conflict* with one or more of the relevant texts the interpretation is supposed to explain. Accordingly, one of the main principles of interpretive adequacy is that of fidelity to the text:

Principle of Textual Fidelity: *No interpretation that is unambiguously contradicted by some relevant text whose meaning is clear can ever be adequate.*

There is always some room for dispute, of course, about whether or not some text "unambiguously contradicts" some proposed interpretation and about which texts are going to count as "relevant" to an interpretation. But the very appearance of such a contradiction to one's proposed interpretation counts as a challenge to it, and those who support such an interpretation must be prepared to meet and disarm all such challenges. Most objections come in the form one would expect from this principle— the citation of texts that seem not to fit with the proposed interpretation. Such challenges may be met by explaining the text or texts that seem not to fit the interpretation (which are often called "recalcitrant texts"), in a way that is consistent with the original interpretation. Of course, another way to meet such challenges is to modify the initial interpretation in such a way as to handle all of the relevant texts in a consistent way.

However, there may be several interpretations that contradict one another, but which all satisfy the criteria we have stated so far. This is obviously most likely to be true where there are very few texts to go on or where the relevant texts are themselves so obscure that considerations of relevance and fidelity cannot be easily weighed. There are several principles that scholars apply that can help to make some judgments in cases such as these. One seems fairly obvious, but it can actually be somewhat tricky in application. According to this principle, no adequate interpretation can be anachronistic:

Prohibition of Anachronism: *No adequate interpretation can provide an understanding of the text that requires the assumption or application of some fact or concept that came about or was generated later in history and would not have been available to or known by the author of that text.*

We shall argue in Chapter 1 that Plato is our primary source of information about the historical Socrates, and it is an adequate interpretation of his early dialogues that we shall be primarily concerned with formulating. Socrates and Plato must be counted among the greatest geniuses and conceptual innovators in all of human history. We might suppose that certain concepts were not available in their time and were only first conceived later in history. But we can also imagine that Socrates or Plato actually anticipated some later conceptual developments and that this had not been noticed before because no one had offered a sufficiently intelligent interpretation of the relevant texts. However, the more conceptual "distance" we find between other Socratic or Platonic views and the one that appears to be guilty of anachronism, the more suspicious we may reasonably be about the apparently anachronistic one. On the other hand, it would not always be unreasonable to speculate about how Socrates or Plato might have thought about some issue, given how that issue relates to some other views they obviously did have, especially where what they would have thought, had they possessed the relevant information, follows from a view we are confident they did hold. Thus, although it is silly to speculate about what Socrates *actually thought* regarding whether one has a moral right to disobey the rulings of a circuit court but not to disobey a court of appeals (for that distinction between types of courts was unknown to him), it may be possible and, indeed, quite interesting, to consider whether something Socrates did believe would entail a view about whether disobedience of one court but not the other is morally permissible.

However, the more evidence we can gather for the contemporary (contemporary, that is, to Socrates or Plato) significance and general acceptance of some concept or historical fact, the more we can feel confident in applying an interpretation to something we find in the text that makes use of or reference to this concept or historical fact. This is what is called "contextualizing" interpretation, because it insists on fitting Socrates or Plato, or both, into their historical and cultural contexts:

Principle of Contextual Coherence: *The better a given interpretation fits the relevant texts to their historical contexts, the more plausible the interpretation is, all other things being equal.*

Just as we found with the *Prohibition of Anachronism*, and for the same reasons, the appeal to contextual coherence can also be tricky to apply, for Socrates and Plato were great innovators, and because they were, they were able to transcend their historical contexts and the conceptions and ways of thinking of their contemporaries.

Another principle—one that is often very controversial both in its conception and in its application—has been called the *Principle of Charity:*

The Principle of Charity: *Other things being equal, the interpretation that provides a more interesting or more plausible view is preferable.*

It does not necessarily follow that the relevant positions have to be *true* for this principle to be satisfied. But it must not be the case that the positions are understood in a way that makes them silly or so implausible as to be unworthy of serious consideration. Of course, there are several ways in which an interpretation might be deemed "more interesting" or "more plausible," however, and some of these come into direct conflict with other interpretive principles. If we decide that the more "modern" a view is, the more "interesting" or "plausible" it is, then we will quickly find that the *Principle of Charity* and the *Prohibition of Anachronism* pull us in exactly opposite directions. In another example, scholars continue to disagree about which aspects of Plato's Socratic dialogues are the most interesting: The dialogues depict philosophical arguments that explore topics, make claims, and have logical structures, so many contemporary philosophers find them especially interesting; the dialogues are also rich in characterization and often have very dramatic elements, which are often more interesting to and are seen to be more significant to literary scholars than to philosophers who want to understand the philosophical views of Socrates. Plainly, one will come up with very different general interpretations, depending on which aspects of the dialogues one pays the most attention to.

But even if the way we are supposed to apply this principle is itself controversial, the basic perception it captures is not particularly controversial. We do not continue to study Socrates in the works of Plato because we find the man or the works in which he appears (or their author) to be trivial, boring, foolish, or mundane. We study Socrates because he is *interesting* and because his positions and arguments usually seem to be at least *plausible*, almost always philosophically significant, and sometimes even exactly right. Other things equal, an interpretation that results in a picture of Socrates, or of Plato's works, that is less interesting or less plausible will be to that degree less satisfying than one that yields a more interesting or more plausible picture, precisely because the less interesting or plausible picture will seem to us to be less accurate concerning the Socrates and Plato we found to merit our attention in the first place. So, part of what scholarly interpretation is supposed to do is to explain *how* and *why* Socrates and Plato are as interesting and why their arguments and positions are as plausible as they are—or better yet, scholarly interpretation should show us that they are even *more* interesting and their positions even *more* plausible than we might initially have supposed.

I.3 Identifying and Solving Scholarly Problems

Although the list of the principles we have just reviewed is hardly complete, it is sufficient for us to begin to see how the goals and guiding principles of scholarship help us to identify the issues and texts that create the need and the opportunity for new inquiry. Plainly, one way in which a problem area might be spotted is to determine where the reader is puzzled by a certain text whose meaning or significance seems unclear. In such a case, one might undertake to survey the interpretive options, to examine the possible meanings, and eventually to offer an interpretation that purports to provide the kind of understanding of the text or passage that was not immediately obvious. The same can be said where one finds a significant lack of understanding of a given text or passage prevalent in what others have written about the troublesome passage.

But other ways in which problem areas can be identified derive directly from the employment of the principles of adequate interpretation, such as those articulated in the last section. Consider, for example, the *Principle of Textual Fidelity*, which holds that interpretations may not be contradicted by relevant texts. Sometimes one finds instances in which the relevant texts seem *themselves* to contain contradictions, for example, where Socrates in one passage seems to commit himself to a certain position on a given topic and in another relevant text or passage seems to hold a conflicting position. Many of the most famous problems of interpretation come from apparent conflicts of this sort, and we will have several opportunities to introduce readers to such problems in this book. In such cases, the texts themselves seem to require interpretation in a way that would violate the *Principle of Textual Fidelity*, but the puzzle can be resolved by an appeal to one or more other interpretive principles.

When conflicting texts are identified, one has several options. One strategy often used is to attempt to nullify the problem by eliminating one of the apparently conflicting texts from consideration. There are several ways of doing this. One might disqualify the text as one that does not count as relevant within the texts or passages to be considered. As we argue in Chapter 1, not all of Plato's dialogues should be counted as relevant to the study of Socratic philosophy—only the "early" dialogues are relevant. Perhaps one of the apparently contradictory texts should be reconsidered as not belonging to this "early" group. Alternatively, one might argue for some more subtle understanding of one of the apparently conflicting texts, according to which the appearance of contradiction is removed. This is why we have been discussing these sorts of cases as ones where the texts *seem* to conflict or as cases of *apparent* conflict—scholars often eliminate the appearance of conflict by explaining how there is no real conflict, once the texts are more carefully interpreted. Of course, the more liberal one is in eliminating the appearance of conflict, the more likely it is that one will face the charge of violating the *Principle of Interpretive Plausibility*. In other words, one will be seen to be offering an interpretation that removes the appearance of conflict only at the cost of failing to provide what looks like a relevant or plausible interpretation of one (or both) of the problem texts. None the less, often a plausible case can be made for some understanding of the text (perhaps deriving from some unanticipated application of the *Principle of Contextual Coherence*) that eliminates or resolves the appearance of conflict, so the initial appearance of conflict should always, at least at first, be treated as an opportunity for scholarly study with the goal of resolution.

Those who are coming to Plato's "Socratic" works for the first time often wonder why more experienced interpreters typically start seeking resolutions to the apparent contradictions one finds in those works rather than simply accepting the apparent conflict at face value. "Why should we assume," they ask, "that Plato or Socrates didn't contradict himself?" There are several considerations that go into this, but all, we believe, go back to what we have called the *Principle of Charity*, which calls for a preference for the more interesting or more plausible interpretation, other things being equal. Contradictions are self-canceling, as it were. There can be nothing less *interesting* and less *plausible* than a contradiction, for precisely because the contradictories cancel each other out, one who contradicts oneself literally fails to articulate any position at all. There can be "meaningful silences," "pregnant pauses," and the like, of course. But contradiction manages to convey no meaning, to accomplish no communication of any kind. It is open to a scholar to claim that the very fact that Plato or Socrates contradicts himself is interesting in some way, but whatever interest there may be in such a strategy cannot be said to provide an interpretation of the relevant *texts*, since the claim that the texts contradict themselves leaves nothing meaningful to interpret, much less anything *interesting* or *plausible* to interpret.

Of course, it is not impossible that Socrates contradicted himself on matters of great importance or that Plato contradicted himself in his attribution to Socrates. But we should reach such a conclusion only after we have exhausted every other interpretive strategy we can. Again, if we too hastily assume that the texts cancel themselves out, we run the risk of missing some edifying, and possibly very interesting and plausible, position that the texts have expressed or identified in a way that only *seems* to be self-contradictory. Good scholars sometimes do come to the conclusion that some irreconcilable conflict may be found in the texts, although the evidence of the last fifty years is that scholarly persistence usually pays off, and a plausible way to resolve the apparent conflict is uncovered.

Most of the opportunities for interpretation we identify in this book derive from apparent conflicts in the relevant texts, but not all do. Some derive more directly from what we have called the *Principle of Charity* itself. The need for interpretation arises whenever the relevant texts seem to commit Socrates to a position that is clear enough but either so implausible or so improbable that explanation is called for by the *Principle of Charity*. In this book, we sometimes have occasion to note that what the text seems to be saying is profoundly implausible, which we will take as a sufficient reason for looking at the text more carefully, in an attempt to find greater plausibility in what we are to attribute to Socrates. Again, though we cannot interpret our texts so loosely as to run afoul of the *Principle of Interpretive Plausibility,* we must always assume that neither Socrates nor Plato is silly or stupid. Thus, when it appears to us that they are, in some case, we are well advised to look more carefully in an attempt to gain a better understanding of what the text is showing us, where "better" simply means an understanding that is more interesting or more plausible, and (hence) sensible. As in the cases of apparent conflict, it is not impossible that Socrates or Plato might have been confused or have said something silly or stupid. It is, however, both silly and stupid to *assume* incautiously and too quickly simply that such great minds have failed in such ways. Again, it is possible that they made obvious conceptual errors that they would not have made had they been more careful. But one should *conclude* that they did so only after trying to find at least good sense behind what they say.

As we said at the beginning, this book is intended to provide an introduction to the philosophy of Socrates. But as we have also noted, the nature of the evidence we have about the historical figure Socrates, as well as the nature of some of the views he apparently held, makes it inevitable that we involve ourselves in the always intriguing but sometimes difficult business of interpreting what we have to go on. In the remainder of this book, as we discuss what we know about Socrates and his philosophy, we identify the texts and issues that have so often raised questions. In a few cases, we have been the first to identify and articulate the relevant problems, but usually this will not be the case. Some of the problems we identify and discuss are notorious among scholars, have been discussed for a long time, often in several different articulations or presentations, and have seen many different attempted solutions. Whenever possible, we survey, at least in some general way, the different ways in which the problems have been identified and the different sorts of solutions that scholars have offered. Typically, we show how and why some of the proposed solutions seem inadequate to us. The *Principle of Textual Fidelity,* together with the *Principle of Charity,* commit us, as a matter of method, to the view that there are *no* problems that cannot be resolved in ways that are both consistent and also interesting, and we propose solutions to every problem we identify in this book. The solutions that we offer, however, may not always (or ever!) convince our readers. Our hope, though, is that when our readers are dissatisfied, they will go to work to provide more plausible, more consistent, or more interesting solutions of their own. Even better, our readers may see problems that require scholarly attention that have gone completely unnoticed. If so, we encourage them to share such problems with us, so that we can all work together in trying to solve them and thus learn even more about the philosophy of Socrates.

I.4 Translations and Citations of Passages

We have intentionally provided our readers with many quotations from primary texts, usually quotations from Plato's early dialogues. We have done so primarily to allow our readers to judge for themselves what Plato, or some other author, actually said and to see for themselves whether we are right about what we claim is being said. We strongly encourage our readers to see if their interpretation of the quotations is in accord with ours. We also encourage our readers to check the contexts in which these quotations occur. To make this possible, we provide at the beginning of each quotation a standard citation, which refers to the numbers and letters that are almost always placed in the margins of translations of complete ancient texts. These numbers and letters refer to page numbers and sections of pages of the edition of Plato's works prepared in 1578 by the French scholar Henri Estienne, who published under the Latin name Stephanus. His collection divided each full page of text into five sections, which were labeled a, b, c, d, and e. Since the publication of the "Stephanus" collection, all subsequent editions of the Greek texts of Plato's dialogues, and most translations from the Greek into other languages, have included in the columns of each of their pages numbers corresponding to the page numbers of the "Stephanus" collection, as well as the letters corresponding to the sections of that collection. This system allows the reader to refer to the text in a way that is convertible to any other edition or translation of the same dialogue or dialogues. Therefore, if we indicate that some passage we have translated occurs at, say, 23c-d of Plato's *Apology*, our readers can look in the margins of virtually any edition or translation of the *Apology* and find those numbers and letters next to the passage we have quoted. This allows our readers not only to compare different translations of the passage but also, and more important, to place the quotation into its context in order to judge carefully what the passage is communicating.

It goes without saying that translations vary greatly in their quality. Some of the most literal translations from Greek into English are virtually unintelligible. Others, in our judgment, take far too many liberties with the text. For the most part, we find those offered in Cooper (1997) to be reliable, and because these are readily available and are the ones most likely to be used by those who might read our book, we have elected to use these translations in this book. In a few instances, where we find some feature of these translations unacceptable, we have substituted our own and have noted this. Translations of works by authors other than Plato, except where noted, are our own. Excerpts from the translations of Plato, *Complete Works* are reprinted by permission of Hackett Publishing Company, Inc., all rights reserved.

A Survey of Our Evidence

1.1 Ancient Evidence and the Socratic Problem

1.1.1 Judging Sources of Information

We know that many ancient writings have been lost, because works from antiquity that have survived refer to them. It is difficult to offer anything like a reasonable estimate of how much has been lost, but it is probably safe to say that only a small fraction of what was written in Socrates' time and shortly after, and only a small fraction of what was written about Socrates himself, has survived the nearly 2,400 years since his death. And what has survived provides historians and philosophers with problematic information. In some cases, the ways in which the ancient texts have come down to us suggest that the texts themselves may have been modified in imperceptible ways. Even if we feel fairly confident that we have an accurate copy of some original text, the authors of these texts themselves may create difficulties, for ancient Greek culture had no "journalistic ethic": These writers had no obvious interest in making sure, when they talked about historical figures or events, that they always got their information exactly right. Even when they did set out to explain some person or event in some way, they felt free to "adjust" the account in ways they supposed were edifying or simply made a better story. For those of us who want to know the whole truth and nothing but the truth, dealing with ancient sources can sometimes be quite frustrating. As a result, at its best and most "scientific," historical reconstruction is to some degree speculative, interpretive, even subjective.

In order to minimize such difficulties, scholars must approach the materials they propose to use with a great deal of caution. Speaking very generally, there are roughly four "grades" of evidence available regarding the ancient world and those who populated it.

- Grade A: Original sources
- Grade B: *Reliable* ancient testimony

- Grade C: *Unreliable* ancient testimony
- Grade D: Later scholarly opinions

Obviously, the best grade of evidence regarding some ancient figure would be anything written by that figure. These sources are called the "original" or "primary" sources, to denote their special significance as evidence. But even these sources do not come with absolute assurances of accuracy. There are not always enough of such materials for judgment, and what does exist may have become corrupted in the later copies that eventually came into our possession. For example, we certainly do not have anything written by Plato himself, only what we believe are more or less accurate copies of his works. We might also doubt the veracity of what certain authors say about their own views: Perhaps such authors have some reason to write a report that distorts or misreports their relevant point of view in some way or ways. In many cases, the authenticity of what are alleged to be original sources is doubtful. For example, *not one* of Plato's works has gone without some challenge to its authenticity in the years since they were written. In some cases (the works now called the *dubia* and *spuria*), works that were attributed to Plato at some time in the past have generally come to be regarded as unauthentic, written by different authors—perhaps later members of the school Plato began in Athens, called the Academy—and often having very different characteristics than authentic Platonic works.[1] But scholars continue to disagree about whether or not several dialogues are authentic, and in this way even the best "grade" of evidence might turn out to be somewhat less accurate than we might wish it to be. Finally, even if we have substantial primary texts and feel we can resolve questions about whether they are authentic and about whether they have been corrupted, we still face interpretive questions. It is certainly not always the case that what an ancient source says is obvious in its meaning.

In the case of Socrates, however, there are no primary texts: According to everything we are told by those who wrote about him, Socrates did not write anything, or if he did, it has not survived. Accordingly, in the case of Socrates, the best we can hope for is "Grade B" evidence—the testimony of reliable ancient sources. These sources are to be distinguished from those that make the next-lower "grade" of evidence ("Grade C" evidence), the *unreliable* ancient sources. Both sorts of sources are called "secondary" sources because they are written from a secondhand perspective; that is, they are written not by the original author or person but by some *second* person writing *about* the original. But how do we distinguish the reliable ancient sources from the unreliable ones? Needless to say, just as there can be scholarly dispute about the issues of textual corruption, authenticity, and interpretation, so there can also be disagreements about which sources are the most reliable ones.

Generally, however, scholars agree that the more historically *proximate* an ancient secondary source is to the primary—in our own case, how proximate the secondary source is to Socrates—the more likely it is that the source is a reliable one. The reason for this assumption is simple: We suppose that those who actually knew Socrates, for example, are in the best position to tell us about who he was, how he behaved, and what he believed. The later sources must rely on the most proximate sources for their information. Thus, the later sources are more likely not to provide "secondhand" evidence, but "thirdhand" or "fourthhand," or even more distant. The problems we face with inaccurate copies, authenticity questions, and interpretation, in original texts, compound with each new transmission in the passage of information through new sets of hands and through the years.

In some cases, we are also able to compare the testimony of later sources to the testimony of the earlier sources from which the later sources received their own information, and in far too many cases, we find that our later sources do not accurately reflect their own sources of information. One example pertinent to our interest in Socrates is the case of Diogenes Laertius, who wrote sometime around A.D. 250 and who often cites the works of Plato as his sources of information but does not always get right what he says he gets from Plato, whose works we can compare to Diogenes Laertius's claims. Diogenes also used other sources, too, and it is not impossible that his own accounts get things right, where Plato got them wrong, on the basis of these other sources. But because these other sources no longer survive, we are not in a position to say whether Diogenes used them in a judicious and accurate way—we can only know for certain that he does not always agree with Plato *even when he seems to be using Plato as his source.* Accordingly, later sources like Diogenes Laertius are not wholly worthless, because they did have access to sources now lost to us; but later sources like Diogenes Laertius must be regarded as *unreliable,* relative to proximate sources like Plato. It is considerations of this sort that scholars use to distinguish reliable from unreliable ancient testimony, yielding two distinct "grades" of evidence.

The final "grade" of evidence also deserves mention, since as your eyes pass over these words, you are actually using such "Grade D" evidence! Works, such as this book and all of the scholarly opinions we survey and offer to you, are only valuable in so far as they have a firm basis in the higher grades of evidence, and help to represent and explain those higher grades of evidence. This is why, in the remaining chapters, we will strive always to provide the passages from the relevant texts that we believe support and motivate the scholarly views we discuss and defend. The words of scholars may (usually) be presumed to represent years of study and learning about the figures and philosophies they discuss, and the value of such study and learning is considerable. But our readers should never forget that our opinions, and all other scholars' opinions, are only as good as the evidence that supports them. However entertaining or intrinsically interesting a scholar's opinions might be, if the other grades of evidence do not support the scholar's opinions, they are simply worthless, as regards the historical facts. We have tried to do our best, in this book, to avoid writing such worthless opinions about Socrates and his philosophy, but we leave it to our readers to decide how far we have succeeded in avoiding such worthlessness!

1.1.2 The Socratic Problem

It is an interesting irony that although Socrates was unquestionably one of the most famous and influential figures in western civilization, what we really know about the man and his philosophical views is quite limited. Of course, there is no good reason to doubt that there was a philosopher by the name Socrates, that he lived in Athens during the fifth century B.C., that he made it his business to engage people in philosophical discussion, often in public places such as the Athenian marketplace, and that he had many devoted friends and an even larger number of implacable enemies. We can also be quite certain that in 399 B.C., when he was well on in years, Socrates appeared before an Athenian court, charged with having violated an Athenian law against impiety, that he was convicted and subsequently executed.

Only the most extreme skeptic would doubt these claims about the actual person, Socrates—"the historical Socrates," as we shall call him. But attempts to go beyond any but the most well-documented, and usually simple, biographical facts about the famous Athenian philosopher are bound to stir controversy. There are a number of reasons for this. In the first place, Socrates himself is of no help. As we have already said, we have no "Grade A" evidence: As far as we can tell, Socrates never wrote anything about himself or his philosophical views. He apparently practiced philosophy exclusively by engaging his contemporaries in discussion. The fact that we must rely on what others said about Socrates is certainly, by itself, no bar to our knowledge of the man or his philosophy. There is nothing, in principle, to prevent someone from providing a far more accurate account of another person's life than could the subject. But where accounts written by others disagree with each other, as we shall see that they do in the case of Socrates, it would be helpful if we had his own testimony about himself and how he understood his own work to help us decide between and among competing accounts of others.

In any event, we are left only with what others wrote about Socrates. Finding references in ancient writings to Socrates and his views is not the problem. On the contrary, ancient literature is replete with such references, some quite extensive. Rather, the problem is determining which, if any, of the many ancient sources gives us reliable information about Socrates, for although ancient sources about Socrates corroborate each other on many key points, on many other key points these accounts are clearly at odds with each other, and it is hardly clear which, if any, of the conflicting sources is accurate.

It is most reasonable for us to attempt to identify which of the many ancient sources look the most likely to qualify as at least "Grade B" evidence, and as we have said, the most likely sources for this are those by people who were in a position to know about Socrates without having to rely on what others said. We know that many things were written about Socrates by persons with very different philosophical temperaments in the years immediately following his death. The philosopher Aristotle refers[2] to these works as *Socratikoi Logoi*, "Socratic writings."[3] But most of these writings have either been completely lost or have survived in the form of only a few fragments.[4] Moreover, what evidence there is strongly suggests that Socrates was an enormously controversial figure and that at least some of those who wrote about him were seeking to condemn him whereas others were trying to defend him. Given the strength of the passions on both sides, we have to wonder how objective any of these accounts could have been.

If we do concentrate mainly on ancient authors whose testimony has survived and who actually knew Socrates sufficiently well to write authoritatively about him and what he believed, we are left with only three authors to consider, each of whom provides us with a substantial amount of evidence to be weighed. First, there is Aristophanes, the famous fifth-century comedy writer, who made a character named "Socrates" one of the main characters in one of his plays and who refers to Socrates in two others. Then there is Xenophon, a historian who wrote extensively about Socrates and who intimates that his writing was informed by a deep friendship with Socrates that extended over many years. Our third principal source is Plato, the famous Athenian philosopher, who also implies that he was one of Socrates' closest friends and who was strongly influenced as a young man by Socrates.

Although these three are doubtless our best candidates for reliable ("Grade B") information about the historical Socrates, we must be careful never to accept uncritically what any of them say. First, it is clear at various points that each of the three is not even trying to write about the historical Socrates but is instead merely attaching the name "Socrates" to an imaginary figure who serves as a kind of mouthpiece through which the author is advancing some agenda of his own that had little or nothing to do with the historical Socrates. Moreover, whether they are intended to be substantially accurate or not, the portraits provided by each of our three principal sources are very different. For reasons we examine in detail below, it is exceedingly difficult to decide which, if any, of these different accounts gives us helpful, accurate information about the historical Socrates.

Fortunately, the testimony of our principal sources does not always conflict. Sometimes they agree, and when they do, surely we have good reason to accept that common testimony as reliable. But as we noted at the beginning of the chapter, except for some biographical information about Socrates, mutually supporting testimony from all three of our sources is fairly unusual. If we restrict ourselves to points of mutual agreement among all three—Aristophanes, Xenophon, and Plato—we shall not get very far in our search.

Accordingly, most scholars are willing to employ a less restrictive interpretive principle: We may accept as accurate the testimony of even a single source—including even later sources, such as Diogenes Laertius—provided, first, that it is not contradicted by another of our sources and, second, that the author has no discernible reason to fabricate what he is saying about Socrates. It is also reasonable to attribute to Socrates any beliefs and attitudes that were universally, or almost universally, held by Athenian males of his day, unless we have good reason from one or more of our sources to think that Socrates rejected such attitudes.

But even the less restrictive principle will not take us very far, because there are a great many contradictions among Aristophanes, Xenophon, and Plato, and commentators are also quick to find reasons for each of our principal sources to indeed stray from the truth about the historical Socrates, especially on matters pertaining to Socrates' philosophy. Nevertheless, before we turn to the question of whether we can apply an even less restrictive principle, which allows us to trust one writer over another when they disagree, we would do well to sketch what we can of Socrates' life, where there is no contradiction among our three sources.

1.2 Relatively Uncontroversial Issues and General Background

1.2.1 Socrates' Life

Socrates was born in the Athenian deme, or district, of Alopece, in 469 B.C. His father was Sophroniscus and his mother was Phaenarete. The financial circumstances of the family into which Socrates was born are in fact somewhat less clear than at least some commentators would have us believe. To be sure, his family was not among the wealthier and more influential in Athens. But just how much money his family had is difficult to say. In one rather famous passage, Plato suggests that Socrates' mother was a midwife (*Theaetetus* 149a). If so, the fact that she had any occupation at all tells us that the family was not well to do, for in the Athens of Socrates' day only relatively poor women would have worked outside the home.[5] All others were virtually confined to the home, where they were expected to manage the household and to have children. Unfortunately, Plato's remark about Phaenarete's occupation is not confirmed by any other of our sources, and the context in which it is made suggests that Plato may not have intended the remark to be taken seriously.

We have even less reason to trust the story that Sophroniscus, Socrates' father, was a stonecutter, or perhaps even a sculptor. Of course, if Sophroniscus did have skill in working with stone, he would have commanded a reasonably good income in the years following the end of the Persian War, for the great building projects that ensued must have created tremendous demand for skilled stoneworkers. But the claim that Sophroniscus was a stoneworker does not come from any of our earliest sources, and their silence on this point makes it impossible to say with any confidence how Sophroniscus earned a living or even if he needed to work for a living. We might think that we can infer that Sophroniscus was a sculptor from the fact that two writers claimed that a group of statues near the Acropolis were actually made by Socrates himself. Since it is reasonable to assume that Socrates did learn his father's trade, for that is the sort of occupational instruction most male children in Athens received, it would follow that Sophroniscus was in all likelihood a sculptor, too. Unfortunately, the authors of these reports lived hundreds of years after Socrates' death,[6] and although they may have sincerely believed what they were told about the creator of the statutes they were shown in Athens, we have no very strong reason to accept what they wrote on this point.

Our principal sources are also silent about Socrates' youth, though we can form a fairly clear, if general, idea of what it was like on the basis of what we know about the history and sociology of the Athens of Socrates' youth. Socrates' childhood was spared the hardships of war. He was born some ten years after the end of the Persian War and was in his forties when the Peloponnesian War, the war between Athens and Sparta and their various allies, broke out. There is no reason to think that the early education of Socrates was in any way exceptional. No doubt, his mother and other women who may have been living in the household told him the familiar folktales and stories about the gods and Homeric heroes. How much or what kinds of instruction outside the home Socrates received is more difficult to say, for there was no publicly supported education in Socrates' Athens. However, most Athenians, even those with relatively meager incomes, did arrange for some kind of schooling for their male children, and instruction from a professional tutor was neither difficult to obtain nor expensive. There is little reason to doubt Plato's suggestion (*Crito* 50d-e) that Socrates' father saw to it that Socrates was educated in "music and gymnastics," as were most Athenian boys. Included in an education in music were such things as elementary grammar, reading, arithmetic, and elementary musical theory. "Gymnastic education" included not only the exercises that we usually associate with that term but also wrestling, boxing, running, and hurling the javelin.[7] It is also likely that Socrates was instructed by his father and any older male relatives in civic institutions and the duties of citizenship. Finally, as discussed earlier, before Socrates passed from boyhood to manhood, he would probably have been given instruction by his father in his father's craft or trade.

1.2.2 Athens and Education in the Time of Socrates

Whether Socrates received any further instruction is a question we must take up in a moment. But we would do well to consider briefly the many changes the city of Socrates' youth underwent. It is not overstating the point to say that the Athens in which Socrates grew to manhood underwent a thorough cultural revolution in what became known as Athens's "golden age." Under the leadership of Pericles, starting in the mid-fifth-century B.C., Athens's political system was transformed into a radical participatory democracy in which every Athenian male citizen could—and was expected to—vote, hold office, and serve on the very powerful Athenian juries.

The fifth century B.C. also saw the physical transformation of Athens. The fortification of the Piraeus, the port of Athens, and the building of a wall around Athens itself was already under way by the time of Socrates' birth. In the mid-fifth century B.C., Pericles argued persuasively that if Athens would only build two "long walls" from Athens to the Piraeus to keep any land army from invading the city, Athens would never have to fear any enemy. He was assuming that the Athenian navy, which emerged from the Persian War as the most powerful in the world, could defeat any enemy and keep the sea lanes open. At the same time the relatively simple temples and public buildings of pre–Persian War Athens were replaced with the magnificent (and magnificently expensive) buildings, such as the Parthenon and Hephaisteion, which adorn the Acropolis and the agora, the large open area at the foot of the Acropolis that constituted the Athenian marketplace and public square. It was during this time, too, that drama and art found new and captivating forms of expression. Left behind were the strictures that made pre–Persian War drama and art lifeless by comparison.

But as profound as these changes were, none could have affected the young Socrates more than the emergence of the practice of calling into question the moral values that Athenians had accepted for so long. The Athenians of Socrates' day assumed, just as their ancestors had assumed, that the best life one could have required the acquisition of what was called virtue, or excellence *(aretē)*. Excellence was not a terribly complicated notion. To have *aretē*, one had to excel in devotion to one's family, city, and the city's gods. A truly good person succeeded in doing great things for the city, strictly obeyed its laws, honored parents and ancestors, scrupulously paid homage to the gods by strictly obeying the conventions governing prayer and sacrifice. The good person never doubted that the gods were the superiors of mortals in intelligence and strength. Even many of nature's most powerful forces were bounded by the will of the gods. These were values one did not need schooling to acquire. Every father was deemed to be responsible for teaching them to his children, and every citizen was responsible for seeing that the law punished those who violated this understanding of the requirements of morality.

However, by the middle part of the fifth century B.C., as Socrates was entering manhood, Athens and the rest of the Greek world witnessed the emergence of a new breed of teachers, the Sophists. Our knowledge of these professional teachers is not all that we would like it to be, for much of the information we have about the Sophists comes from Plato, who made little attempt to disguise his contempt for sophistic education and some of the most prominent and influential Sophists of Socrates' day. Fortunately, a number of excellent recent studies of the Sophists, relying on various other sources, have helped to lessen our need to rely so heavily on Plato.[8] In any case, it seems clear that the Sophists, some of whom traveled from city to city, lectured about a variety of subjects, some quite esoteric and specialized. They often charged substantial fees, and consequently, only the sons of Athens's wealthier families were able to attend their lectures. Some of the Sophists, apparently, acquired great reputations for their wisdom and, as a result, amassed enormous personal wealth.

We may divide the Sophists into two broad groups. Some, men like Anaxagoras, were sometimes referred to as "nature-philosophers." They typically professed theories about such fundamental questions about nature as "Is there a basic substance out of which everything else is composed?" "Why does change in nature occur?" or "What is the shape of the universe?" Many of their views strike us today as little more than crude speculation. But insofar as they sought naturalistic explanations for natural phenomena, they undermined the traditional explanations of natural change in terms of what the gods ordained. Because they questioned the traditional role of the gods as the governors of the universe, the nature-

philosophers came to be seen not as harmless crackpots but as the enemies of Athenian religion as it was practiced by most people.

The other major group of Sophists was interested in more human matters. We refer to this group as the humanistic Sophists. Like the nature-
philosophers, the humanistic Sophists were a mixed lot. Sophists such as
Hippias of Elis and Gorgias of Leontini claimed to be able to teach their
students not how to find and present the truth but how to be persuasive
and, hence, how to be able to be influential, truthfully or dishonestly,
right or wrong, just or unjust. The threat these men posed for the traditional values of most Athenians of Socrates' day is obvious. At the same
time, as more and more Athenians saw the Assembly and the law courts
as places where they could advance their interests, members of this group
of humanistic Sophists were increasingly viewed as teachers of a valuable
but very controversial skill.

Among others, Protagoras made his fortune teaching students that
there are no moral absolutes and that what appears to be true to an individual or accepted within a given society is true only for that individual
or within that society. The implications of Protagoras's relativism for the
conventional understanding of *aretē* are also obvious. Equally brazen in
its attack on the conventional morality was the central teaching of Thrasymachus, who taught that the truly excellent individual is the one who has
the power to get what he wants. It would hardly have been surprising,
then, if in the eyes of many Athenians, the humanistic Sophists encouraged and enabled those who sought to advance their own interests at the
cost of what is best for the community.

1.2.3 Socrates and the Sophists

Just what influence the Sophists may have had on Socrates' thinking is
difficult to assess. In one dialogue, the *Phaedo* (96a–97b), Plato seems to
imply that when the historical Socrates was young, he took a serious interest in certain aspects of nature-philosophy but that he abandoned these
concerns when he became convinced that they could not explain why
even the most mundane things are the way they are.[9] Whether or not
Plato's remarks in this connection are historically accurate is a matter of
dispute. Although much of the *Phaedo* was written years after Socrates'
death and almost certainly discusses philosophical doctrines that *Plato*
had come to accept and that the historical Socrates could not have known
about, some scholars believe that Plato had no reason to fictionalize what
appears to be a brief biographical report about the historical Socrates.
One might argue, however, that Plato did indeed have a reason to fictionalize what he has the character "Socrates" say in the dialogue about the
poverty of naturalistic explanations, for in the *Phaedo*, Plato plainly

wanted to show that another sort of explanation was superior to that of the nature-philosophers. Accordingly, it is entirely possible that Plato would have Socrates say that he had studied naturalistic explanations and found them wanting. Because we have already said that it is best that we not use the testimony of just one of our authors if we can discern a plausible motive for fictionalizing, we will be on firmer ground if we say we just do not know whether the historical Socrates ever took a serious interest in nature philosophy.

Often passed over is the equally interesting question of whether the historical Socrates ever seriously studied under the tutelage of any of the Sophists. The only serious candidate for having been a sophistic teacher is Prodicus, one of the humanistic Sophists, who professed to be an expert on the meanings of words. The question should be raised because there is at least one place in Plato's work (*Meno* 96d) where Socrates is described as having been the pupil of Prodicus, and we have no reason to think that Plato is just making up the claim.[10] The evidence here is slight indeed. But even if Socrates did actually study with Prodicus for a period, we have no reason to think that Prodicus was interested in undermining the traditional Athenian conception of *aretē* or that Socrates ever accepted any of Prodicus's specific moral teachings.

Although we can be sure that Socrates was never a student of any of the more malignant humanistic Sophists, Socrates' friends who wrote about him after his death consistently represent him as the implacable foe of those who challenged the notion that morality expresses objective truths. Nevertheless, there is a sense in which even these Sophists exercised a positive influence on Socrates, for like anyone who must contend with intellectually powerful adversaries, as some of these men must have been, Socrates was doubtless forced to think through his own views with greater care in order see how his sophistic adversaries and their arguments might be defeated. Although it would be a mistake to say that Socrates' interest in moral philosophy was merely a reaction to the moral skepticism and relativism of some of his adversaries, it would also be a mistake to think that Socrates' thought was not shaped, at least to some extent, by the formidable opposition these views presented.

1.2.4 Socrates the Soldier

Much of Socrates' adult life must be understood against the background of Athens at war with its longtime rival, Sparta. Although the actual war did not actually break out until 431 B.C., when Socrates was not quite forty, tensions between the two great Hellenic powers had been growing for many years as Athens became increasingly rich and powerful and arrogant. Athens's rise to power began innocently enough. Shortly after the end of the Persian threat to Greece, Athens took the position of leadership in a confederacy of cities and islands, perhaps as many as two hundred at one point.[11] The Delian League, as it was initially called, was originally formed to provide for its members' mutual protection in the event of a renewed Persian threat to the region. At its inception, all of the members were equal. But because Athens's large and powerful navy was left intact when the Persians retreated and because there was no other member to rival Athens's military power or prestige, the Athenians gradually assumed control of the Delian League, which meant that economic and military policies that governed members tended to favor Athens. In time, members were forced to pay what amounted to a tax to Athens, ostensibly to pay for protection from any future Persian threat, but in reality the money collected went to support Athens's increasingly expensive appetite for civic adornments and military domination. Eventually, Athens moved the treasury of the Delian League from the island of Delos to Athens for "safekeeping."

Once it became clear that the Delian League really existed only to serve the economic and military interests of Athens, some member islands tried to leave it. To block such attempts and perhaps to keep others from getting similar ideas about leaving the league, Athens put down these revolts with the full force of its navy. If the case of Samos was typical,[12] those who challenged Athenian dominance were reduced to being mere subjects of Athens. The decision of Pericles and his democratic allies in the Assembly to glorify the city of Athens at the expense of its formerly trusting allies fully demonstrated the truth that power corrupts.

According to the historian Thucydides, Sparta did not really recognize the full extent of Athenian political and military ambitions until it witnessed Athens's willingness to use its power to crush any opposition to its wishes.

T1.1 Thucydides, *The History of the Peloponnesian War* 1.118.2:

It was in these times [the period after the end of the Persian War] that the Athenians established their more unyielding rule and they advanced their power to greatness. But when the Spartans saw this, they did not thwart it, except for a short time, but instead they remained undisturbed most of the time, since they did not quickly go to war unless they were forced to and they were bringing an end to their own internal wars. But before long the power of the Athenians was clearly on the rise, and they were choking their allies. Then when the situation was no longer tolerable, they made war on the exalted Athenians, but attempting it in the most zealous way with the most destructive force which they were able to assemble.

As a result, in 431 B.C. the two great Hellenic powers, Athens and Sparta, began a death struggle that continued off and on until 405 B.C. When the fighting finally stopped, Athens had been thoroughly defeated. In the end, Athens's treasury had been exhausted and its navy, which had been the source of the city's military power, had been all but destroyed. The judgment of history has not been kind to Athens during this period, for its ruthless imperialistic practices and voracious appetite for wealth led to the most egregious excesses. But whether Socrates would have agreed that his city's cause was unjust is difficult to say. Aristophanes sometimes jokes that Socrates may have been sympathetic to the Spartans, and Xenophon consistently represents him as hostile to certain features of Athenian democracy.[13] However, there is no reason to doubt Plato's claims that Socrates remained in the city and fought, probably in the ranks of the hoplite class,[14] on behalf of the city. In fact, Plato reports that Socrates took part in three major campaigns—Potidaea (in 432 B.C.), Delium (in 424 B.C.), and Amphipolis (in 422 B.C.) and that he distinguished himself for his endurance in the face of great hardship in the first and for his great courage in the second. Even if Plato exaggerated Socrates' fierce courage on the battlefield and phenomenal ability to endure hardship, it is unlikely that Plato would have so conspicuously mentioned Socrates' presence in these campaigns had Socrates not actually been there and fought bravely.

Socrates' role in one of the most wrenching episodes in Athenian history, however, in the aftermath of the Peloponnesian War, is more controversial. When Athens surrendered to Sparta, the Athenians were offered a remarkably generous peace accord, according to which Athens would continue to have political independence, provided that the Athenians agreed not to engage in further military or defensive buildup. Within a year of signing the accord, however, Athens violated one of the provisions by attempting to rebuild its defensive walls. Using this as a pretext, a Spartan general forced Athens to abandon the democracy in favor of an oligarchy that was known as the "Thirty" (or sometimes, the "Thirty Tyrants"). The Thirty remained in power only a brief time (roughly eight months), but during their reign, the Thirty committed an appalling number of atrocities in their efforts to consolidate and increase their power. Many of those who were loyal to the democracy of Athens went into exile and were able to organize themselves into a fighting force sufficient to overthrow the Thirty before a full year was out. But Socrates did not leave Athens during the reign of the Thirty, and although both Plato and Xenophon (as well as other later writers) tell us that Socrates came into dangerous conflict with the Thirty, some scholars have found Socrates' decision to remain in the city a sign that his political sympathies may have been disloyal to the democracy. We consider this issue in more detail in Chapter 6.

1.2.5 Socrates' Appearance and Socrates as "Gadfly"

Our primary sources are in remarkable agreement about Socrates' appearance. A broad, snub nose, bulging eyes, bald head, and thick lips hidden behind a full beard made him decidedly unattractive. His squat body only added to his physical unattractiveness, in a culture that even more than our own revered and elevated beautiful people. Plato and Xenophon both compare him to a silenus: a half man, half goat. He may also have had some usual mannerisms that, apparently, created a somewhat comic effect, at least in the eyes of some. In time, he must have become something of a spectacle, as he made his way through Athens with his belly stuck out and his eyes rolling from side to side. His habit of going barefooted, even in the winter, or of wearing the same cloak day in and day out could only have added to the comic effect. He may also have been somewhat disheveled, perhaps even dingy.[15]

It is worth noting that no one reports that Socrates ever held a job, though as noted above, it is very likely that he had been trained in the sort of work that his father did. Plato gives us a reason for why Socrates did not work, at least later in life. According to Plato, Socrates told the jury at his trial that "the god" (presumably Apollo) had made him like "a gadfly attached to the city just as to a large and noble horse that is sluggish because of its size and needs to be aroused by a stinging" (*Apology* 30e). What Socrates meant is that he believed the god recognized the false presumption of his fellow Athenians that they understood what moral excellence is and so did not need to inquire into its nature. The god, then, had given Socrates what amounted to a "divine mission," commanding him to question his fellow citizens about the nature of *aretē* and about how they thought they ought to live generally. And when he found that they did not really know what they thought they did, the god commanded him to chastise them and to exhort them to engage in philosophical reflection. Whether Socrates really believed that he had such a duty or whether Plato simply portrays him as a servant to the god is a question we shall turn to shortly. But there can be little doubt that Socrates did carry on philosophical discussions in the agora and various other public settings and that he had already gained considerable notoriety with the Athenian public as an eccentric intellectual of some stripe by the time he was in his mid-forties.[16]

1.2.6 Socrates' Family

At some point, Socrates married a woman named Xanthippe. Her name at least suggests that she came from an aristocratic family, but we know nothing about her personal history. Presumably with Xanthippe, Socrates had three sons: Lamprocles, Sophroniscus (named for Socrates' father), and Menexenus. Almost nothing is known of Socrates' relationship with his wife, including how they came to marry.[17] According to one of our principal sources, Xenophon, the marriage of Socrates to Xanthippe was not entirely a happy one, for Socrates was absent from the home too often to suit Xanthippe and, Xenophon tells us, Xanthippe was difficult to get along with. However, neither of our other sources confirms this, and Plato, when he mentions her, seems sympathetic and respectful. The fact that our evidence on this point is so scant and mixed should incline us away from drawing any firm conclusion about Xanthippe's character or about whether the marriage of Socrates and Xanthippe was a happy one.

It is equally impossible to know whether those ancient sources who claim that Socrates was actually married twice are correct. According to these tales, Xanthippe was actually Socrates' second wife, his first being a woman named Myrto, who was the granddaughter of a man known as Aristeides the Just.[18] Beyond the mere assertion that there was a first wife, these ancient sources tell us very little. But because our principal sources are silent on the matter, a fact that seems telling in itself, we cannot regard them as anything but interesting stories.

1.2.7 Socrates' Daimonion

Two of our principal sources are emphatic that Socrates firmly believed that, from time to time, he had some sort of uncanny experience, which he referred variously to as a "voice" or "sign," or as his *daimonion* (a "divine something"), that in some way guided his actions when he heard it. On the one hand, Plato tells us that Socrates first started hearing the voice in childhood and that when it came to him, the voice only turned him away from what he was about to do but never guided his actions in any positive way. Xenophon, on the other hand, claims that the *daimonion* also directed Socrates to perform certain actions. Plato and Xenophon agree that Socrates made no attempt to conceal this experience. On the contrary, he talked openly about it and about the divine communications he took his "sign" to represent. And both agree that Socrates' apparent conviction that a divinity of some sort spoke to him was at least part of the motivation for bringing him to trial in 399 B.C. Although, as we shall see, the prosecution doubtless had other reasons as well to have Socrates brought before a court, it is significant that no ancient source contradicts the claim Plato and Xenophon make about the importance of the *daimonion* to Socrates' eventual prosecution. In any event, there is general agreement among commentators that his *daimonion* was well known to the general public, although the extent to which the general public thought it was a benign eccentricity is a matter of considerable dispute.[19]

1.2.8 Socrates' Associates

Two of our principal sources, Plato and Xenophon, give us good reason to believe that Socrates attracted a following of young men who enjoyed listening to him. It should be stressed, however, assuming we can discount the testimony of Aristophanes, for reasons we discuss below, that Plato and Xenophon agree that Socrates' following was in no sense a school. On the contrary, it seems to have consisted of young men who were free to join Socrates and others in conversation from time to time, as they saw fit. Thus, some were more closely associated with Socrates than others, depending upon how much time they spent in his presence. In any case, one of the most curious facts about Socrates' life is how different some of his closest friends turned out to be. Plato indicates that by the time of Socrates' death, he had become one of Socrates' close friends,[20] as were a number of others who were thoroughly committed to the importance of the philosophical life. Of these, some were, doubtless, more gifted than others. Since we know that some of these young philosophers went on to develop quite distinctive philosophical views of their own, it is possible that philosophical discussion within the Socratic circle was not limited to discussion of what the "master" thought.

Other members of this group, however, did not turn out so well. Plato indicates that at least some of these men (*Apology* 23c) followed Socrates primarily because they found his questioning and inevitable refutations of others to be amusing. It is curious that Plato never suggests that Socrates saw anything harmful, or even potentially harmful, about allowing these men to mimic him, even if they were doing no more than sharpening their skill at argument. This is puzzling because three men, who were each known to have been closely associated with Socrates at some point in their life, turned out to be among Athens's most unscrupulous and dangerous enemies. First, there was Alcibiades, a man some twenty years younger than Socrates. Alcibiades was born into one of Athens's wealthiest families and was, by all accounts, blessed with uncommon intelligence and extraordinary good looks. According to Plato, Socrates' friendship with Alcibiades was very close and very well known. Indeed, Plato tells us that at least in some sense, the two were lovers (*Gorgias* 481d, *Protagoras* 309a), though not, perhaps, in the physical sense (*Symposium* 215a–219d). Socrates even saved Alcibiades' life during the battle at Potidaea.[21] Alcibiades, however, went on to become one of Athens's most notorious traitors, spending periods of time working with Sparta during the Peloponnesian War, and later with the Greeks' ancestral enemies, the Persians.

Then there were Critias and Charmides, members of one of Athens's most conservative families (Plato's own family: Critias was an uncle, and

Charmides was Critias's cousin—see Plato's *Charmides* 154a-b). These two men, too, were well known to have been Socrates' friends, and though under different circumstances, they also proved themselves to be traitors to the city, like Alcibiades. Critias is generally regarded as the leader of the bloody Thirty Tyrants, and Charmides was also one of this group. We shall have more to say about these three when we discuss Socrates' politics in Chapter 6. Suffice it to say now, though, that at least some of those who enjoyed Socrates' company turned out to be very bad men indeed.

1.3 Socrates' Trial

1.3.1 What We Know About the Trial

Without doubt the single fact about Socrates' life about which we can be most confident is how it ended. In 399 B.C., some five years after the end of the Peloponnesian War and three years after the restoration of the democracy, Socrates was charged by a man named Meletus with having violated a vague law forbidding irreligious conduct. Diogenes Laertius, the third-century A.D. biographer, reports that Favorinus saw the actual charges against Socrates posted in the Metroon, a temple in the agora that housed the city archives.[22] The indictment, we are told, was as follows.

T1.2 Diogenes Laertius, *Lives of the Eminent Philosophers* 2.4:

> Meletus, the son of Meletus, of the deme of Pitthos wrote this indictment and takes this oath against Socrates, the son of Sophroniscus of Alopece: Socrates is guilty of not believing in the gods that the city believes in, and of introducing other, new divinities; and he is guilty of corrupting the youth. The penalty is death.

Although Meletus was the one who actually brought the charges against Socrates, he was supported in the prosecution by two other Athenians, Anytus and Lycon. In their capacity as assistants, or *sunēgoroi*, Anytus and Lycon helped prepare the case against Socrates and, along with Meletus, gave speeches supporting the charges. It is unfortunate that no version of what any of these men actually said against Socrates has come down to us.[23]

There is virtually nothing known about Meletus and Lycon other than their participation in the prosecution of Socrates. We do have a little independent information about Anytus. A master tanner by occupation, he appears to have been, in the words of one commentator, "one of the two or three leading statesmen of the time."[24] Anytus was associated with the moderate democratic faction in Athens and must have been working diligently to restore the traditional democratic institutions in the chaos that followed the end of the Peloponnesian War. It is of some importance to our understanding of the trial that we recognize Anytus as one of the principal proponents of an amnesty passed in 403 B.C., which (with the exception of the Thirty themselves) forbade any prosecutions for crimes alleged to have been committed before 403 B.C.[25] Perhaps more important is the fact that because of his leadership of the opposition to the reign of the Thirty, Anytus must have been regarded as something of a hero in Athens at the time of Socrates' trial.

Before the case against Socrates actually proceeded to trial, Socrates was obliged to appear before the king-archon, a public official whose task it was to decide whether particular charges of impiety had sufficient merit on their face to go before a jury. The law required that any person charged with impiety be tried in what was called an *"agōn timētos,"* a trial in which the penalty for conviction was not established by law. Rather, the prosecutor stipulated what penalty he sought at the end of the indictment, and the defendant, if convicted, was required to offer a "counterpenalty." After hearing what counterpenalty the defendant offered to pay, the jury was then required to take a second vote, in which it decided between the prosecutor's proposal and the defendant's proposal.

We do not know the exact number of jurors who decided Socrates' fate in 399 B.C. Jury sizes during this period tended to vary, from several hundred into the thousands. A typical jury for a trial such as that of Socrates, however, was made up of five hundred, and so it is likely, though by no means certain, that this was the number of jurors Socrates addressed. Jurors were assigned randomly to different courts on trial days. We cannot say that the jury represented a true cross-section of the citizen body, however. Because jurors were paid,[26] it is likely that a disproportionate number of them were older citizens and no longer working or laborers who would have enjoyed taking a day off from work.

The trial itself began in the morning and, by law, had to be completed by the end of the day. It was presided over by the king-archon. Because Athenian legal procedure contained no rules of evidence, the king-archon's function would have been little more than seeing that the appropriate law was read to the jury, keeping the peace as best he could, calling on the various parties to give their speeches and seeing that neither side used up more than its allotted time. It is likely that the prosecution had the morning hours to present its speeches, to call witnesses, and to offer evidence. The defendant was given an equal amount of time in the afternoon to do the same. We might note in passing that although both prosecution and defendant were free to consult professional writers about what would be most effective in court, Athenian law required that the speeches be given by the principals themselves. Advocates or attorneys, as we think of them today, were not allowed to speak to the jury on behalf of anyone.

1.3.2 More Controversial Issues About the Trial

Whether or not Socrates was really guilty of the charges or whether he should even have been brought to trial remained a hotly debated topic for decades after the trial took place and continues to be debated today. Some writers have even produced "accounts" of what Socrates actually said or perhaps could have said in defense. Two of our principal sources, Plato and Xenophon, have provided us with complete works, though they appear to be attempting to accomplish different things. Plato's *Apology*, on its face, appears to report what Socrates actually said to the jurors, though it seems highly unlikely that it could be a word-for-word transcript. Xenophon's *Apology*, by contrast, claims to be an explanation of why Socrates spoke in such an apparently inappropriately haughty way at his trial. Whether either really tells us much about what Socrates said is a matter that scholars continue to debate, although most commentators think that of the two, Plato's version is more likely to be accurate. After all, Plato twice indicates that he was present at the trial to hear what Socrates said, whereas Xenophon was away from Athens at the time of Socrates' trial, leading a Greek military expedition in Persia. Moreover, most scholars have found Plato's version to provide more insight into what might have led to Socrates' prosecution and conviction. But Xenophon's account does provide a certain amount of evidence about what some of those who wrote about the trial were trying to achieve. Xenophon makes it clear that he was *not* writing about what Socrates *could* have said or *should* have said. He was writing down what he was told by someone who did witness the trial, and he tells us that he was doing so in order to set the record straight. Plainly, Xenophon, at least, believed that other accounts were represented as what Socrates actually said. Unfortunately, Xenophon does not mention Plato explicitly, and we cannot even be sure that Plato had completed his version of the speech when Xenophon wrote his. But the single piece of evidence we have in this regard—Xenophon's comment about what he hoped to accomplish, that is, to recount what *was* said and not merely what Socrates *might* have said, reflects a principal goal of those who wrote versions of Socrates' speech.

If Plato's version is faithful at least to the substance and general tenor of the speech Socrates actually gave, Socrates began by explaining why he thought so many people in Athens regarded him as a troublemaker. He had been for many years, he said, the victim of falsehoods that made him out to be either an atheistic nature-philosopher or a humanistic Sophist, who taught students how to lie convincingly. Socrates singled out Aristophanes, whose comedy the *Clouds* features a confused and unprincipled Sophist by the name of "Socrates," as one of the reasons so many people in Athens looked on him with suspicion. But otherwise, Socrates said, he was unable to name any of those who had defamed him for so many years.

According to Plato, Socrates then conceded that there was a sense in which he was indeed a wise man, a fact he came to realize through no less an authority than the oracle of Apollo at Delphi. It seems that once his friend Chaerophon traveled to Delphi to ask the god whether there was anyone wiser than Socrates, and the oracle responded that indeed no one was wiser.[27] In trying to uncover what the oracle could possibly mean, for Socrates said he was unaware of possessing any special wisdom at all, he discovered that there was no shortage of people who thought that they knew what, as Socrates' interrogations inevitably showed, they did not know. Of course, some of those Socrates questioned—the craftsmen—did indeed possess important knowledge: They knew how to practice their crafts. Nevertheless, about the most important of all things, how best to live, they also thought they had knowledge. From these interrogations, Socrates told the jury, he came away convinced that even though he knew nothing, he was wiser than those who did know many wonderful things but who also thought they knew how to live when they did not.

Once he realized that so many people lived in the most shameful ignorance, believing mistakenly that they knew how to live, Socrates undertook what he says was nothing less than a "mission on behalf of the god," whose purpose was to free people from their disastrous pretense of wisdom about the most important of all matters and to exhort them to care about acquiring real wisdom and, through that, the perfection of their souls. That his real purpose behind his philosophizing was to "serve the god" was, according to Plato, the centerpiece of Socrates' defense. Indeed, it was a post he could never willingly leave. After dedicating his life to the service of the god, a service that won him only poverty, the fact that he was being charged with denying the existence of the gods and being a Sophist was an especially bitter irony.

Plato reports that the vote to convict Socrates was quite close, so close in fact that had only thirty more jurors voted for acquittal, Socrates could have returned to his mission, which he vowed he would do if set free (*Apology* 29c-d). If we assume a jury of 500 members, the vote to convict was 280 to 220, since ties were counted as going to the defendant. As noted previously, because Socrates' trial was an *agōn timētos*, Socrates was given the opportunity after his conviction to offer a counterpenalty to Meletus's proposal that he be killed. It is entirely possible that those responsible for bringing Socrates to trial never intended to have the jury vote to execute him. They could very well have thought that Meletus's proposal of death would force Socrates to propose exile or to promise that he would avoid any further engagement in philosophical discussion as his counterpenalty and that the jury would agree to the less harsh way of bringing an end to what they saw as Socrates' corruptive influence on the young.

If Plato's version is to be believed, Socrates began by telling the jury that even though they had just convicted him, he still regarded himself as Athens's greatest benefactor, a fact that, he said, merited his receiving "free meals in the Prytaneum," an honor reserved for Athens's greatest heroes (*Apology* 36d–37a). He then went on patiently to explain why he would not offer any of the counterpenalties the members of the jury were probably expecting him to offer. Imprisonment or imprisonment until a fine could be raised were out of the question, since each would have prevented him from carrying out his "service to the god." The same reasoning precluded the possibility of going into exile. In Plato's account, Socrates told the jury that if his fellow Athenians could not endure his manner of questioning others, surely people in other cities would not endure it either. Going from one city to the next, never welcome anywhere, he says, would be an intolerable life (*Apology* 37c-d).

Socrates did, however, offer a counterpenalty.[28] According to Plato, he initially offered to pay a fine of one mina, which was equal to 100 silver drachmas, well over a pound of silver. He said that, being a poor man, that was all he could afford to pay. That amount was raised to thirty minas by Plato himself and three of Socrates' friends.[29] Many scholars have assumed that Socrates' initial offer and even the subsequent offer were insignificant, perhaps even insulting amounts and Socrates must have known that the jury would not accept either offer. The latter point may well be true, for Socrates had already explained that his mission would require that he return to his questioning of others if he were released and he must also have known that the jury would not convict him of a crime and then release him to go back to doing the very thing that they had just determined by their vote to be a serious crime. But the first point—that even the thirty minas was insignificant and could not have been offered as a serious alternative—is mistaken.[30]

First, we must keep in mind that Socrates had already explained that he would not enter prison voluntarily until an even larger fine was raised. Thus, his friends must have been able to produce the thirty minas immediately. But second, and more importantly, thirty minas was roughly the equivalent of eight and one-half years' wages for a typical Athenian worker—and actually something like twice as much as his jurors were making in pay for their service as jurors. Seen in this light, the counterpenalty Socrates offered could not very well have been seen by the jury as insulting or trivial. Finally, recall that Socrates had made it as clear as he could that he had acted as he had all of those years not because he enjoyed antagonizing people but because he thought he was ordered to engage his fellow citizens in philosophy by the god. This was a duty from which he could not release himself. Assuming, as we think we must assume, that Socrates thought piety required that he do as the god had commanded him, he must have tried to do everything in his power, short of doing anything unjust, to continue to serve the god. His duty to continue to carry out his mission, then, together with his commitment to have the jury decide the case in the way that would serve justice and his conviction that he was utterly innocent of the charges, forces us to conclude that Socrates could not have been indifferent to the outcome of the trial.

Even less plausible is the view sometimes advanced (presumably at least partly on the basis of Xenophon's testimony) that Socrates was actually *trying to goad* the jury into convicting him. On the contrary, the logic of Plato's version of the speech, with the emphasis it places on Socrates' refusal ever to abandon his mission, requires Socrates' trying to gain his acquittal in a way that did no damage to his principles.

Of course, Socrates was unsuccessful and the jury voted, by what margin we cannot say with certainty, to condemn him to death, the penalty Meletus called for.[31] Ordinarily, the penalty would have been carried out the next day. But if Plato is to be believed, the sentence was actually delayed for a period of time because the Athenians were in the midst of their annual festival to commemorate the return of the legendary Theseus to Athens and it was illegal for any executions to take place during this commemoration. Assuming that Plato is to be believed on this point, the delay in executing Socrates is perhaps further evidence that neither Socrates' prosecutor nor the king-archon expected Socrates to offer to pay a fine as his counterpenalty, which, therefore, all but insured his execution upon conviction. Had either Meletus or the king-archon realized how uncompromising Socrates was about his duty to the god to philosophize, one or the other would very probably have scheduled the trial for another time.

In any case, Plato tells us that the brief reprieve allowed Socrates to spend his final days engaging in philosophical discussion with his friends. On his last day, when he was brought a cup containing hemlock extract, a powerful poison, he drank it without hesitation. Plato tells us that as the poison was starting to take effect, Socrates spoke his final words to his old friend Crito: "We ought to make a sacrifice to Aesclepius. See to it and do not forget" (*Phaedo* 118a). Aesclepius was the god who looked out for those who practice the art of healing. Socrates' final remark, then, was that he regarded the end of his life actually to be a blessing. Of course, Plato's account of Socrates' final moments is probably apocryphal, intended to portray the philosopher's bravery in the face of uncertainty. But it is likely that whatever his actual last words were, he was unworried about what death held for him, for he told those jurors who voted for his acquittal: "No harm comes to a good man in life or in death, nor are his affairs neglected by the gods" (*Apology* 41c-d).

1.4 Assessment of the Principal Sources

1.4.1 Aristophanes' Socrates

Socrates' appearance and way of living seems to have provided material for a number of the comic poets in Athens in the fifth century B.C.[32] But as far as we know, Aristophanes made a character named "Socrates" a significant figure in only one of his plays, the *Clouds*, which was first produced in 423 B.C., when Socrates was in his mid-forties. Until fairly recently, commentators have tended to regard the *Clouds* as a complete distortion of the historical Socrates, and thus Aristophanes was usually dismissed as a significant source of information about the historical Socrates. Recently, however, this assessment was significantly revised when scholars began to notice the ways in which details of Aristophanes' portrait match those of the Platonic portrait.

The production of the *Clouds* treated the audience to a wickedly biting satire in which the character "Socrates" and his friend, a character named "Chaerophon" (recall that this was the name of Socrates' friend who asked the oracle at Delphi about him), are presented as operating a school—a *phrontisterion*, or thinking shop, as Aristophanes calls it. A chorus of clouds, which "Socrates" and his students worship as if they were divinities, provide commentary as the action develops. The play turns on the desire of a foolish father, an Attic farmer named "Strepsiades" to have his only son, Pheidippides, educated in the "new logic" of the day, which aims not at establishing truth but at persuasion by whatever means possible. Strepsiades wants his son to master the art of persuasion so that Pheidippides can fend off the creditors who have been hounding Strepsiades to pay off Pheidippides' considerable betting losses. When Pheidippides balks, Strepsiades decides to attend the school himself, where he studies such ridiculous matters as how to measure how far a flea can jump or why gnats hum. For his part, Aristophanes' "Socrates," who makes his entrance suspended in a basket (because the air away from the ground helps him think more clearly, he says), professes a crude brand of naturalism that reduces the powers of the gods to so many natural forces. Consider the following exchange between Socrates, who has just explained that everything can be understood by scientific principles alone, and Strepsiades, who holds the conventional view that gods are the masters of all nature.

T1.3 Aristophanes, *Clouds* 365–378:

SOCRATES: These [referring to scientific principles], then, are the only gods, the rest [i.e., the Olympian deities] are nonsense.

STREPSIADES: What? Is not Zeus an Olympian god?

SOCRATES: What Zeus? Don't be stupid. There is no Zeus.

STREPSIADES: What are you saying? Then who makes it rain? You most explain this to me before anything else.

SOCRATES: These clouds here, and I'll prove it with convincing evidence. Does rain ever fall without clouds in the sky? And yet [according to you], Zeus can make it rain on a bright clear day, when the clouds are away.

STREPSIADES: By Apollo, you're right. I used to think it came from Zeus, pissing through a sieve. But who makes it thunder? That makes me shiver.

SOCRATES: While rolling along, these [i.e., the clouds] make it thunder.

STREPSIADES: How so? Oh, you are daring.

SOCRATES: Whenever they are filled with a great deal of water and are forced by necessity to be carried along and are hung up in the sky filled with water, they produce rain by necessity, and then weighted down and falling into each other, they are ripped apart and go boom!

Although Strepsiades is not entirely sure that he is doing the right thing, he prevails upon his son to begin his study at Socrates' school. Potential student and father are treated to a contest between two unusual characters, Just Logic and Unjust Logic, with the winner gaining Pheidippides as a student. Just Logic appeals to the traditional Athenian values of piety and justice, whereas Unjust Logic argues for pleasure unfettered by moralistic concerns. Here is what Aristophanes has Unjust Logic tell young Pheidippides about being virtuous:

T1.4 Aristophanes, *Clouds*, 1071–1080:

Consider, young man, all that come with this thing self-control, what pleasures you will have to turn your back on—sex, women, gambling, feasting, drinking—why is life worth living if you are bereft of these things? And, what about your natural needs: Well, suppose you commit adultery or you seduce someone, and you get caught. [If you are a follower of self-control], you're ruined. You're not able to speak on your behalf. But by following me, you do what your nature tells you—play and laugh, and think nothing is ever disgraceful.

With such arguments as these, Unjust Logic wins, and Pheidippides is turned over to Socrates to learn how to use it.

Although initially Strepsiades is thoroughly pleased with what he and his son have learned, since he is able to send away two creditors unpaid, his joy soon turns to disgust when Pheidippides, in a shocking display of disrespect, strikes his own father during a disagreement. At the end of the play, Strepsiades comes to the realization that the real culprits in the corruption of his son are the purveyors of the new way of thinking, "Socrates" and his group. The play concludes with Strepsiades burning down the *phrontisterion* and putting an end to Socrates' corruption of his students.

Before we turn to asking why Aristophanes chose to tie the actual Socrates so closely to the action of the play and what we may learn about the historical Socrates from the "Socrates" of the *Clouds,* we must first understand that Aristophanes was using his "Socrates" to stand for virtually the whole group of nature-philosophers and Sophists we discussed earlier. Much of the play, then, is a barely disguised send-up of nature-philosophers, like Anaxagoras, who taught that all natural phenomena occur through the workings of purely mechanical, naturalistic principles. The heavenly bodies, including the sun and the moon, are nothing more than great pieces of effulgent rock, and the earth itself is nothing more than a great mass of rock floating on a bed of air. Although the views of nature-philosophy put into the mouth of Aristophanes' "Socrates" are thoroughly absurd, it is important to understand that Aristophanes was taking on a serious threat to established Greek religious views: As we saw, to the extent that nature-philosophy removed the divine from explanations of the workings of nature, nature-philosophy seemed to support atheism, something that most Athenians in the fifth century B.C. would have found unsettling, to say the least.

The barbs hurled by Aristophanes at the humanistic Sophists were no less sharp. The treatment of father and son in search of a way to make quick money is hilarious. In Aristophanes' hands, the humanistic Sophists are nothing but a collection of avaricious charlatans who prey on the gullible. But as with the treatment of the nature-philosophers, not far beneath the surface of the play is an issue that many conventionally minded Athenians continued to treat with the utmost seriousness: How can one make one's children moral? To these people, who made up the majority of Aristophanes' audience, it was unthinkable that anyone would actually pay a stranger to teach his sons how to be acquisitive and deceitful.

That Aristophanes could have successfully used a single character to stand for such a dizzying array of different views tells us something important about how all the new intellectuals were regarded in Athens.

Whether they were nature-philosophers or humanistic Sophists, they must have been seen as posing a common threat to the moral fabric of Athenian society. Part of Aristophanes' comic brilliance is that he could articulate in such an economical way an idea that may have been not fully formed in the minds of his audience: Although they talk about such different things, all of these new intellectuals are out to destroy the values of right-minded Athenians.

But if Aristophanes could count on his audience's seeing how all of the new intellectualism could be symbolized by just one character, why did he choose the name "Socrates" for that character? Clearly, Aristophanes' "Socrates" could not have been merely a symbol for the "new intellectualism." The whole point of the play is to make fun of the nature-philosophers and Sophists. For the play to work, the audience had to readily grasp the connection between the character "Socrates" and the historical Socrates and between the historical Socrates and the new intellectuals. But what was the latter connection? In what way could the historical Socrates be easily recognized by Aristophanes' audience as one of the new intellectuals?

In trying to answer this question, we should begin by setting forth the likely dissimilarities between the character and the historical person, for unless we are prepared to dismiss altogether the testimony of Plato and Xenophon, the two were very different indeed. For instance, unlike the "Socrates" of the *Clouds,* the "Socrates" we find in the pages of both Plato and Xenophon is a pious believer in the gods. Their "Socrates" never had a school and never accepted pay for his teachings, nor did he ever hold the amoral notions that Aristophanes puts into the mouth of his "Socrates." In these important ways, Aristophanes' "Socrates" fails to fit what every other ancient source says about him. And the suggestion that Socrates would actually have taught others how to distort the truth in order to win a case at law is anathema to the person described in the pages of Plato and Xenophon. Finally, there is the greatest irony of all: The testimony of Plato and Xenophon is solid on the point that Socrates considered the Sophists to be the most pernicious influence in all of Athens.

In what ways, then, were the character and the historical Socrates alike? Ancient sources agree that the historical Socrates cared little for his appearance and for money. No doubt, this is true, but similarities of this sort only explain how the character was like the man. We must see why the audience would have readily seen the historical person as a representative of the whole of the new intellectualism. Part, but only a part, of the answer *may* be found in a reference in Plato's dialogue, *Phaedo* (97c). As we have seen, some commentators argue that Plato is describing the interest the historical Socrates had early in his life in nature-philosophy, which would help to explain why Aristophanes could successfully skewer him as a nature-philosopher in *Clouds*. But even if this passage in the *Phaedo* does provide an accurate account of one stage in the intellectual development of the historical Socrates and even if Socrates' interest in natural science had been notorious (a questionable assumption), we still have no explanation for why Aristophanes' audience could easily identify Socrates with the other major characteristic of the new intellectuals—their immoralism.

To understand this, we must first notice that Plato's and Xenophon's "Socrates" is like Aristophanes' character and many of the most notorious of the Sophists in the following respect: All of our principal sources, to varying degrees, reveal a Socrates who questioned the traditional notion of *aretē* and how it was to be instilled. Of course, Plato and Xenophon insist that he vehemently rejected the sophistical alternative. But insofar as he made it known that most fathers were not able to make their sons virtuous, he was indeed *like the Sophists,* and thus, he really did pose a threat to the commonly accepted view of how to improve the youth of the city. Moreover, in Plato's account, Socrates shared yet another important view with the Sophists. Like them, he thought that *aretē* was a kind of moral expertise and that it could be acquired through the expertise of another. Of course, Socrates never found anyone who possessed that expertise and so regarded the Sophists who professed to have it as frauds.

It is difficult to assess the value of Aristophanes' testimony to a search for the historical Socrates precisely because exaggeration and slander were essential to Aristophanic comedy. But we cannot infer, as some scholars have, that Aristophanes was actually inverting the truth.[33] Aristophanes never treats his other characters, such as the politician Cleon, who was perhaps his favorite target, in that way. To be sure, Aristophanes was able to make his audiences laugh by making them recognize the difference between the actual person they knew and the exaggeration they saw on the stage. Nevertheless, there had to have been at least the perception on the part of a large portion of the audience, and hence, on the part of the Athenian public at large, that the actual person had many of the characteristics that were being exaggerated. Otherwise, making the caricature stand for the actual person simply would not have achieved the desired comic effect. If this is right, we can infer that Aristophanes must have been trading on the fact that there was already at the time of the production of the *Clouds* the widespread perception that Socrates was one of the new intellectuals. No doubt, part of the perception was due to Socrates' concerns with argument and the improvement of people. But if what we have argued is correct, Aristophanes was right in suggesting that Socrates did indeed break with the traditional view of how virtue should be acquired and that he did so in a way that, at least in this respect, correctly placed him in with the Sophists he detested so much in other respects. If so, the study of Aristophanes' "Socrates" will repay careful study.

1.4.2 Xenophon's Socrates

Xenophon was born in Athens around the time that hostilities broke out between Athens and Sparta. He first earned distinction not as a history writer or Socratic apologist but as a military leader. He tells us in the *Anabasis* of his military mission fighting on behalf of Cyrus in a civil war in Persia. Xenophon was instrumental in leading ten thousand Greeks who had been trapped deep in Persia to the sea and, thus, to safety. Later, after serving as an adviser to the Spartans, he retired to Corinth, where he wrote on recent Athenian history, his exploits in the mission in Persia, his interest in horsemanship, and of course, the life of Socrates. But whatever his merits as a writer and though he must have been a devoted friend of Socrates, Xenophon was *not* a philosopher, which helps explain why his account of Socrates' conversations appear philosophically dull.

In spite of the paleness of his portrait of Socrates and even though none of the other principal sources ever mentions Xenophon as one of Socrates' associates, we can be quite confident that before he left Athens in 401 B.C. to join the expedition of Greeks fighting on behalf of Cyrus (see *Anabasis* 3.1.5), Xenophon had been on friendly terms with Socrates for a number of years. But regardless of how well Xenophon knew Socrates, there is some reason to think that Xenophon did not undertake his "Socratic writings" until many years after Socrates' death and then only after a substantial Socratic literature had already been produced to which Xenophon was in part reacting. Of course, even if we accept that Plato began his writing about Socrates shortly after the death of his beloved friend and that Xenophon waited much longer, perhaps as long as thirty years, it does not necessarily follow that Plato's must be the more reliable account. Even if it could be shown, as some have thought, that Xenophon's account is drawn in part from Plato's, this does not prove that Plato's is the more accurate on those points where they disagree. In assessing the accuracy of Xenophon's portrait, we must also ask how well it explains the two most extraordinary facts we do know about the historical Socrates: that Socrates counted as among his closest companions enormously gifted young minds and that Socrates was seen by some as posing such a great danger, at least in some respect, that he was tried and executed by an Athenian jury.

Xenophon writes about a "Socrates" in four different works, and although each of the four is strikingly different in certain respects, none of them fits well with either of the two facts about the historical Socrates we just mentioned. In Xenophon's *Oeconomicus*, for example, Socrates is concerned primarily with dispensing advice about various aspects of farm management. There, "Socrates" is presented as having engaged an old farmer in a lengthy and often tedious conversation about such things as how to prepare a horse to be ridden in combat, how to reward servants to get the most work out of them, and how deep to plant an olive tree. The closest this "Socrates" comes to being a philosopher is when he remarks (in passing) about the value of asking the right questions if one wants a student to learn anything (*Oeconomicus* 10.9.14–15). In the *Oeconomicus*, we see nothing of the powerful mind that would attract young men who wanted to spend their time in *philosophical* discussion, as we know, of course, the historical Socrates did. Indeed, so different is the portrait of Socrates in the *Oeconomicus* that many scholars today have concluded that it was never even intended to reflect the values or interests of the historical Socrates. In that respect, the "Socrates" of that work probably bears less resemblance to the historical Socrates than does the "Socrates" of the *Clouds*. Instead, in the *Oeconomicus* at least, Xenophon is merely using the name of his honored friend as a literary device by means of which Xenophon could set down in writing his own reflections about some of his favorite topics regarding the management of an estate. But this fact only makes the search for the historical Socrates more difficult, for it shows that at least one of Socrates' intimate friends thought it appropriate to create a *character* by the name of "Socrates" who bears little or no resemblance to the historical person.

However, as we noted above, Xenophon's *Apology* makes an explicit attempt to set down for posterity what Socrates' motives were when he spoke as he did at his trial (*Apology* 1). Xenophon, as noted above, was away from Athens serving in the army of Cyrus at the time of the trial and so had to rely, he says, on what he had been told by a certain Hermogenes, a friend of Socrates, who did witness the trial. According to Xenophon, others who had written about Socrates' defense failed to explain Socrates' haughtiness, his *megalēgoria*, before the jury. The explanation, says Xenophon, is that Socrates *wanted* to alienate the jury to insure that they would vote to condemn him, for in that way, he could escape the ravages of old age.

Unlike Plato, who provides us with what seems intended to be a complete version of Socrates' speeches to the jury, Xenophon's account of the speech is sketchy and, in places, disorganized. But in spite of its shortcomings as an account, there is good reason to think that even Xenophon's limited discussion of Socrates' motives at his trial misses the mark at which Xenophon says he is aiming. Whatever else is true of the historical Socrates, he was greatly admired by a host of young men, including Xenophon, for his unshakable commitment to moral virtue. But it is impossible to see how the person Xenophon describes in *Apology*, who

puts his desire to die to escape the infirmities of old age ahead of exhorting others to pursue virtue, would have won the devotion of so many
young philosophers. Unless it can be shown how manipulating the jury
into putting him to death somehow serves the aims of virtue, Xenophon's
account of the stance Socrates took at his trial and why he took it is not to
be believed. At any rate, neither Xenophon nor Plato gives us any reason
for supposing that Socrates suffered from any noticeable loss of his faculties—he may have been seventy years old at the time of his trial, but nothing in Plato or Xenophon reveals any lack of vigor or energy on Socrates'
part. Accordingly, for this reason as well, Xenophon's "explanation" that
Socrates wished to die at this time, because of impending old age, does
not ring true.

The third work of Xenophon centering around a person named
"Socrates" bears the same name as one of Plato's most famous works,
the *Symposium*. Although the two works obviously share a number of
features that could not very well be coincidental, it is impossible to say
with absolute confidence which was written first. Most commentators,
however, now think that Plato's is more likely to have been the original
and that Xenophon was in some sense inspired by the Platonic work
rather than the other way around. Like the Platonic work, Xenophon's
Symposium centers around the speeches Socrates and his acquaintances
give on a common theme, in this case, what each has done to promote
the welfare of the city. That Xenophon's is not representing some scene
that actually took place seems clear. But it is also clear from the number
of ways Xenophon's descriptions fit well with those of Plato[34] that both
men were in a position to know when they were describing accurately
and that Xenophon was trying in earnest to provide an account of how
his friend comported himself among his friends. Although Xenophon's
Symposium provides us with yet more evidence that at least one of our
principal sources was *trying* to capture the historical Socrates,
Xenophon's *Symposium*, at best, tells us in the most general terms about
some of the historical Socrates' most basic commitments.

The fourth work, the *Memorabilia*, can be divided into two parts of un-
equal length: The first part is an explicit defense of the historical Socrates
against the charges he faced in 399 B.C. The second and by far longer part
is a loose collection of Xenophon's reminiscences about Socrates. Like the
first part, it is clearly intended to portray Socrates in a favorable light,
though Xenophon says he is doing so not to answer any specific charges
but to show that Socrates "benefitted his companions, revealing himself
as he was in what he did and by what he discussed with them" (*Memorabilia* 1.3.1). Xenophon's account of Socrates' character is sometimes rich in
detail and often accords well with what other sources say about Socrates.

For example, in the *Memorabilia*, Xenophon goes to some length to convince the reader that Socrates maintained rigid control over his desires at all times.

T1.5 Xenophon, *Memorabilia* 1.3.5–6:

> He educated his body and soul in a way of living in which anyone who followed it, unless he were a spirit, would lead a courageous and safe life and would not worry about his needs. He lived so cheaply that one does not know if anyone could do so little that it would not handle what Socrates needed to be satisfied. He needed only such food that gave him pleasure. And for this he was so prepared that his appetite was the seasoning. Any drink was pleasant to him because he did not drink if he was not thirsty. But if he was invited and wanted to go to dinner, he guarded without difficulty against what is the most common temptation for most people, to be filled beyond one's limit. He counseled those who were not able to do this to guard against what persuades them to eat when they are not hungry and to drink when they are not thirsty. For they destroy the stomach, and the head, and the soul.

This characterization fits well with some of the descriptions we find in Plato,[35] and we have no reason to dismiss them. But the defense of Socrates in the *Memorabilia* against the legal charges he faced at the end of his life is simply not very convincing. Recall, for example, that two of the charges against Socrates were that he did not "believe in the gods the city believes in but introduced new divinities." To this charge, Xenophon's defense in the *Memorabilia* is simply to claim that the charge is false, and obviously so, to anyone who knew Socrates at all.

T1.6 Xenophon, *Memorabilia* 1.1.2–4:

> By what sort of proof did they try to show that? He was often seen sacrificing at home, and often at the common altars of the city, and he didn't hide his use of divination. It was commonly reported that Socrates says that he was guided by a divine sign. It was from this they seemed to me to charge him with introducing new divinities. But he introduced nothing newer into the city than any of the others, who believe in divination and use birds, oracles, omens, and sacrifices. They understand that it is not the birds and the people they happen to meet who know what benefits those who use divination, but that it is the gods, who are giving signs through them; and that's what Socrates thought, too.

Later, Xenophon closes his remarks about Socrates' attitude toward religion as follows.

T1.7 Xenophon, *Memorabilia* 1.1.19–20:

> I am amazed at how the Athenians were at that time persuaded that Socrates was not temperate regarding the gods, for he neither said nor did anything that constituted impiety about the gods, but he said and did those things which anyone by saying and doing them would be and would be thought most pious.

Xenophon's Socrates is *so* conventional, at least with respect to the charge of irreligion, that it is impossible to see why anyone would have thought he posed a threat to the city and, hence, why Meletus, Anytus, and Lycon thought they could make the charges against Socrates stick.

The same objection can be made to the way Xenophon responds to the remaining charge, that Socrates "corrupted the youth."

T1.8 Xenophon, *Memorabilia* 1.2.1–8:

> But it is also amazing to me that some were convinced that Socrates corrupted the youth. He was in the fullest control of all human beings of his passions and appetites, and he had the most endurance when it came to heat and cold and every hardship, and he was trained to need moderation so that he needed quite little and was easily satisfied. Since he was this sort of person, how did he make others impious, lawbreakers, gluttons, philanderers, and weak, and soft with regard to hardship? On the contrary, he stopped many of them and created a desire for virtue, giving them hope that if they cultivated themselves, they would be good and noble. And yet he never undertook to be a teacher of this, but rather it is evident that by being the sort of person he was, he made those with whom he spent his time hope that by imitating him they would become such a person, too. Moreover, he did not fail to care about his body and he did not approve of those who did neglect theirs. He rejected overexertion and then overeating, whereas he approved of sufficient exertion that the soul enjoys. He said that such was conducive to a healthy disposition and the care of the soul. He was neither pretentious nor a showoff about fine garments or shoes, or his way of living, nor did he endow his friends with a love of money. He kept the desires of others in check, he did not create his own desire for money . . . he was confident that those of his companions who demonstrated what he approved would be his friend and friends with each other throughout their entire lives. How could such a man corrupt the youth, unless concern for virtue is corruptive?

The "Socrates" we find in the *Memorabilia* is such a model of decorum, according to the average person's sense of what morality requires, that it is impossible to see why any Athenians would have wanted him silenced, much less put to death. At best, then, we would have to say that Xenophon's attempt to reveal the character and activities of the historical Socrates is distorted and incomplete. It leaves out precisely what the historical record requires: an explanation for why the Athenians found it necessary to put Socrates to death in the first place.

Xenophon's portrait in the *Memorabilia* also fails to explain why fine young minds would have been attracted to Socrates in the first place. Rarely do we find the "Socrates" of the *Memorabilia* approaching moral issues as philosophical issues. On the contrary, as a number of commentators have pointed out, Xenophon's "Socrates" tends to accept uncritically conventional Athenian moral values and to preach to his friends about the importance of embracing those values. Raising questions about the relationship between morality and the good life or about what moral virtue consists in seems, for the most part, foreign to the man Xenophon commends to us. And when Xenophon's Socrates does present arguments, they are typically uncontroversial and uninspiring. The following exchange in the *Memorabilia* between Socrates and Euthydemus, one of his companions, is typical.

T1.9 Xenophon, *Memorabilia* 4.2.24–30:

Socrates said, tell me, Euthydemus, have you ever gone to Delphi?

And he said, yes, by god, twice.

And did you take note of the inscription somewhere on the temple, "Know Thyself"?

Yes.

And did you pay attention to the inscription or did you take heed of it and try to figure out who you are?

No, by god, I didn't, he said. I think I know this well enough already. I think I could scarcely know anything else if I did not know myself.

Do you think one knows himself if one knows only his name, or is he like those who buy horses who do not think they know what they want to know before they consider whether the horse is docile or hard to train or strong or weak or whether it is quick or slow and how he is with respect to all the other things that make a horse useful or useless, that is, does the one who knows himself in considering what sort of usefulness he has as a human, does he know what his powers are?

It seems to me, then, that one who does not know what his own powers are does not know himself.

Is it obvious, he said, that through knowing themselves men enjoy many good things, and through being mistaken about themselves, they suffer many evils? Those who know themselves know what is useful for them and grasp what is in their power and what is not, and by doing what they understand they are able to do, they acquire what they need and do well, and avoiding what they do not understand, they avoid doing what is evil. By being able to test other men, and through their acquaintance with other men, they acquire good things and guard against evils . . . .

Euthydemus said, you can be sure that it is clear to me that one must work hard to know oneself.

What is so disappointing about this brief interchange is not Socrates' definition of self-knowledge as knowledge of what one is able to do and not do, though Plato's Socrates rejects this definition in the *Charmides*. Rather, what is so disappointing is the picture of Socrates as a teacher who is convinced he knows the right answers, who does nothing to examine the obvious objections that might be raised to such a thesis, and who simply *tells*, in this case, a not very inquisitive Euthydemus, the right answer. It is ironic, to say the least, that here we find Xenophon's Socrates *telling* a disciple that it is through the *testing* of other men that one gains real benefit. Yet rarely in Xenophon do we ever find Socrates actually engaging in the activity he claims provides the consummate rewards for its practitioner. To the powerful and incisive philosophical minds that we know were attracted to the historical Socrates, the "Socrates" of the *Memorabilia* appears ploddingly dogmatic and arbitrary.

1.4.3 Plato's Socrates

If Xenophon's "Socrates" makes us wonder why Socrates was ever considered a serious threat to the city and why serious philosophers would have been attracted to him, Plato's "Socrates" makes the answers to these questions perfectly obvious. Like Xenophon, Plato knew and admired Socrates, although just how and when Plato became acquainted with Socrates is not known. One colorful story about their first meeting is told by Diogenes Laertius (3.5–6). According to Diogenes, when Plato was a young man of about twenty, he was intent on becoming a tragic poet. After listening to Socrates only one time, however, he proceeded to burn his poetry and resolved to follow Socrates. Unfortunately, because Diogenes is our only source, we have no good, independent reason to think that the first encounter of the two great men really happened in this way at all.

We must exercise special caution, however, when we refer to "Plato's Socrates," for Plato made many of his dialogues revolve around a character named "Socrates." The problem is that the character seems to hold very different, sometimes even incompatible, views in different dialogues. Which, then, if any, of the views expressed by "Socrates" in Plato's dialogues most closely resembles the philosophical views of the historical Socrates? Fortunately, the problem is not as daunting as it may at first appear. For many years, commentators have noticed that certain philosophical and stylistic features are found in some dialogues and not others. This is not surprising, given that Plato's career as a writer continued for over half a century. On the basis of such differences in the dialogues, there has come to be a fairly broad agreement among commentators (though never without dissent) that based on similarities in style and thematic content, three fairly distinct groups emerge, with a number of dialogues, apparently, marking transitions between groups. In recent years, the validity of dividing the dialogues into groups has been bolstered by careful, computer-assisted analysis of Plato's style of writing.[36] Of course, this much would not tell us the order in which the three groups were written. But if we assume that the *Laws*, which was unfinished, was written toward the end of Plato's career and the *Apology* was written relatively early in Plato's career, we can order the groups chronologically as follows:

The early group: *Apology, Crito, Charmides, Euthyphro, Greater Hippias, Lesser Hippias, Ion, Laches, Lysis, Protagoras,* and Book I of the *Republic.*

The first transitional group: *Cratylus, Euthydemus, Gorgias, Menexenus,* and *Meno.*

The middle group: *Symposium, Phaedo, Phaedrus,* and Books 2–10 of the *Republic.*

Second transitional group: *Parmenides* and *Theaetetus.*

The late group: *Sophist, Politicus, Philebus, Timaeus, Critias,* and *Laws.*

We should note that most scholars have given up on trying to order the dialogues within a period chronologically. Moreover, the fact that Plato's dialogues can be grouped in this way does not, by itself, tell us whether any of the groups contains dialogues with a character named "Socrates" who was intended by Plato to represent the views of the historical Socrates. That the views of the historical Socrates can be found in the pages of Plato's early and first transitional stage dialogues, however, is the conclusion defended by Gregory Vlastos, the most influential figure among those who have seriously searched for the historical Socrates.[37] Vlastos detailed a number of differences between the character Socrates (whom Vlastos calls "Socrates$_e$") in the early and first transitional dialogues and the character Socrates (whom Vlastos calls "Socrates$_m$") who came later. Although some of these differences had long been noted before, Vlastos's work showed just how many and striking these differences really are. If Vlastos is right, there are ten salient characteristics of the Socrates of the early and first transitional groups (Socrates$_e$) that are missing from the subsequent groups.

Several examples of these differences will suffice for our purposes: First, Socrates$_e$ is concerned almost exclusively with moral issues such as the nature of justice or courage. But though various important metaphysical and epistemological issues are never far below the surface, Socrates$_e$ seems to have no interest in uncovering them and subjecting them to scrutiny. Socrates$_m$, however, is interested in virtually the entire spectrum of philosophical issues, from questions about ethics and politics to questions about the most abstruse metaphysical and epistemological issues.

In the *Apology*, Socrates$_e$ recounts for the jury the story of how his friend Chaerophon once inquired of the Delphic oracle whether there was anyone wiser than Socrates, and the oracle, to his utter surprise, replied that no one was wiser. Socrates says that he was perplexed because he was "not aware of being wise in any way, great or small" (21b). He goes on to say that he subsequently discovered that he was indeed wiser than many, for at least he was aware that he did not know anything of real importance, whereas the others whom he questioned thought they possessed moral knowledge and, of course, did not. Such professions of ignorance, which are common in the early works,[38] have sometimes been dismissed as examples of Socrates' famous irony. But as we will see, regardless of whether we think we can draw any inference from what the Socrates of the early dialogues says about his lack of knowledge about the historical Socrates, there is excellent reason to believe that Plato intends the professions of ignorance in the early works to be sincere. Moreover, because Socrates is the "wisest of human beings," it is clear that he is deeply skeptical about our capacity to have such knowledge. As a result, Socrates insists that he is not a teacher (*Apology* 33a).

Socrates$_m$, however, argues that moral knowledge is possible and offers several accounts as to how it might be attained. Moreover, although he still does not ever claim to have such knowledge himself, he is often willing to teach others in quite substantive ways. In the following passage from Book 4 of the *Republic*, written as part of the middle period, Socrates virtually *tells* his interlocutor, Glaucon, what he, Socrates, takes justice to be.

T1.10 Plato, *Republic* 4.433a-b:

(Socrates speaking) [In our earlier discussions] we stated, and often repeated, if you remember, that everyone must practice one of the occupations in the city for which he is naturally best suited.

(Glaucon responds) Yes, we did keep saying that.

Moreover, we've heard many people say and have often said ourselves that justice is doing one's own work and not meddling with what isn't one's own.

Yes, we have.

Then, it turns out that this doing one's own work—provided that it comes to be in a certain way—is justice.

A third striking contrast can be seen in the different philosophical methods employed in the early and middle periods. In the early works, Socrates$_e$ philosophizes by using a style that has come to be known as the "elenchus" or "elenchos" (from the Greek word *elenchos*, which means "to examine" or "to refute"). When someone with whom Socrates$_e$ is talking makes a moral claim, Socrates$_e$ will put the interlocutor to the test by asking questions and insisting that the interlocutor answer in accordance with his own sincere beliefs. Using these answers as premises, Socrates$_e$ constructs the elenchos, whose conclusion contradicts the interlocutor's initial moral claim. In the middle and late dialogues, however, the elenchos virtually disappears. In the transition between the two periods, Plato seems to have come to the conclusion that knowledge can be achieved—though not easily—if we can gain a cognitive "vision" of the transcendent realities he calls the "Forms." The ultimate goal of inquiry, upon which all knowledge depends, is what Socrates$_m$ calls the "unhypothetical first principle of everything" (*Republic* VI. 510b, 511b), which most scholars take to be the Form of the Good. Obviously, the philosophical method of the middle period is far more optimistic and ambitious in its scope than is the elenchos we find used as Socrates$_e$' only approach to philosophical questions. What explains Plato's confidence that the philosopher can acquire knowledge is an elaborate metaphysics and epistemology that Plato seems to have developed some twenty years after Socrates' death, probably as the result of Plato's having met philosophers and mathematicians during travels in Italy. Whereas these doctrines are absolutely central to the philosophy of the middle dialogues, they are nowhere in evidence in the early period works.

That Plato's thought underwent significant changes as Plato matured few scholars would dispute. But this hardly warrants any inference about the relationship between Socrates$_e$ and the historical Socrates. After all, one might argue, some of the historical Socrates' most philosophically acute associates, men such as Aeschines and Aristippus, developed quite distinctive views of their own. Why might it not be the case, then, that Plato's early dialogues represent nothing more than Plato's first philosophical explorations and that he simply chose to name the character around whom each of these works revolved after his beloved friend Socrates? If so, Plato's early works may really express little more of the philosophical outlook of the historical Socrates than do those middle and late period works in which Socrates also appears as the central character. Plainly, we would need some additional, *independent* reason to say that we have learned something significant about the historical Socrates from the character "Socrates" of Plato's early dialogues.

Some scholars think we can obtain just the confirmation we need from what Aristotle says about the historical Socrates. Aristotle was born in remote northern Greece in 384 B.C., some fifteen years after the death of Socrates. But even though Aristotle did not know Socrates, it can be argued, he was surely in a position to know the difference between what the historical Socrates believed and what some highly fictionalized character in Plato's early works is made to say, for Aristotle must have known Plato quite well, having lived at Plato's Academy first as a student and later as an instructor for nearly twenty years. And when Aristotle started his own school, around 332 B.C., he was surrounded by philosophers and intellectuals of all sorts who were in a position to distinguish between what the historical Socrates thought and what Plato put into the mouth of a character named Socrates. Commentators who see the historical Socrates in Plato's early dialogues argue that Aristotle distinguishes between what he attributes simply to "Socrates," appearing to be referring to the historical Socrates, and what he attributes to "the Socrates" (using the definite article "the") who appears in Plato's middle and later period works. And what he says about (the historical) Socrates fits remarkably well with what we find in Plato's early dialogues. Moreover, although Aristotle was clearly interested in showing why his own views were superior to all others, including those of the historical Socrates, were he to have distorted the views of the historical Socrates too greatly, many others, who also knew what the historical Socrates actually thought, would have been in a position to discredit Aristotle's remarks.

This argument, however, does not enjoy universal acceptance.[39] Skeptics point out that there is really very little evidence that Aristotle was relying on any evidence other than the early dialogues in making his claims about what the historical Socrates, as opposed to Plato's Socrates, believed. On the contrary, what evidence he does cite in favor of a distinction seems to be drawn exclusively, or almost exclusively, from Plato's early dialogues. Even if Aristotle was "in a position to know" what the historical Socrates actually thought, there is no evidence that he relied on testimony other than Plato's. Thus, when Aristotle refers to what "Socrates" believed, Aristotle may just be reporting Plato's initial views after all, whether Aristotle realized it or not.

Of course, even those who fail to share this skepticism would be quick to point out that all of Plato's dialogues—including those of the early period—are to some extent works of fiction. Even the staunchest supporters of the view that we see the historical Socrates in the pages of Plato's early dialogues agree that the dialogues are hardly verbatim reports. In fact, with the exception of the conversation Socrates has with Meletus in

Plato's *Apology*, there is no reason to think that Socrates actually held any of the conversations Plato writes about.[40] Even if we are persuaded by Vlastos's argument, we can say at best only that the historical Socrates probably did hold the doctrines we find him defending in the early dialogues of Plato and that the historical Socrates is not entirely lost in the darkness of ages gone by. But neither can we say we really *know* what this philosopher, who inspired so many to take up the philosopher's life, really believed.

Although we shall refer to "Socrates" and "his views" in what follows, we are really exploring the views of Plato's Socrates$_e$, the Socrates of Plato's early dialogues. To what extent Plato's character expresses the views of the historical person, we do not presume to say beyond what we have just speculated. But as we hope to show, Plato's Socrates$_e$ maintains a fascinating and powerful philosophy, one that is well worth our careful attention regardless of its faithfulness to the views of the great philosopher and Plato's friend of the same name.

Notes

1. The most recent published collection of Plato's works includes not only all of the dialogues now generally regarded as authentic (called the "canonical dialogues") but also all of the *dubia* and *spuria*, which are noted as such. See Cooper (1997).

2. Aristotle, *Poetics* 1447b11.

3. For an interesting, though somewhat speculative, discussion of some of the Socratic writings, see Clay (1994), 26–32.

4. Whether we can draw inferences about Aeschines' views from the small fragments that remain of his writings remains a topic of scholarly dispute. Those interested in a detailed defense of the position that we can draw such inferences should consult Kahn (1994), 87–106.

5. For more on the status of women in fifth-century B.C. Athens, see Roberts (1984), 22–26.

6. The two authors in question are Pausanius (1.22.8, 9.35.2) and Diogenes Laertius (2.19). Both of these writers lived and wrote in the middle of the third century A.D.

7. An excellent discussion of elementary education in fifth-century B.C. Athens can be found in Roberts (1984), 94–101.

8. Excellent detailed discussions of the sophistic movement in Athens and of individual sophists can be found in Guthrie (1971b) and Kerford (1981).

9. Plato is not the only Socratic writer who claims that Socrates once took a serious interest in nature-philosophy. Diogenes Laertius says that Socrates was at one time the pupil of Archelaus, a fifth-century B.C. nature-philosopher (2.16, 2.19, and 2.23) and reports other testimony that Socrates had been the pupil of Anaxagoras, another fifth-century B.C. nature-philosopher (2.19). As we have seen, however, we have no good reason to accept any of Diogenes' specific claims.

10. In Plato's *Cratylus* (384a-c), however, Plato may well be simply joking when he has Socrates say that he, Socrates, could afford only Prodicus's one-drachma course.

11. For an excellent brief discussion of the rise of the Athenian Empire, see Roberts (1984), 82–93.

12. Thucydides, *The History of the Peloponnesian War*, 1.17.3.

13. See Xenophon, *Memorabilia* 2.6.26, 3.14, 3.7.5–9, and 3.9.10. We discuss Socrates' attitude toward Athenian democracy in Chapter 6.

14. The fact that Socrates served in the army as a hoplite, a heavily armed soldier, certainly suggests that he was not impoverished, at least at the time of the Battle of Delium in 424 B.C. (see Plato, *Symposium* 220e–221a), for the full armor was relatively expensive and Athens's truly poor could not afford to serve as hoplites. On the other hand, it is possible that the armor may have been a gift from someone, though were this true, it is odd that no one refers to it.

15. For a more detailed discussion of Socrates' appearance, see Brickhouse and Smith (1989), 14–15.

16. We believe that this can be inferred from the fact that Aristophanes' *Clouds*, the play in which one of the central comic characters is named "Socrates," was first performed in 423 B.C. Calling the character in the play "Socrates" would not have been amusing had not the historical Socrates already gained a reputation in Athens as a somewhat eccentric intellectual.

17. See Roberts (1984), 22–24.

18. Myrto is mentioned only in later, and hence unreliable sources. Reference to the marriage is made in Diogenes Laertius (2.26), Plutarch, *Aristeides* 27, and Athenaeus 555D–556A. More credible sources, however, say nothing about the woman.

19. We discuss Socrates' *daimonion* in greater detail in Sec. 7.4.

20. We can infer this from the fact that Plato tells us (*Apology*, 38a) that he was one of the four persons who were willing to put up a substantial sum of money for Socrates to pay as a fine after his conviction and that had he not been ill, he would have been present when Socrates was executed (see *Phaedo* 59b).

21. The story of Socrates saving the life of Alcibiades during the campaign at Potidaea is recounted in Plato's *Symposium* 220d-e.

22. We have good reason to think that this statement of the charges is accurate because it very closely resembles the statement we find in Plato's *Apology* (24b-c). As we argue below, Plato would have known what the actual charges were and would have no reason to change them in his version of Socrates' speech.

23. For reasons we explain further in Chapter 6 (see Sec. 6.3.4), it is important not to confuse the *Accusation of Socrates* attributed to Polycrates with any of the speeches made at the actual trial.

24. Burnet (1924), 99.

25. According to A. E. Taylor, the legislation of 403 B.C. also called for the complete recodification of the laws, a process that was not completed until 401–400 B.C. See Taylor (1953), 102–103. This may explain why Anytus did not move against Socrates earlier.

26. At about the time of Socrates' trial, jurors were paid three obols a day, not a large sum but enough to allow laborers to take time off from work to serve on ju-

ries, which many apparently did. For more on this point, see MacDowell (1978), 34–35.

27. In Xenophon's version of the story, when questioned about Socrates, the oracle announced that no one was "more free, more just, or more temperate" (*Apology* 14). Xenophon makes no attempt to show how the oracle may have influenced Socrates to do anything that led to his trial, however.

28. In Plato's account, at least. According to Xenophon's version, Socrates refused to offer a counterpenalty, on the ground that doing so would be tantamount to an admission of guilt. According to Xenophon, Socrates actually wanted to be convicted and executed, since he had decided that at his age, his life could only become a misery of poor health and loss of faculties, and it would be better to die as a martyr than to live into such decrepitude.

29. In the much later account given by Diogenes Laertius, Socrates first offered to pay a small fine (Diogenes reports two different versions of the actual amount) but then changed his mind and offered free meals in the Prytaneum as his actual proposal. Several aspects of Diogenes' account of the end of the trial, however, are inconsistent.

30. A detailed account of the purchasing power of thirty minas can be found in Brickhouse and Smith (1989), 225–234.

31. Diogenes Laertius reports that the margin of votes going against Socrates was actually greater in the second vote than in the first, the vote to convict (2.42). This requires the very unlikely supposition, however, that some of those who were prepared to allow Socrates to go entirely unpunished (by finding him innocent in the first vote) somehow decided to condemn him to death in their next vote. Some evidence, from Plato, can be given for supposing that the second vote was exactly the same as the first vote, which makes more sense. See Brickhouse and Smith (1989), 231–232.

32. Brickhouse and Smith (1989), 16.

33. This point is developed in Arrowsmith (1969), 6.

34. For more on this point, see Guthrie (1971a), 24.

35. See, for example, Plato's description of Socrates' mastery of his appetites in the *Symposium* 219b–220c.

36. A good introduction to employment of "stylometric" technique is Brandwood (1992).

37. Vlastos (1991), 45–106.

38. There are many passages in Plato in which Socrates professes to lack wisdom. See, for examples, *Apology* 20c, 21d, 23b; *Charmides* 165b-c; *Euthyphro* 5a-c, 15c; *Laches* 186b-c; *Lysis* 212a; *Republic* 1.337e. We discuss Socrates' many disavowals of knowledge in Chapter 3.

39. For searching criticisms of Vlastos's account, see J. Beversluis (1993), and Debra Nails (1993).

40. The *Apology* may well be an exception, for as we have noted, Plato (and others who wrote about the trial) may have thought that what Socrates said to the jury should be written down. But even if that was part of Plato's motivation in undertaking to write the *Apology*, his version presumably only captures the substance of what Socrates said at his trial. To the best of our knowledge, however, there is nothing said or done in Plato's *Apology* that could not have been said or done at the actual trial.

Suggested Readings

On the "Socratic Problem"

The magisterial work of the late Gregory Vlastos (1991) provides perhaps the most comprehensive and compelling argument for the identification of the historical Socrates with the Socrates we find in Plato's early dialogues. Those who follow Vlastos's lead on this issue include Kraut (1992, 1–50) and Irwin (1995). Skeptical responses to Vlastos's specific argument may be found in Beversluis (1993) and Nails (1993). A position that is the opposite of Vlastos's may be found in Montuori (1981), who argues that *none* of our sources on Socrates are reliable and so all that remains of Socrates is what he calls "a myth." Lacey (1971) inclines to the identification of the historical Socrates with the Socrates of Plato's early dialogues but warns that "no source can be trusted or ignored entirely, and no source can be assumed to be equally reliable throughout" (49). Defenders of the reliability of the Aristophanic portrait include Nussbaum (1980) and Edmunds (1985). A defense of the reliability of Xenophon (which also critiques Vlastos's arguments) can be found in Morrison (1988).

On the Trial of Socrates

Strikingly similar accounts of Plato's version of Socrates' defense (in the *Apology*) are offered in Brickhouse and Smith (1989) and Reeve (1989). Both treat Plato's account as at least historically possible and even plausible. A very different assessment can be found in de Strycker and Slings (1994), which argues that Plato's *Apology* is best viewed as a literary creation by Plato. Brickhouse and Smith (1989) offer extensive reviews of the legal and historical circumstances of the trial as well.

What Socrates Does, and How He Does It

2.1 Socrates as a Teacher

2.1.1 Does Socrates Use the "Socratic Method" of Teaching?

Socrates is widely regarded as one of the great teachers of all time. There is even a "method" of teaching named after him—the so-called Socratic method, in which one teaches by asking leading questions that guide students to discovering the subject matter rather than simply telling the students what they need to know. It is easy to understand why this method of teaching is known as "Socratic," for in Plato's dialogues, what we see Socrates doing most is asking questions. Only rarely do we find him "lecturing" to anyone, though we do see something like this in Plato's *Apology*, in which Socrates gives three speeches to the jurors at his trial. Yet even in the *Apology*, we find Socrates asking questions (from 24b to 28a), when he cross-examines his prosecutor, Meletus. In much of the rest of his presentation to the jurors, he talks about how he has spent his life asking questions (and how his doing so has so often annoyed those questioned). Moreover, only rarely do we find Socrates answering others' questions. There are brief episodes in which he does; for example, Socrates is questioned by Polus in Plato's *Gorgias* from 462b to 466e and then again from 470b to 474c. Polus quickly proves not to be up to the task of turning the tables on Socrates, however, and soon ends up answering Socrates' questions. In other cases, Socrates answers questions he imagines someone asking him; for example, in the *Crito*, he "submits" to being questioned by an imaginary personification of the laws of Athens (50b-c; see also **T2.5**, below). But, of course, even here it is actually Socrates asking all of the questions.

But is Socrates a practitioner of what we have come to call the "Socratic method" of teaching? There are several reasons for thinking that he was not. First, those who employ the "Socratic method" of teaching already know all of the answers to their questions and simply try to lead or guide their students, via the questions, to these answers. But in Plato's dialogues, every time the issue comes up, Socrates explicitly denies knowing the answers to his own questions.

T2.1 *Charmides* 165b-c:

(Socrates speaking) [Y]ou are talking to me as though I professed to know the answers to my own questions and as though I could agree with you if I really wished. This is not the case—rather, because of my own ignorance, I am continually investigating in your company whatever is put forward. However, if I think it over, I am willing to say whether I agree or not.

T2.2 *Laches* 186e:

SOCRATES: Socrates denies having any knowledge of the matter or being competent to decide which of you speaks the truth, because he denies having been a discoverer of such things or having been anyone's pupil in them.

T2.3 *Laches* 200e–201a:

SOCRATES: Indeed, Lysimachus, I should be very wrong in refusing to aid in the improvement of anybody. And if I had shown in this conversation that I had a knowledge which Nicias and Laches have not, then I admit that you would be right in inviting me to perform this duty, but as we are all in the same perplexity, why should one of us be preferred to another?

T2.4 *Lysis* 212a:

(Socrates speaking) When I see you and Lysis together, I'm really amazed; I think it's wonderful that you two have been able to acquire this possession so quickly and easily while you're so young. Because you have, in fact, each of you gotten the other as a true friend—and quickly too. And here I am, so far from having this possession that I don't even know how one person becomes the friend of another.

T2.5 *Greater Hippias* 286c-d:

SOCRATES: But now answer me a short question about that; it's a fine thing you reminded me. Just now someone got me badly stuck when I was finding fault with parts of some speeches for being foul, and praising other parts as fine. He questioned me this way, really insultingly: "Socrates, how do *you* know what sorts of things

are fine and foul? Look, would you be able to say what the fine is?"
And I, I'm so worthless, I was stuck and I wasn't able to answer
him properly. As I left the gathering I was angry and blamed
myself, and I made a threatening resolve, that whomever of you
wise men I met first, I would listen and learn and study, then
return to the questioner and fight the argument back. So, as I say,
it's a fine thing you came now. Teach me enough about what the
fine is itself, and try to answer me with the greatest precision
possible, so I won't be a laughingstock again for having been
refuted a second time.

T2.6 *Meno* 71b-d:

MENO: Socrates, do you really not know what virtue is? Are we to
report this to the folk back home about you?

SOCRATES: Not only that, my friend, but also that, as I believe, I have
never yet met anyone who did know.

MENO: How so? Did you not meet Gorgias when he was here?

SOCRATES: I did.

MENO: Did you then not think that he knew?

SOCRATES: I do not altogether remember, Meno, so that I cannot tell
you now what I thought then. Perhaps he does know; you know
what he used to say, so you remind me of what he said. You tell me
yourself, if you are willing, for surely you share his views.

Today, when we say that someone uses the "Socratic method," we assume that the person is teaching (or at least attempting to teach) *something,* that is, the person is attempting to lead or guide to an understanding of some subject that they do not have. Socrates not only invariably
denies being a teacher (**T2.7**, **T2.8**; see also **T2.3**, above), he also often
claims to engage those he proposes to question not as their teacher but as
their student (**T2.9**, **T2.10**, **T2.11**; see also **T2.4**, **T2.5**, **T2.6**, but compare
T2.2, above) and says not that he gives those he questions new knowl-
edge or understanding but only reveals to them their lack of such knowledge or understanding (**T2.12**, **T2.13**, **T2.14**).

T2.7 *Apology* 19d (immediately follows **T7.7**):

(Socrates speaking) If you have heard from anyone that I undertake to teach
people and charge a fee for it, that is not true either.

T2.8 *Apology* 33a-b (immediately precedes **T2.13**):

(Socrates speaking) I have never been anyone's teacher. If anyone, young or old, desires to listen to me when I am talking and dealing with my own concerns, I have never begrudged this to anyone, but I do not converse when I receive a fee and not when I do not. I am equally ready to question the rich and the poor if anyone is willing to answer my questions and listen to what I say. And I cannot justly be held responsible for the good or bad conduct of these people, as I never promised to teach them anything and have not done so. If anyone says that he has learned anything from me, or that he heard anything privately that the others did not hear, be assured that he is not telling the truth.

T2.9 *Euthyphro* 4e–5a (overlaps with **T3.9**)[1]:

SOCRATES: Whereas, by Zeus, Euthyphro, you think that your knowledge of the divine, and of piety and impiety, is so accurate that, when those things happened as you say, you have no fear of having acted impiously in bringing your father to trial?

EUTHYPHRO: I should be of no use, Socrates, and Euthyphro would not be superior to the majority of men, if I did not have accurate knowledge of all such things.

SOCRATES: It is indeed most important, my admirable Euthyphro, that I should become your pupil.

T2.10 *Lesser Hippias* 369d-e:

SOCRATES: Hippias, I don't dispute that you are wiser than I, but it is always my custom to pay attention when someone is saying something, especially when the speaker seems to me to be wise. And because I desire to learn what he means, I question him thoroughly and examine and place side-by-side the things he says, so I can learn. If the speaker seems to me to be some worthless person, I neither ask questions nor do I care what he says. This is how you'll recognize whom I consider wise. You'll find me being persistent about what's said by this sort of person, questioning him so that I can benefit by learning something.

T2.11 *Lesser Hippias* 372a-c:

SOCRATES: You see, Hippias, that I'm telling the truth when I say that I'm persistent in questioning wise people. It may be that this is the only good trait I have and that all the others I have are quite worthless. I make mistakes as to the way things are, and don't know how they are—I find it sufficient evidence of this that when I am with one of you who are highly regarded for wisdom, and to whose wisdom all the Greeks bear witness, I show myself to know nothing. [. . .] But I have one wonderfully good trait, which saves me: I'm not ashamed to learn. I inquire and ask questions and I'm very grateful to the one who answers, and I've never failed in gratitude to anyone. I've never denied it when I've learned anything, pretending that what I learned was my own discovery. Instead, I sing the praises of the one who taught me as a wise person, and proclaim what I learned from him.

T2.12 *Apology* 23b (part of longer quote in **T2.20**):

(Socrates speaking) So even now I continue this investigation as the god bade me—and I go around seeking out anyone, citizen or stranger, whom I think wise. Then if I do not think he is, I come to the assistance of the god and show him that he is not wise.

T2.13 *Apology* 33c (immediately follows **T2.8**; immediately precedes **T7.12**):

(Socrates speaking) Why then do some people enjoy spending considerable time in my company? You have heard why, gentlemen of the jury, I have told you the whole truth. They enjoy hearing those questioned who think they are wise, but are not. And this is not unpleasant.

T2.14 *Euthyphro* 15c-e:

SOCRATES: So we must investigate again from the beginning what piety is, as I shall not willingly give up before I learn this. Do not think me unworthy, but concentrate your attention and tell the truth. For you know it, if any man does, and I must not let you go, like Proteus, before you tell me. If you had no clear knowledge of piety and impiety, you would never have ventured to prosecute your old father for murder on behalf of a servant. For fear of the gods you would have been afraid to take the risk lest you should not be acting rightly, and would have been ashamed before men, but now I know well that you believe you have clear knowledge of piety and impiety. So tell me, my good Euthyphro, and do not hide what you think it is.

Socrates, then, unlike one who uses the "Socratic method" of teaching, claims not to know the subject he asks questions about, claims not to be teaching when he asks his questions, claims that he asks more as a student seeking knowledge than as a teacher who has it, and the most obvious result of his questioning is not that those he questions come to possess some new knowledge or understanding. Instead, Socrates reveals that some knowledge or understanding those questioned claimed to have was only confusion, ignorance, or pretense. But each of these points raises several questions.

2.1.2 Socrates' Claims Not to Know and the Irony Problem

One problem with the way Socrates characterizes himself is often noted by those who read Plato's early dialogues: For someone who claims only to be a seeker of knowledge, who claims not to know the answers to his own questions, Socrates is extraordinarily good at finding just the right issues to pursue and just the right questions to ask to confound his interlocutors and reveal their ignorance. If he does not have the knowledge he finds lacking in his interlocutors, how can he be such a virtuoso at revealing others' ignorance? In the *Apology*, we actually find Socrates himself explicitly acknowledging this suspicion about what he does.

T2.15 *Apology* 22e–23a (immediately precedes T2.19):

> (Socrates speaking) As a result of this investigation, gentlemen of the jury, I acquired much unpopularity, of a kind that is hard to deal with and is a heavy burden; many slanders came from these people and a reputation for wisdom, for in each case the bystanders thought that I myself possessed the wisdom that I proved my interlocutor did not have.

There have been a variety of ways in which scholars have attempted to deal with Socrates' disclaimers of knowledge. One way, which is often expressed or suggested by Socrates' interlocutors themselves, is simply to understand Socrates' professions of ignorance as a pose, designed to entrap his interlocutors into making their own claims, which Socrates can then expose as ignorance.

T2.16 *Republic* 1.336e–337a:

> (Socrates speaking) . . . Don't be too hard on us, Thrasymachus, for if Polemarchus and I made an error in our investigation, you should know that we did so unwillingly. If we were searching for gold, we'd never willingly give way to each other, if by doing so we'd destroy our chance of finding it. So don't think that in searching for justice, a thing more valuable than even a large quantity of gold, we'd mindlessly give way to one another or be less than completely serious about finding it. You surely mustn't think that, but rather—as I do—that we're incapable of finding it. Hence, it's surely far more appropriate for us to be pitied by you clever people than to be given rough treatment.
>
> When he [Thrasymachus] heard that, he gave a loud, sarcastic laugh. By Heracles, he said, that's just Socrates' usual irony. I knew, and I said so to

these people earlier, that you'd be unwilling to answer and that, if someone questioned *you*, you'd be ironical and do anything rather than give an answer.

That's because you're a clever fellow, Thrasymachus.

Socrates never endorses or admits to the characterization of himself as an "ironist" in this or any other passage in Plato's early dialogues; but, of course, if Socrates is what Thrasymachus claims, we might well expect him never to come out of his "ironical" pose. There are several serious interpretive problems here, and scholars have been very interested in the way or ways Socratic "irony" might be understood.

In a recent and very influential study of various features of Socratic philosophy, the late Gregory Vlastos devotes the entire first chapter to an analysis of Socratic irony.[2] Vlastos's very careful analysis begins by noting that the Greek word *eironeia* is, indeed, the etymological root of our word "irony." But the connection in meaning between the two concepts is not entirely exact. Examples of "irony" may be found when someone says something other than, often exactly the opposite of, what is actually meant. A student brings home a report card filled with low grades, and the student's parent, surveying the disaster, remarks, "Great job!"; or a coach, watching a new recruit dribble the basketball off his foot, proclaims, "I think we have a real talent on our hands here!" But these are only the most direct (Vlastos calls them "the most artless"[3]) forms of irony. Vlastos asks us to consider another, more subtle example: "Mae West explains why she is declining President Gerald Ford's invitation to a state dinner at the White House: 'It's an awful long way to go for just one meal.'"[4] In the most direct forms, we recognize that we are supposed to understand the exact opposite of what is specifically stated in the irony; in the Mae West example, all we can be entirely sure of is that Mae West has not given her real reason for declining Ford's invitation, or at least not the main reason. She might well think it is a long way to go, but no one turns down an invitation from the White House just because it is a "long way to go for just one meal." As Vlastos puts it, West is implying: "If you are not an utter fool you'll know this isn't my real reason. Try guessing what that might be."[5] Accordingly, we might say that this is a "riddling" sort of irony.

Since not all irony is direct (or "artless") irony, the real intentions or thoughts of the ironist are not always obvious or easily discerned. And, of course, some people *are* "utter fools" and will not "get it" even when the irony is obvious. Moreover, the more subtle the irony, the more likely it is that it will not just be "utter fools" who do not detect the irony. Vlastos claims that one big difference between our notion of irony and the Greeks' *eironeia* has to do with deception: "[T]he intention to deceive, so alien to our word for irony, is normal in its Greek ancestor."[6] The victims of irony may *be* deceived, of course; but deception must not be the *intended* aim of the ironist, in Vlastos's view. But deception, he claims, is at the heart of the original Greek uses of *eironeia*. He goes on to note, however, that what begins as a secondary use in Greek does not seem to have the same implication, and in this use, *eironeia* is better understood as something more like "pretending," where the connotations do not have to be especially negative. Vlastos even credits the figure of Socrates himself (and "Socratic irony") with the eventual elimination of the original primary use of *eironeia* as deception in favor of the secondary use, turning *eironeia* into a high form of playful pretense,[7] so that by the time Cicero invents the Latin form of the word *(ironia)*, the connotations are ones of "urbanity, elegance, and good taste."[8]

Missing from Vlastos's characterization of the differences between "irony" and *eironeia* are what we might call examples of "mocking" irony, in which there is an intent to deceive.[9] In some cases, after all, ironies are designed to be detected only by those with "inside information": Imagine members of a secret club of racists struggling to hold in malicious laughter as they watch one of their leaders hyperbolically praise the virtues of interracial marriages to an unsuspecting antiracist audience. We do not have to suppose that the "victims" of such an irony must be "utter fools" to miss the "joke," though perhaps the most perceptive might begin to feel that something is amiss. The whole point of this category of ironies is to amuse the "inside" audience by mocking the victim or target of the irony, who is not "in on the joke." One can easily imagine similar cases where such ironies are not for anyone's sake but the ironist—where the only one "in on the joke" is the one making the "joke." The "joke" and its intention remain the same; the only difference is that now the intended audience is reduced to one: the one engaging in irony.

At any rate, we cannot simply assume, from the fact that Thrasymachus refers to Socrates' "well-known *eironeia*" that he means to say that Socrates says things other than he means or believes, intending no deception. It seems more likely that Thrasymachus really is accusing Socrates of malicious trickery that has the direct intention of deception—he thinks Socrates is mock-modest, not genuinely modest; he thinks that Socrates' profession of ignorance is simply a pose intended to entrap his interlocutors into answering his questions. But if this is what Socrates' "well-known *eironeia*" consists in, we must not take Thrasymachus's accusation to refer to "irony" in our sense—we wouldn't call simple mock-modesty "irony" at all. Of course, Thrasymachus may think it is more complicated than this—he may also take Socrates to be engaging in what we have called mocking irony, feigning modesty while also attempting to ridicule others.

This is still different from other forms of deception. There are many reasons for deception: The confidence artist (or "con man") deceives in order to trick victims out of money or other valuables; the professional magician deceives as a kind of performance for those deceived to enjoy; the teller of "white lies" deceives in order to spare the feelings of those deceived. The mocking ironist, however, deceives as a kind of sport or joke, where the main (or perhaps the sole) point of the deception is to have a laugh (outward or inward) at the expense of the one deceived. The mocking ironist enjoys and finds a kind of humor in the position in which the irony has put the victim—in so far as "knowledge is power," the mocking ironist leaves the victims in a powerless state, in contrast to the ironist's own empowerment.

If we are to understand Socrates as an ironist, it is important to be as clear as we can about what sort of irony we take him to be engaging in, and we have noted one form of irony that seems closer to the negative connotations of the Greek concept of *eironeia*. Is this, then, what we should understand Socrates as doing? This question actually has two sides: (1) Is this what Thrasymachus is accusing Socrates of doing, and (2) regardless of whether or not Thrasymachus is accusing Socrates of this, does Socrates do this?

The first question may be answered simply by looking at what Thrasymachus is complaining about. Thrasymachus thinks that Socrates is trying to gain an unfair advantage in his conversations. He may also worry that one intended product of Socrates' tactics will be that everyone gets a malicious laugh at Thrasymachus's expense. But the main focus of Thrasymachus's complaint makes it clear that he thinks of the situation more as if Socrates were cheating at a high-stakes game in which the loser will suffer a certain degree of humiliation in defeat (indeed, when Thrasymachus is himself defeated, his humiliation is evident; see *Republic* 1.350c-d). Thrasymachus never accuses Socrates of finding humor in his adversary's defeat; instead, Thrasymachus thinks that Socrates dishonestly uses unfair tactics just to avoid being defeated himself (this understanding is confirmed when Thrasymachus again criticizes Socrates' manner of arguing at 340d, 341a). Thus, it is not mocking irony that we find at the heart of Thrasymachus's complaint—though Thrasymachus clearly thinks that Socrates is not being sincere. Thrasymachus's real complaint, as we see at the end of T2.16, is that Socrates is cheating by refusing to say what he really believes.

Another instance of this sense of *eironeia* may be found in the *Apology*. T2.17 *Apology* 38a (immediately precedes T2.21):

(Socrates speaking) If I say that it is impossible for me to keep quiet because that means disobeying the god, you will not believe me and will think I am being ironical (*eironeumen i*).

Socrates is not imagining that the jury thinks he would say such things as ironies or *jokes* or merely to have a kind of mocking laugh at their expense. Socrates thinks that they would suppose he was just trying to deceive them.

But Thrasymachus is not the only one who accuses Socrates of *eironeia*, and in at least one other case, there is the strongest sense that Socrates' *eironeia* is for the sake of a kind of mockery.

T2.18 *Symposium* 216d-e:

> (Alcibiades speaking) You can't imagine how little he cares whether a person is beautiful, or rich, or famous in any other way that most people admire. He considers all these possessions beneath contempt, and that's exactly how he considers all of us, as well. In public, I tell you, his whole life is one big game—a game of irony.

We are not likely to find any clearer accusation of what we have been calling mocking irony than this.

Moreover, if we return to the episode with Thrasymachus, it turns out that there may even be some element of mocking irony in what Socrates says. Notice that the last thing that Socrates does before Thrasymachus makes his accusation is to characterize himself as inept and to say that he deserves only pity, and then the first thing he does after Thrasymachus's accusation is to heap praise on Thrasymachus for his wisdom. Might not Thrasymachus's accusation simply be the result of a misunderstanding of something that Socrates really *is* doing that is out of the ordinary? Thrasymachus might sense that in characterizing himself as inept and pitiable, Socrates was, in part, actually mocking others, including especially Thrasymachus himself.

There are very good reasons, other than Alcibiades' characterization of Socrates, to suppose that Socrates makes a habit of this sort of irony, even if we understand it as charitably as we can and suppose that those whom he deceives in this way richly deserve the mockery inherent in Socrates' deception. Look again at those cases in which Socrates claims to want to have others teach him. In some cases, the malicious or mocking irony is fairly gentle, as we see in **T2.4** and in **T2.6**. But in others, it is almost ferocious, as it is with Euthyphro in **T2.9** and **T2.14** and with Hippias in **T2.5**, **T2.10**, and **T2.11**.

The fact is that Socrates has a very low opinion of what he calls "human wisdom."

T2.19 *Apology* 23a-b (immediately follows **T2.15** and immediately precedes **T2.20**):

(Socrates speaking) What is probable, gentlemen, is that in fact the god is wise and that his oracular response meant that human wisdom is worth little or nothing, and that when he says this man, Socrates, he is using my name as an example, as if he said: "This man among you, mortals, is wisest who, like Socrates, understands that his wisdom is worthless."

Recall that in **T2.6** Socrates goes so far as to say that he has never met anyone who knew what virtue is. Accordingly, we would expect from his low opinion of human wisdom that any time we find Socrates calling one of his interlocutors "wise," attributing knowledge to him, or saying that he hopes to become the other's "student," what we have called mocking irony is at work. In fact, not one of our texts conflicts with this expectation. And Socrates' mockery seems to increase in sharpness in proportion to the interlocutor's presumptuousness. Those guilty of the most extreme or dangerous pretensions (such as Euthyphro and Hippias) are given the most lavish ironical praise. Those whose presumptions are more innocent Socrates only gently teases with his mocking irony.

We have thus found at least one form of irony that Socrates commonly uses, which we have called mocking irony. We began our inquiry into Socratic irony by asking whether or not Socrates' profession of ignorance was an example of irony of some sort, as Thrasymachus seemed to assume. What we have found, however, is that Thrasymachus may have sensed such irony, but if so, he misunderstood it as something else. The one form of irony we have found Socrates using—mocking irony—does not fit the Socratic profession of ignorance. There does seem to be clear mocking irony when Socrates calls others wise or "recognizes" them as ones who have the knowledge that he, himself, claims to lack. But the mockery does not work by his own disclaimer of such things; the irony is in the mocking compliments and flattery Socrates lavishes on others. So Socrates is not guilty of mock-modesty; his modesty is genuine. His praise of others, however, is often mock-praise and not at all sincere— there is mockery in such praise.

At least part of the irony in Socrates' mock-praise of others is in the *contrast* between the customary Socratic disclaimers of knowledge and wisdom, on the one hand, and the acknowledgments of others' knowledge and wisdom, on the other. But notice that such a contrast does not require us to assume—as Thrasymachus seems to assume—that Socrates actually supposes that he possesses the knowledge and wisdom he claims to lack, whereas his interlocutors lack the knowledge and wisdom they claim to have. The contrast works, instead, by highlighting the interlocutor's presumption that there is some significant contrast of knowledge and wisdom between Socrates and the interlocutor. It is this presumption that

Socrates mocks as false and unwarranted. If neither has the knowledge the interlocutor imagines that he has, then there is, in fact, no contrast of the sort Socrates makes, when he compares his own ignorance with the "great wisdom" of his interlocutor. The contrast, instead, is between one who recognizes his own lack of wisdom and one who does not.

Therefore, nothing we have seen so far in Plato's texts supports the idea that mocking irony undercuts or nullifies Socrates' profession of ignorance, even if we have found that we should certainly think there is mocking irony at work when Socrates flatters others for their knowledge and wisdom. Moreover, Thrasymachus's reference to Socrates' "well-known *eironeia*," which often comes out in translations as "well-known irony," also does not support the idea that Socrates' profession of ignorance is *irony*. Of course, we might decide simply to agree with Thrasymachus that in professing ignorance, Socrates is simply being manipulative and dishonest, or as we said at the beginning, we might decide that the profession of ignorance is some other sort of irony.

Both of these alternatives, however, have very serious consequences for the project of interpreting our texts, and despite the apparent differences between the two alternatives, the problems they create turn out to be of the same sort. Let us take up Thrasymachus's charge first. We have already said that we nowhere find Socrates admitting to being the kind of manipulator Thrasymachus accuses him of being. Thus, if Socrates is attempting to deceive when he claims to be ignorant, then we must suppose that he is attempting to deceive every time we find him making such a claim, and we must also admit that at least *this* lie is one he tells *very* often in our texts.[10]

If you recall the principles of interpretation we discussed in the introduction to this book, however, it is easy to see that this interpretation is in direct conflict with the *Principle of Textual Fidelity*, which stated that no interpretation that is unambiguously contradicted by some relevant text can ever be adequate. The problem is that this interpretation seems to be unambiguously contradicted by *many* relevant texts!

It might be objected that all the cases of mocking irony we have noted would also run afoul of this principle, since Socrates quite often does identify his interlocutors as wise and knowledgeable. In this claim, however, we judged Socrates to be saying something other than what he believes, because we also found texts in which he broke from this pose and admitted that he thought no one was wise or had the kind of knowledge we found him elsewhere granting to his interlocutors. Accordingly, and given support from a text in which Alcibiades accuses him of such things, we supposed that Socrates' praise in such cases was mocking irony. In this way, we resolved what would otherwise have been a problem in the texts: some texts proclaiming that Socrates has never met anyone with a certain kind of wisdom and some in which he seems very eager to recognize such wisdom in others. Recall that what we call the *Principle of Charity*, which requires an interpretation to provide a view that is as interesting and as plausible as possible, makes inconsistency in our texts or interpretations unacceptable, other things being equal.

It turns out that there *are* some texts in which Socrates seems to claim to have knowledge and others in which he seems to grant that others also have knowledge. Indeed, these texts and the obvious problems they create both for Socrates' profession of ignorance and for what he says about others' lack of knowledge and wisdom will be the focus of our discussion in the next chapter. Thus, we cannot provide any final decision on whether or not Socrates' profession of ignorance is sincere until we have solved these problems. But we can now note that the standard reason given to explain *why* Socrates would lie when he professes ignorance seems not to provide an adequate interpretation of these professions. We said earlier that one reason Socrates might lie about his own knowledge would be to entrap unsuspecting interlocutors into answering his questions—feigning ignorance so that they would be willing to "educate" him. This, however, conflicts with what we call the *Principle of Interpretive Plausibility*, which requires that an adequate interpretation must unproblematically and plausibly account for the text(s) it proposes to interpret. The problem is that Socrates sometimes makes his customary disclaimer of knowledge and wisdom when there is *no* possibility that in doing so he might be luring some interlocutor into the relevant kind of trap. Specifically, the profession of ignorance is at the heart of Socrates' defense in his first speech in the *Apology* (see 20c, 21d, 23b), a circumstance in which none of those to whom he is making his profession (the jurors) could possibly have been lured into a discussion with Socrates. If Socrates is being dishonest in these cases, then, it must be for some other reason.

Problems of this same sort also arise if we imagine that Socrates' profession of ignorance is some form of irony other than mocking irony (which, we have argued, it does not seem to be). For it to be direct (or what Vlastos calls "artless") irony, Socrates would have to be saying the exact opposite of what he means, where the reversal of meaning is intended to be transparent. But again this does not seem to be a plausible option, especially when he makes the profession of ignorance central to his defense in the *Apology*. Too often, such a reversal of meaning is anything but obvious, and the profession itself seems easily taken (both by Plato's reader and by Socrates' audience) to be sincere.

But there was another form of irony we have recognized—the form we found in Mae West's "explanation" of why she turned down Gerald Ford's dinner offer at the White House: "It's an awful long way to go for just one meal." Even if we detect the irony, we recognize it as "riddling" irony, for her real reasons for not going to the dinner are not only not stated but are not obvious. Certainly no simple operation (such as is available in direct or "artless" irony) will explain it. But again, if we suppose that it is this riddling sort of irony that Socrates uses in disclaiming knowledge, we will not be in a good position to satisfy the *Principle of Textual Fidelity* or the *Principle of Interpretive Plausibility*, for if what Plato's Socrates says is riddling irony, he does not really mean what he has said. What he does really mean is, however, a matter for speculation.

Of course, it might be fun to speculate about all kinds of tantalizing and curious hidden meanings in what Socrates says. But since we do not know of any limit to the kinds of speculation that might be equally possible, it seems foolish to pursue any of these lines of interpretation much further—at least as long as we think that the more direct interpretation, which holds that Socrates' profession of ignorance is sincere, can be made to suffice. As we have said, we cannot make any final decision on this issue until we have confronted the texts in which Socrates makes and grants to others claims of knowledge. But we can at least tentatively conclude at this point with a general observation about what consequences flow from any assumption that abandons the most straightforward sense of what Socrates says. If we suppose that Socrates is willing to be dishonest or intentionally unclear about whether or not he has knowledge and wisdom, then we will have at least some reason to be suspicious about any other claim he might make as well. Once we convict someone of being a liar or a riddler on one issue, we will have no clear reason to accept the person's apparent meaning in any other case. One can imagine an aggressively "deconstructive" stance, in which literally every claim Socrates makes or seems to make is subjected to such doubt, with endless varieties of fantastical speculations about what his *real* views (which are now never those he actually gives or argues for) might be—or even if he *has* any such views. If we convict Socrates of misleading presentations of his own views, therefore, we are obviously at serious risk of losing any value we hoped to get from reading these texts to begin with, since what they actually say is now to be ignored and no longer constrains how we must understand them and it now appears possible that indefinitely many and conflicting interpretations of their "hidden" meanings will all have equal claims of adequacy. If this is what we are led to, we are probably better off simply abandoning our texts altogether and discussing other matters.

We have surely not given anything like a full list of the different forms of irony, but before we turn to another topic, we should consider one more form, which we have not yet mentioned and which we believe is present in our texts and also present in Socrates' profession of ignorance. It is a form of irony, however, that does not require us to disbelieve what Socrates actually claims. What we have in mind is what is often called "tragic" irony, in which one means exactly what one says, but one's meaning actually resonates with deeper connections and meanings that convey a kind of tragic meaning in context. In his defense in the *Apology*, Socrates tells the story of the oracle at Delphi (see **T2.19**), which proclaimed that no one is wiser than Socrates. The oracle is not direct (or "artless") irony—it is not saying the exact opposite of the truth. Nor is this mocking irony, in which the one(s) to whom the oracle is given is supposed to be deceived through a form of mockery or argumentative entrapment. Nor, indeed, is this an example of riddling irony. Once Socrates comes to understand the oracle, he realizes that it is literally true—no one is wiser than he is. But Socrates also realizes that there is tragedy here— the oracle is true despite the fact that Socrates counts his own wisdom as "worthless." The irony, in this case, does not require the literal meaning of the oracle's claim to be false. Instead, the irony is in the very tragic way in which the oracle's claim is true.

The same kind of irony, in a sense, can be found in Socrates' profession of ignorance and in his many disclaimers of wisdom. Socrates is a man who says he has been on a mission given to him by the god, but it is no easy burden for him.

T2.20 *Apology* 23b (immediately follows **T2.19**; repeats and then continues **T2.12**; immediately precedes **T2.24**):

> (Socrates speaking) So even now I continue this investigation as the god bade me—and I go around seeking out anyone, citizen or stranger, whom I think wise. Then if I do not think he is, I come to the assistance of the god and show him that he is not wise. Because of this occupation, I do not have the leisure to engage in public affairs to any extent, nor indeed to look after my own, but I live in great poverty because of my service to the god.

Socrates pronounces what are probably his most famous words in his second speech to the jurors, in the *Apology*.

T2.21 *Apology* 38a (immediately follows **T2.17**):

> (Socrates speaking) I say that it is the greatest good for a man to discuss virtue every day and those other things about which you hear me conversing and testing myself and others, for the unexamined life is not worth living for men . . . .

Socrates has devoted his life—at least since he received the oracle about his wisdom—to this "mission" and to leading what he calls "the examined life." But despite this, and all his years of effort, his wisdom continues to be "worthless." In disclaiming wisdom and knowledge, we suggest, Socrates tells nothing but the truth; but there is tragic irony in this truth. It is the same tragic irony we find in the oxymoron Socrates uses to identify what is at the heart of this truth, in the kind of "wisdom" in which he is truly unexcelled—in his "human wisdom." Socrates' "wisdom" is none other than his sincere disclaimer of wisdom.

We believe that this kind of irony can often be found in Plato's early dialogues, but let us give just one more example. At the end of his final words to his jurors, before he is led away to the prison in which he will end his days, Socrates makes a plea to those who have condemned him.

T2.22 *Apology* 41e–42a:

(Socrates speaking) This much I ask from them: when my sons grow up, avenge yourselves by causing them the same kind of grief that I caused you, if you think they care for money or anything else more than they care for virtue, or if they think they are somebody when they are nobody. Reproach them as I reproach you, that they do not care for the right things and think they are worthy when they are not worthy of anything. If you do this, I shall have been justly treated by you, and my sons also.

Does Socrates really wish his jurors would do this to his sons? Of course he does; but he knows that there is no chance at all that they will do as he has asked. In telling the truth as he sees it, his words resonate with tragic irony.

Many scholars have been very eager to find various "ironies" in the words and actions Plato gives to Socrates, and often the interpretations that feature such alleged ironies are very appealing and subtle—indeed, as appealing and subtle as irony itself can be. But we have suggested that the more subtle and "ironical" the interpretation is, the more it risks putting us in a position of losing any objective grounds for accepting any interpretation over any other. As soon as some interpreter claims that Plato's Socrates does not really mean what he has said, therefore, one should insist that the interpreter explain how this claim can still retain the principles of interpretation that require us to take what the text itself says very seriously and as straightforwardly as possible. We have suggested that our principles of interpretation are not violated by finding mocking irony in Socrates' praise of others' knowledge and wisdom. However, we are also strongly inclined to think that our interpretive principles require us to see no dishonesty and only the tragic form of irony in Socrates' disclaimers of knowledge and wisdom. If this is so, then at least one feature of Socrates' claim not to be a teacher is that he does not think of himself as knowing anything worth teaching to others. We return to this issue in the next chapter, for some passages in our texts seem to provide contrary evidence.

2.1.3 Socrates' Claims Not to Teach

The teacher who uses the "Socratic method" of teaching, we have said, actually has something to teach and does at least attempt to *teach* something, whereas Socrates claims not to know anything worth teaching and claims not to have taught anyone anything. We have already found tragic irony in Socrates' disclaimer of knowledge and wisdom, but there is additional tragic irony in his claim never to have taught anyone anything. Those who read through Plato's early dialogues are often struck by how little success Socrates actually enjoys in convincing anyone of anything. The *Apology* gives several good examples of Socrates' failures: After his first speech, in which he argues that he has devoted his life to the pious service of the god, the jury convicts him of impiety; after his second speech, in which he argues for a penalty other than death, the jury gives him the death penalty; and finally, as we noted in **T2.22**, Socrates ends his appeal to the jurors with a hopeless plea on behalf of his sons. The same can be said for virtually every other dialogue: Even when his interlocutors end up agreeing with him, one senses that the agreement is not entirely secure and might at a later time be reversed or abandoned. Certainly, his most aggressive interlocutors, even when they are bested in the argument, do not show any signs of conversion to the point of view Socrates represented to them; at most, they fall into a kind of resentful passivity. (We have in mind the ways in which Euthyphro and Polus and Callicles and Thrasymachus give in to Socrates at the end of their conversations—no obvious changes in their convictions are evident, even if they have ceased trying to defend their positions.) Moreover, no one who reads Plato's dialogues can miss the powerfully moral figure Socrates represents in them, but it is also true that many of those with whom Socrates is shown to speak are known to have gone on to notorious careers as criminals or traitors. Perhaps the most calamitous of these is the man whom Plato's Socrates openly professes to love: Alcibiades (see *Gorgias* 481d), whose infamies are alleged to include impiety, treason, fraud, and adultery (for details, see Plutarch's *Life of Alcibiades*). For all the respect we might suppose Plato has for Socrates, the dialogues do not show Socrates to have had much success in convincing others of his moral views.

However, we are often left with the strongest impression that Socrates does lead his interlocutors in a way that certainly looks like teaching. Even if the interlocutors almost always end up failing to "get the message," their failures often appear to be more the result of some fault in the student, as it were, rather than in the teacher, Socrates. It is, after all, entirely possible that Socrates could be a teacher but never have much success with his students.

There are three groups that might be seen as Socrates' students. The most obvious group, which we have already mentioned, includes Socrates' interlocutors, the men he actually "examines" with his questions. The Athenian general, Nicias, gives his view of what it means to be subjected to Socratic "examination" in Plato's *Laches*.

T2.23 *Laches* 187e–188a:

> (Nicias speaking) You don't appear to me to know that whoever comes into close contact with Socrates and associates with him in conversation must necessarily, even if he began by conversing about something quite different in the first place, keep on being led about by the man's arguments until he submits to answering questions about himself concerning both his present manner of life and the life he has lived hitherto. And when he does submit to this questioning, you don't realize that Socrates will not let him go before he has well and truly tested every last detail.

In **T2.20**, we learn that Socrates sees himself as on a religious mission to target putatively wise people for such examination, and in **T2.6**, we see that Socrates thinks he has never met anyone who could "pass" his examinations. Plato often depicts these sorts of conversations in his early dialogues. It is no wonder that such conversations inevitably end in perplexity: Socrates targets those who have a reputation for wisdom and reveals their ignorance. Because the approach is negative, we should not expect Socrates' interlocutors in such exchanges to come away with a new positive doctrine as much as a chastened sense of their own position vis-à-vis knowledge and wisdom.

Is this teaching? Certainly it is, in a sense. One of Socrates' interlocutors could certainly respond to a Socratic examination by claiming to have learned about his own ignorance from Socrates and thus for Socrates to have shown him ("taught him") to recognize his own ignorance. Socrates never denies doing *this* kind of teaching; indeed, in so far as *this* is teaching, Socrates plainly says he has made it his "mission" to teach such things.

As pleasing as this result might be, however, not all of his interlocutors end up with even this much of a benefit from their encounter with Socrates. At the end of Plato's *Charmides*, for example, the young Charmides acknowledges that he is unsure about his own wisdom and temperance (see 176a-b). Nicias and Laches, too, at the end of Plato's *Laches*, acknowledge their own lack of knowledge (see 200a-d). Sometimes, one senses that even if the conversation ends in a friendly way, the interlocutor remains essentially unmoved from his original presumption (see, for example, Protagoras in Plato's *Protagoras* 361d-e). But in too many cases, Socrates' interlocutors are left more angry than chastened (see, for example, Anytus, in Plato's *Meno* 94e–95a; Socrates characterizes this result as common at *Apology* 22e–23a). Even where we find Socrates succeeding in his "mission," Plato's readers would recognize a certain instability in Socrates' "successes," for the most obviously successful cases of this sort are not men whose eventual careers turned out particularly well: Charmides later became a member of the notorious Thirty who briefly overthrew the Athenian government in a bloody oligarchic revolution; Athens's terrible defeat at Sicily in the Peloponnesian War is credited to Nicias; Laches ended up being charged with embezzlement of public funds. It would be unreasonable to fault Socrates because these men did not turn out better. After all, some must have been blindly arrogant before they met Socrates, and it is highly unlikely that such men would have changed their impression of their own worth after only one meeting with Socrates. Even those who spent considerable time with him may have done so only because they found his interrogations amusing. Thus, when they left his company to go on to other pursuits, they quickly returned to their habits of failing to examine their beliefs about how to live. If we count only Socrates' interlocutors in Plato's dialogues, we find little evidence of success even in his most "negative" mode of "teaching," in which he reveals others' ignorance to them.

Socrates mentions yet another group that might qualify as his "students" in some sense: those, especially the younger men, who watch as Socrates practices his "mission" on those who are reputed to be wise. Socrates talks about such "witnesses" in the *Apology*.

T2.24 *Apology* 23c-d (part of longer quote in **T7.10**; immediately follows **T2.20**; see also **T2.13**):

> (Socrates speaking) The young men who follow me around of their own free will, those who have the most leisure, the sons of the very rich, take pleasure in hearing people questioned; they themselves often imitate me and try to question others. I think they find an abundance of men who believe they have some knowledge but know little or nothing.

In a later passage in the *Apology* (at 34a), Socrates lists Plato himself as one of those who has spent time with Socrates in this way. Might Socrates count as a teacher to those who watched him question others? It seems impossible to deny that Plato would regard Socrates as a kind of teacher, and through Plato, Socrates made contact with yet another group: those of us who read Plato's dialogues. In reading Plato, does Socrates not also become *our* teacher? There is at least some reason to think that the students in Plato's Academy—a school founded and run by Plato in Athens—were required to read and discuss these dialogues.

But what did Plato and Socrates' other younger followers learn from him, and what do Plato's readers learn? This question is remarkably difficult to answer, and any answer is likely to be unsatisfactory to some. After Socrates' death, several very different philosophical movements trace at least some of their principles back to Socrates: the Cynics; the Cyrenaics; the Skeptics; the Stoics; and, of course, Plato and the members of his Academy. Moreover, the accounts of Socrates we get from those who spent time with him, as we said in Chapter 1, vary widely and make extremely problematic the whole idea of giving some positive account of "Socratic teachings." In Sections 2.2 and 2.3, we discuss ways in which Plato's Socrates, at least, would claim that whatever we learn in our contact with him, we really get from ourselves, more than from him. Perhaps this is the truth of the matter, which would explain why his most immediate followers did not form a unified group of thinkers. It would also help to explain the great diversity of opinions about Socrates among scholars today.

In **T2.21**, we found Socrates advocating what he calls the "examined life." In Socrates, we find a man so exceptional and so relentlessly dedicated to the life of inquiry that we are inclined to call him a "teacher" because our own attitudes toward philosophy as a lifelong commitment are changed, deepened, and amplified through our contact with Socrates. Even if all we "learn" from Socrates is to value reasoned inquiry much more than we ever did before, it is fair to call him an important teacher. But we should realize that it was not *this* kind of teaching Socrates ever denied doing, and when we think of him as a teacher of this sort, we do not thereby regard him as being what he claimed not to be.

2.2 Socratic Doctrines and Positive Teachings

2.2.1 Positions We Can Unproblematically Attribute to Socrates

So far, we have been focused almost exclusively on Socrates' refutative style, which seems ill suited to his being a teacher in any directly positive sense. Still, one does not have to spend much time reading Plato's early dialogues to find Socrates advocating specific positive positions. He tells his jury in no uncertain terms that he regards their hierarchy of values to be mistaken.

T2.25 *Apology* 29d–30b:

> (Socrates speaking) . . . as long as I draw breath and am able, I shall not cease to practice philosophy, to exhort you and in my usual way to point out to

any one of you whom I happen to meet: Good Sir, you are an Athenian, a citizen of the greatest city with the greatest reputation for both wisdom and power; are you not ashamed of your eagerness to possess as much wealth, reputation and honors as possible, while you do not care for nor give thought to wisdom or truth, or the best possible state of your soul? Then, if one of you disputes this and says he does care, I shall not let him go at once or leave him, but I shall question him, examine him and test him, and if I do not think he has attained the goodness that he says he has, I shall reproach him because he attaches little importance to the most important things and greater importance to inferior things. I shall treat in this way anyone I happen to meet, young and old, citizen and stranger, and more so the citizens because you are more kindred to me. Be sure that this is what the god orders me to do, and I think there is no greater blessing for the city than my service to the god. For I go around doing nothing but persuading both young and old among you not to care for your body or your wealth in preference to or as strongly as for the best possible state of your soul, as I say to you: "Wealth does not bring about excellence, but excellence brings about wealth and all other public and private blessings for men, both individually and collectively."[11]

In the *Gorgias*, Socrates is aggressively willing to articulate his own views, and some of these certainly do not seem to be mere platitudes to his interlocutors. Consider just one example, in his discussion with Polus.
T2.26 *Gorgias* 472e–473a:

SOCRATES: On my view of it, Polus, a man who acts unjustly, a man who is unjust, is thoroughly miserable, the more so if he doesn't get his due punishment for the wrongdoing he commits, the less so if he pays and receives what is due at the hands of both gods and men.

POLUS: What an absurd position you're trying to maintain, Socrates!

SOCRATES: Yes, and I'll try to get you to take the same position too, my good man, for I consider you a friend.

Contrast what we see here with Socrates' vivid denial that he is a teacher, which is worth quoting again.
T2.8 (Repeated) *Apology* 33a-b:

(Socrates speaking) I have never been anyone's teacher. If anyone, young or old, desires to listen to me when I am talking and dealing with my own concerns, I have never begrudged this to anyone, but I do not converse when I receive a fee and not when I do not. I am equally ready to question the rich and the poor if anyone is willing to answer my questions and listen to what I say. And I cannot justly be held responsible for the good or bad conduct of these people, as I never promised to teach them anything and have not done so. If anyone says that he has learned anything from me, or that he heard anything privately that the others did not hear, be assured that he is not telling the truth.

Is Socrates' posture regarding Polus, in **T2.26**, and with the Athenians in general, in **T2.25**, not a clear example of Socrates teaching in precisely the way that he claimed never to teach in **T2.8**?

To sort this problem out, we must be clear on what is to count as evidence that contradicts Socrates' claim in **T2.8**. To begin with, Socrates could have all sorts of opinions, even the most strongly held convictions and yet sincerely deny that he *teaches* anything. After all, many of us have beliefs and convictions, though we never teach anyone. To be a teacher, one must put oneself in the recognizable position as a promoter or promulgator of the relevant opinions.

Of course, now there is a "teaching profession," in which people can be identified as teachers simply by working at certain jobs. In Socrates' time, there were no schools of the sort so common today, but there were paid professional teachers of various kinds, and Socrates is certainly consistent in denying that he ever took payment for his philosophizing (see **T2.7** and **T2.8**, for examples), which would be one sign of his being a teacher in the professional sense. But there are certainly other teachers than these, and Socrates could not honestly make the claim he makes in **T2.8** unless he was no one's teacher in the sense of "teacher" he expects his audience to have in mind as including any of the standard examples. In the last section, we argued that the refutative aspect of Socratic philosophizing would not make him a "teacher" in the standard sense and was compatible with his denial in **T2.8**. But even his willingness to express positive commitments of various forms does not make him a teacher in the standard sense. His behavior with Polus, however, really does begin to look like more than just an ordinary (i.e., a nonteaching) form of expressing his own views. Let us look more closely at what Socrates thinks he is doing, to see if he is or is not teaching Polus and others with whom he talks in his normal way.

2.2.2 Constructivism and Nonconstructivism: Two Scholarly Views

In 2.1.2, we asked whether or not we had reason to suppose that Socrates knew the answers to his questions, and our interpretation of the relevant texts led us to the conclusion that (at least in most cases) he did not. His profession of ignorance, we concluded, was sincere and genuine, and ironical only in the tragic sense. But Socrates is also the one who claimed that the "unexamined life is not worth living" (in **T2.21**). Is the only benefit of "the examined life" what Socrates calls "human wisdom" (in **T2.19**), namely, the understanding that one's actual "wisdom" is "worthless"? Or does Socrates think that "the examined life" can also bring positive benefits as well?

Scholars have divided over this question. What has come to be known as the "nonconstructivist" position[12]—which claims that Socrates does not take his characteristic questioning of others to do any significant "constructive" work in discovering or deriving positive philosophical doctrines—may seem to be obviously correct. Socrates thinks that he continues to be ignorant, despite a life of searching for wisdom. He claims his "mission" in life has been to expose the pretense of wisdom for the ignorance it invariably is. Moreover, and perhaps most important, Socrates' elenchos (the Greek word that Socrates often uses—and scholars now always use—to refer to Socrates' questioning might be translated as "cross-examination"), his own style of philosophizing, is purely negative: He "examines" others by having them say what they think they know, and then, by asking his questions, Socrates identifies other beliefs they have that are not consistent with their original claim.

But Socrates makes several claims about what he does that also seem to point to a more constructive aspect of his use of the elenchos. At the beginning of 2.2.1, we gave two such examples (in **T2.25** and **T2.26**), where Socrates seems to be prepared to defend certain positive positions in a more constructive way. And yet his practice of philosophy, at least as we find him in the pages of Plato, is limited to the construction of elenctic arguments—arguments that seem only to yield negative conclusions. George Grote, perhaps the best known of the nineteenth-century English-speaking Platonists, claims that Socrates' endorsement of various positive views, on the one hand, and his elenchos, on the other, were unrelated: "The negative cross-examination, and the affirmative dogmatism, are . . . two unconnected operations of thought: one does not lead to, or involve, or verify, the other."[13] The problem with this position is obvious, however. For one thing, Socrates would have to hold his positive views—some of which, as we shall see, are quite counterintuitive—as a matter of sheer dogmatism.

A more promising account was also advanced in the nineteenth century by Eduard Zeller, who claimed that Socrates did his philosophical work by "deducing conceptions from the common opinions of men."[14] Zeller's thesis has also been endorsed by several contemporary scholars, at least partly because this form of argumentation, known generally as "dialectical argumentation," has a distinguished history in Greek moral thought and becomes the basic form for Aristotle's method of inquiry in ethics. However, there are at least two major problems for this thesis as well, for Socrates both shows a complete lack of respect for "the common opinions of men" and seems very willing to rely on premises that he recognizes are directly contradictory to what is commonly believed.

T2.27 *Crito* 44c-d (= **T7.25**):

> SOCRATES: My good Crito, why should we care so much for what the majority think? The most reasonable people, to whom one should pay more attention, will believe that things were done as they were done.

> CRITO: You see, Socrates, that one must also pay attention to the opinion of the majority. Your present situation makes clear that the majority can inflict not the least but pretty well the greatest evils if one is slandered among them.

> SOCRATES: Would that the majority could inflict the greatest evils, for they would then be capable of the greatest good, and that would be fine, but now they cannot do either. They cannot make a man either wise or foolish, but they inflict things haphazardly.

T2.28 *Crito* 49c-d:

> SOCRATES: One should never do wrong in return, nor injure any man, whatever injury one has suffered at his hands. And Crito, see that you do not agree to this, contrary to your belief. For I know that only a few people hold this view or will hold it, and there is no common ground between those who hold this view and those who do not, but they inevitably despise each other's views.

If Socrates thought that his own views had to conform to "the common opinions of men," he would have to retract everything he says in **T2.25**, **T2.26**, **T2.27**, and **T2.28**, where he advances positions that conflict with those of most others. Of course, some of the premises from which Socrates derives his own views may also be what most people think. But Socrates never holds a view *because* most people hold it.

A more recent constructivist account, offered by Richard Robinson, characterizes the logical form of the elenchos as consisting in reducing some stated hypothesis to self-contradiction.[15] As "negative" as this may sound, it is actually a very powerful proof procedure for the negation of the "stated hypothesis," so if Socrates' views derive from a method that does this, it would seem that every elenctic argument provides a decisive proof for the falsehood of every position Socrates targets for refutation and, hence, for the truth of the negation of each of the targeted positions.

Unfortunately, there are also at least two problems with this view: (1) It does not accurately represent the way that Socrates' elenctic arguments actually work (which we will describe in detail in the next section), and (2) it conflicts with Socrates' attitudes toward his own conclusions, which at least in some cases seem deeply skeptical (see **T2.41**, **T2.42**, **T2.43**, and **T2.44**, below).

2.2.3 Vlastos's Deductivist Constructivism

Dissatisfied with each of the above interpretations, and yet unwilling to concede the nonconstructivist position, perhaps the most famous Socratic scholar of the twentieth century, Gregory Vlastos, sought to provide a very different solution.[16] Vlastos begins by characterizing the actual form of what he calls "the standard elenchus"[17]:

- (1) The interlocutor asserts a thesis, *p*, which Socrates considers false and targets for refutation.
- (2) Socrates secures agreement to further premises, say, *q* and *r* (each of which may stand for a conjunct of propositions). The agreement is *ad hoc:* Socrates argues from *(q, r)*, not to them.
- (3) Socrates then argues, and the interlocutor agrees, that *q & r* entail *not-p*.
- (4) Socrates then claims that he has shown that *not-p* is true, *p* false.[18]

Vlastos identifies what he calls "*the* problem of the elenchus" as follows:

How can Socrates claim, as I shall be arguing he does claim in "standard elenchus," to have proved that the refutand is false, when all he has established is its inconsistency with premises whose truth he has not tried to establish in that argument: they have entered the argument simply as propositions on which he and the interlocutor are agreed. This is *the* problem of the Socratic elenchus.[19] (Vlastos's italics)

The agreement Socrates secures with his interlocutor, to premises *q* and *r*, is always *ad hoc* (see step [2] in Vlastos's account of how the elenchos works). Socrates does not secure these premises; as Vlastos says, "Socrates argues from *(q, r)*, not to them." But Vlastos notes that Socrates is very persistent in insisting that each of the premises in an elenctic argument must satisfy what Vlastos calls the "say what you believe" requirement: Socrates always insists that his interlocutors must agree only to premises that they themselves accept and believe are true (see also **T2.28**).[20]

T2.29 *Protagoras* 331c:

(Protagoras speaking) It's not so absolutely clear a case to me, Socrates, as to make me grant that justice is pious, and piety just. It seems a distinction is in order here. But what's the difference? If you want, we'll let justice be pious and piety just.

(Socrates speaking) Don't do that to me! It's not this "if you want" or "if you agree" business I want to test. It's you and me I want to put on the line, and I think the argument will be tested best if we take the "if" out.

T2.30 *Gorgias* 495a:

> CALLICLES: Well, to keep my argument from becoming inconsistent if I say that they're different, I say they're the same.

> SOCRATES: You're wrecking your earlier statements, Callicles, and you'd no longer be adequately inquiring into the truth of the matter with me if you speak contrary to what you think.

T2.31 *Gorgias* 500b:

> SOCRATES: And by Zeus, the god of friendship, Callicles, please don't think that you should jest with me either, or answer anything that comes to mind, contrary to what you really think, and please don't accept what you get from me as though I'm jesting!

T2.32 *Republic* 1.345b:

(Socrates speaking) . . . first, stick to what you've said, and then, if you change your position, do it openly and don't deceive us.

T2.33 *Republic* 1.346a (part of longer quote given as **T5.11**):

(Socrates speaking) Please don't answer contrary to what you believe, so that we can come to some definite conclusion.

T2.34 *Republic* 1.350d-e:

(Thrasymachus speaking) I could make a speech about it, but, if I did, I know that you'd accuse me of engaging in oratory. So, either allow me to speak, or, if you want to ask questions, go ahead, and I'll say, "All right," and nod yes and no, as one does to old wives' tales.

(Socrates speaking) Don't do that, contrary to your own opinion.

Indeed, so important is this condition to Socrates that he is even willing to allow an interlocutor to withdraw premises, after assenting to them, if the interlocutor decides that he no longer believes them or that the premises did not assert the interlocutor's real beliefs correctly.

T2.35 *Gorgias* 461d (see also: *Euthyphro* 11b, 13c-d; *Crito* 49d-e; *Protagoras* 354e–355a; *Gorgias* 462a, 480e [**T2.47**, below]):

> SOCRATES: And if you think we were wrong to agree on it, I'm certainly willing to retract any of our agreements you like . . . .

According to Vlastos, in the *Gorgias*, Plato makes clear that he himself has become disturbed over how the standard elenchos could ever possibly achieve the desired results, that *p* is proved false and that *not-p* is proved true. In the pre-*Gorgias* dialogues, all Socrates could reasonably have expected to show with the standard elenchos is that his interlocutor (and Socrates himself, if he, too, accepts all of the premises of his argument) must consider *p* false and *not-p* true, given their mutual but undefended beliefs in premises *q* and *r*. For Vlastos, the signal that Plato in the *Gorgias* intends to place the standard elenchos on firmer ground is to be found in the strength of the claims Socrates makes about the outcome of elenctic arguments. For the first time, Vlastos says, Socrates can be found claiming to have "proved" a proposition true.

T2.36 *Gorgias* 479e (part of longer quote at **T2.46**):

> SOCRATES: Hasn't it been proved that what was said is true?

Convinced that this passage requires an account of how Socrates could think he has proved anything with the elenchos, Vlastos identifies two extraordinary assumptions that he argues Plato gives to Socrates for the first time in the *Gorgias*.

[A] Whoever has a false moral belief will always have at the same time true beliefs entailing the negation of that false belief.[21]
[B] The set of elenctically tested moral beliefs held by Socrates at any given time is consistent.[22]

In Vlastos's account, [A] explains why Socrates is so insistent that the interlocutor accept only premises that the interlocutor himself actually believes. Evidence for [B], Vlastos claims, can be seen in Socrates' elevation of consistency "to a supreme desideratum in his own search for truth" in the *Gorgias*.[23]

T2.37 *Gorgias* 482b-c (= **T6.18**; immediately follows **T2.50**):

(Socrates speaking) I think it's better to have my lyre or a chorus that I might lead out of tune and dissonant, and have the vast majority of men disagree with me and contradict me, than to be out of harmony with myself, to contradict myself, though I'm only one person.

Of course, strictly, this passage says only that Socrates would not wish to hold inconsistent beliefs—it does not actually affirm that he has achieved his wish. But Vlastos claims that Socrates has reason to make such an affirmation because of his long experience with elenctic arguments:

> The consistency of the set is being inferred from its track-record in Socrates' own experience: in all of the elenctic arguments in which he has engaged he has never been faulted for inconsistency. This is a very chancy inference, for the results of elenctic argument are powerfully affected by the argumentative skill of the contestants; since that of Socrates vastly exceeds that of his interlocutors, he is more effective in finding beliefs of theirs which entail the negation of their thesis than are they when trying to do the same to him. So his undefeated record need not show that his belief-set is consistent; it may only show that its inconsistencies have defied the power of his adversaries to ferret them out. Socrates could hardly have been unaware of this unavoidable hazard in his method. This must contribute to the sense of fallibility which, I believe, is the right clue to his profession of ignorance.[24]

Vlastos's [A] and [B] entail a powerful conclusion in the case of Socrates himself: Since all of Socrates' elenctically tested moral beliefs are consistent (as per [B]), it must be that they are all *true*, since if any of them were false, Socrates would have other beliefs that entailed the negation of the false one (as per [A]), which would yield an *inconsistent* set of beliefs, which, again, [B] rules out. Socrates, accordingly, can claim to have *proved* *p* false and *not-p* true, in every case in which he, himself, accepts all of the premises of the argument that yields *not-p*, since those premises (*q* and *r*) turn out to be true (as being part of Socrates' own consistent and all-true belief-set).

2.2.4 Criticisms of Vlastos's Deductivist Constructivism and the Nonconstructivist View

But just how compelling is Vlastos's "solution" to "*the* problem of the elenchus" as he calls it? Let us first look at Vlastos's principle [A]. Does Plato's Socrates actually assume this? It is certainly true that Socrates operates, in his elenchos, in a way that suggests something like this, but we believe principle [A] commits Socrates to far more than our texts—or the Platonic Socrates' own actions—supply. The main problem with [A] is that it requires that the beliefs to which Socrates can refer, in the interlocutor's own belief set, which entail the negation of some false belief Socrates has targeted for elenctic refutation, must all be *true*. On what basis could Socrates decide that all of the relevant beliefs are *true* ones? Vlastos's answer, in the end, is that Socrates can feel confident that these beliefs (those, that is, that supply the additional premises *q* and *r*, from which *not-p* follows) are true because Socrates himself also holds these beliefs. If this were true, we should not find Socrates using premises unless he is willing in every case to affirm the truth of those same premises (or at least, his own belief in their truth).

However, we all too often find Socrates perfectly willing to use premises his interlocutor willingly affirms, which we have at least some reason to suppose that Socrates himself does *not* believe. Consider, for example, the way Socrates argues with Euthyphro at 6a and following in the *Euthyphro*.

T2.38 *Euthyphro* 5e–6b:

EUTHYPHRO: . . . These people themselves believe that Zeus is the best and most just of the gods, yet they agree that he bound his father because he unjustly swallowed his sons, and that he in turn castrated his father for similar reasons. But they are angry with me because I am prosecuting my father for his wrongdoing. They contradict themselves in what they say about the gods and about me.

SOCRATES: Indeed, Euthyphro, this is the reason why I am a defendant in the case, because I find it hard to accept things like that being said about the gods, and it is likely to be the reason why I shall be told I do wrong. Now, however, if you, who have full knowledge of such things, share their opinions, then we must agree with them, too, it would seem. For what are we to say, we who agree that we ourselves have no knowledge of them? Tell me, by the god of friendship, do you really believe these things are true?

EUTHYPHRO: Yes, Socrates, and so are even more surprising things, of which the majority has no knowledge.

In this passage, Socrates makes it clear that he does *not* share the same beliefs about the gods that Euthyphro holds, and yet we also find Socrates ready and willing to use Euthyphro's beliefs as premises in the ensuing argument, which, in fact, ends up in inconsistency precisely because of the premises that Euthyphro did—and Socrates did not—believe (see *Euthyphro* 8a-b). A similar argument, perhaps, may be found in the *Protagoras* (351c–358c), where Socrates relies on the identification of goodness with pleasure—an identification he expressly argues against in the *Gorgias* (see esp. 500a).

There are not many such examples, however, where we have very explicit evidence for supposing that Socrates is using premises that he himself does not accept. Thus, we might suppose that we could isolate the examples we do find and regard these examples as exceptions to what is still a significant rule of Socratic inquiry. But some passages suggest that there may be many other "exceptions" and raise serious questions about whether we can count on Socrates' acceptance of premises as anything like a rule.

T2.39 *Euthyphro* 14c (immediately follows **T5.10**):

SOCRATES: . . . the lover of inquiry must follow his beloved wherever it may lead him.

T2.40 *Republic* 1.348e–349a:

(Socrates speaking) That's harder, and it isn't easy now to know what to say. If you had declared that injustice is more profitable, but agreed that it is a vice or shameful, as some others do, we could have discussed the matter on the basis of conventional beliefs. But now, obviously, you'll say that injustice is fine and strong and apply to it all the attributes we used to apply to justice, since you dare to include it with virtue and wisdom.

(Thrasymachus speaking) You've divined my views exactly.

(Socrates speaking) Nonetheless, we mustn't shrink from pursuing the argument and looking into this, just as long as I take you to be saying what you really think. And I believe that you aren't joking now, Thrasymachus, but are saying what you believe to be the truth.

In these passages, we find Socrates discussing his own situation as a "lover of inquiry." Given the "say what you believe" rule, Socrates must always "follow out the logic of the inquiry," even when he does not agree with what his interlocutor might be willing to accept as premises, and sometimes, as he suggests to Thrasymachus, this will require him to accept (for the sake of the inquiry) even very *un*conventional principles and premises. We saw above, moreover (see **T2.35**), that Socrates is always willing to allow his interlocutors to retract any premise they have accepted earlier, if it later seems to them that they should not have accepted this premise.

But if Socrates is not always committed to the premises in the elenctic arguments with which he examines the beliefs of his interlocutor, then even if Vlastos's [A] and [B] were correct, it would not follow that any specific elenctic argument was actually a proof of the truth of its conclusion unless we could be very sure that each premise of that argument was one that Socrates himself believed. There are cases where Socrates seems clearly to express his own opinions, as we have already said, and there are other cases where Socrates introduces premises in ways that make it seem plausible to suppose that he does accept such premises as true. But such cases are not frequent or common enough for us to feel much trust in the idea that Socrates thinks he typically proves the truth of some conclusion he reaches.

At any rate, precisely because there are cases in which Socrates is willing to use as premises certain of his interlocutor's beliefs that Socrates thinks are false, we cannot help but be skeptical about whether Socrates really would be prepared to assume anything as strong as [A]. Surely, Socrates practices the elenchos in a way that always finds him attempting to secure agreement to premises *(q* and *r)* that will be revealed as inconsistent with the interlocutor's initial thesis *(p)*. But because Socrates often suspects that these premises are (also) false, all he may have strong evidence for, from his long history of elenctic argumentation, is a far weaker version of [A]:

[A'] Whoever has a false moral belief will always have at the same time some other (true or false) beliefs entailing the negation of that false belief.

Any argument, however, that relies on some (other) false beliefs to entail the negation of some original false belief cannot qualify as a proof of the sort Vlastos finds in our texts.

If we turn to Vlastos's principle [B], we confront several texts that seem to picture Socrates in ways that directly conflict with Vlastos's account. Socrates often not only professes ignorance, as we have already seen (see **T2.12**, **T2.13**, **T2.14**), but also sometimes says he is perplexed and confused about the issues he is discussing.

T2.41 *Meno* 80c:

SOCRATES: . . . I myself do not have the answer when I perplex others, but I am more perplexed than anyone when I cause perplexity in others.

T2.42 *Euthyphro* 11b-d:

EUTHYPHRO: But Socrates, I have no way of telling you what I have in mind, for whatever proposition we put forward goes around and refuses to stay put where we establish it.

SOCRATES: Your statements, Euthyphro, seem to belong to my ancestor, Daedalus. If I were stating them and putting them forward, you would perhaps be making fun of me and say that because of my kinship with him my conclusions in discussion run away and will not stay where one puts them. As these propositions are yours, however, we need some other jest, for they will not stay put for you, as you say yourself.

EUTHYPHRO: I think the same jest will do for our discussion, Socrates, for I am not the one who makes them go round and not remain in the same place; it is you who are the Daedalus; for as far as I am concerned they would remain as they were.

SOCRATES: It looks as if I was cleverer than Daedalus in using my skill, my friend, in so far as he could only cause to move the things he made himself, but I can make other people's move as well as my own. And the smartest part of my skill is that I am clever without wanting to be, for I would rather have your statements to me remain unmoved than possess the wealth of Tantalus as well as the cleverness of Daedalus.

T2.43 *Lesser Hippias* 372d-e (continues **T2.11**):

SOCRATES: So indeed now, I don't agree with what you are saying but disagree very strongly. But I know very well that this is my fault— it's because I'm the sort of person I am, not to say anything better of myself than what I deserve. To me, Hippias, it appears entirely the opposite of what you say: those who harm people and commit injustice and lie and cheat and go wrong voluntarily, rather than involuntarily, are better than those who do so involuntarily. However, sometimes I believe the opposite, and I go back and forth about all this—plainly because I don't know.

T2.44 *Lesser Hippias* 376b-c:

HIPPIAS: I can't agree with you in that, Socrates.

SOCRATES: Nor I with myself, Hippias. But given the argument, we can't help having it look that way to us, now, at any rate. However, as I said before, on these matters I waver back and forth and never believe the same thing. And it's not surprising at all that I or any other ordinary person *should* waver. But if you wise men are going to do it, too—that means something terrible for us, if we can't stop our wavering even after we've put ourselves in your company.

No one who speaks about himself in this way could simply *assume* that all of his beliefs were true, or even consistent (see also *Protagoras* 361a-d).

Recall that it was Socrates' claim in **T2.37** that led Vlastos to identify what he called "*the* problem of the Socratic elenchus," which was how Socrates could take himself to be *proving* anything with arguments that used premises whose own truth was unsecured.[25]

T2.36 *Gorgias* 479e (repeated):

SOCRATES: Hasn't it been proved that what was said is true?

Earlier, Socrates made very clear what he meant in making this claim and what it is that he is seeking to accomplish with Polus.

T2.45 *Gorgias* 475e–476a:

SOCRATES: So you see, Polus, that when the one refutation is compared with the other, there is no resemblance at all. Whereas everyone but me agrees with you, you are all I need, although you're just a party of one, for your agreement and testimony. It's you alone whom I call on for a vote; the others I disregard. Let this be our verdict on this matter, then.

The kind of "proof" Socrates is giving to Polus, then, is entirely conditioned upon the "testimony" of Socrates' single witness, Polus himself. Moreover, as he goes on, immediately after claiming to have won his "proof" at 479e, he makes very clear that the entire result of the argument is conditioned on what Polus has agreed to in the argument itself.

T2.46 *Gorgias* 480a-b:

SOCRATES: Hasn't it been proved that what was said is true?

POLUS: Apparently.

SOCRATES: Fair enough. If these things are true then, Polus, what is the great use of oratory? For on the basis of what we're agreed on now, what a man should guard himself against most of all is doing what's unjust, knowing that he will have trouble enough if he does. Isn't that so?

POLUS: Yes, that's right.

SOCRATES: And if he or anyone else he cares about acts unjustly, he should voluntarily go to the place where he'll pay his due as soon as possible; he should go to the judge as though he were going to a doctor, anxious that the disease of injustice shouldn't be protracted and cause his soul to fester incurably. What else can we say, Polus, if our previous agreements really stand?

Notice how Socrates repeatedly reminds Polus that the "proof" they have achieved is conditioned upon their earlier agreements. Moreover, when Polus shows that he has found Socrates' alleged "proof" anything but convincing, Socrates immediately makes his customary offer to have Polus disavow some premise he had agreed to earlier (see **T2.35**).

T2.47 *Gorgias* 480e (immediately follows **T5.24**):

> POLUS: I think these statements are absurd, Socrates, though no doubt you think they agree with those expressed earlier.
>
> SOCRATES: Then either we should abandon those, or else these necessarily follow?
>
> POLUS: Yes, that's how it is.

From the way Socrates conceives of his "proof," therefore, it is clear that he does not take himself, in his argument with Polus, to have demonstrated anything as simply and conclusively true; he has only revealed to Polus the consequences of various premises to which Polus was at least initially willing to agree, and he is ready to have Polus disavow those premises and make very different claims. This is hardly the behavior of anyone who takes himself as having "proved" anything in a way that would give rise to what Vlastos calls "*the* problem of the Socratic elenchus." It seems, then, that "*the* problem of the Socratic elenchus" is not a problem at all, unless we overestimate considerably, and thus misunderstand, the strength of Socrates' claim in **T2.37** to have "proved" something to Polus. Of course, it may well be that Socrates actually does accept each of the premises of his argument with Polus, in which case the argument would also provide Socrates with deductive support for the conclusion. Indeed, Socrates never gives us any reason to doubt this. But even so, such a "proof" would not give rise to what Vlastos has called "*the* problem of the elenchus," for Socrates' commitment to the truth of these premises may not be a matter of unconditional conviction, so much as a matter of quite provisional acceptance—acceptance that he would gladly submit to critical scrutiny, and that he could well imagine changing, if good reasons for doing so were presented.

Accordingly, there is no special reason to suppose that Socrates counts any of his arguments as "proofs" in the unconditional sense assumed in Vlastos's account. But does this mean that Socrates only exposes inconsistencies in his interlocutors' belief systems, as the nonconstructivist claims? Does Socrates achieve no constructive results in his lifelong experience with elenctic argument?

2.2.5 Inductivist Constructivism

A deductive proof is one in which the conclusion will always be true, wherever the premises are true. Proofs of geometric theorems are one kind of deductive proof. Vlastos's approach to the Socratic elenchos began with the perception that Socrates' elenctic arguments are deductive in form, and so—if the inferences made within these arguments are valid ones—it will be the case that the conclusions he reaches with his interlocutors will be true when the premises are true. The problem with Vlastos's view is that he seems to think that it is by way of these deductions that Socrates derives moral knowledge. But this would be the case only if Socrates always—or at least for the most part—thought that he was in a position to know the truth of the premises he uses. For the reasons we have given, we doubt that Socrates really did suppose he was in such a position, and we doubt that it was ever a requirement even that he actually believe all of the premises of his arguments, though sometimes perhaps he did.

These doubts, then, take us back to the question of Socrates' own views and what reason or support or warrant he might suppose that he had for believing what he believed. That he has certain opinions—even some for which he seems prepared to argue (as in the *Gorgias*) and even (as in the *Crito*) to die—is something we noted in section 2.2.1. If Socrates did not think he had proofs for these positions, then where and how did he come to hold them? And if the elenchos does not *prove* its conclusions, can the elenchos give anyone reason to believe anything?

Nonconstructivists argue that all Socrates ever claims to do with the elenchos is to reveal the ignorance of those who think they know when they do not. But the elenchos certainly does more than this, for it shows the logical links between the premises the interlocutor accepts and the conclusions the interlocutor usually finds so surprising. The interlocutor asserts that p, but then Socrates gets the interlocutor to assent to q and r (where these may be conjunctions of several propositions), then shows that q and r entail *not-p*. In so far as the interlocutor feels committed to the truth of q and r, Socrates has revealed to the interlocutor reasons (accepted by the interlocutor himself) for believing *not-p*, instead of p. As we have said, this is not a *proof* of *not-p*, for the premises q and r are not themselves known to be true and may even be false.

Socrates' interlocutors often end up in perplexity, not knowing what to do, because they find themselves in a position of having some reasons (namely, q and r) for believing *not-p*, whereas they had also supposed they had reason to believe that p. Thus, they find their beliefs do not form a consistent set, and this is what the elenchos is so good at revealing. But it may not be at all clear to the interlocutor which belief, in the inconsistent belief set *(p, q, r)*, should be jettisoned for the sake of consistency in his beliefs. Socrates, however, may be in a much better position than his interlocutors in this case, for as Vlastos also notes, Socrates has spent a substantial part of his life engaging in elenctic arguments with others. In a famous passage in the *Gorgias*, Socrates makes his customary disclaimer of knowledge but then reveals that his experience in argument has shown him something none the less:

T2.48 *Gorgias* 509a (part of longer quote at **T3.8**):

> SOCRATES: . . . I don't know how these things are, but no one I've ever met, as in this case, can say anything else without being ridiculous.

Throughout the *Gorgias*, we find Socrates making claims and arguing for certain positions, which are then challenged by his interlocutors. Each new challenge Socrates turns aside, despite the fact that each new challenge comes with a somewhat different set of premises. No doubt, Socrates has encountered many different belief sets while pursuing his "mission" in Athens, but in **T2.48** he shows that no matter what else others have believed, certain beliefs (in this case, the belief that it is better to do than to suffer injustice) have always turned out to get those who believed them into the kind of trouble that Callicles (Socrates' interlocutor at this point in the *Gorgias*) now finds himself in. Thus, Callicles—like Socrates' other interlocutors—may find himself in perplexity and not know which of his beliefs he should give up; but Socrates, given his experience with elenctic argument, feels quite confident that it is the original thesis that is the problem.

In the next chapter, we consider the issue of whether enough experience of the relevant sort would be sufficient for Socrates to claim to *know* what his elenchos, over time, shows in this way. For now, it is enough to say that extensive experience with elenctic argument, which allows him to examine many different belief sets for consistency, can generate constructive results—that is, reasons to accept certain propositions and to reject others. Moreover, in the *Crito*, we find Socrates arguing in a way that makes explicit reference to convictions he has derived from his discussions with others.

T2.49 *Crito* 49a-b:

> SOCRATES: Do we say that one must never in any way do wrong willingly, or must one do wrong in one way and not in another? Is to do wrong never good or admirable, as we have agreed in the past, or have all the former agreements been washed out during the last few days? Have we at our age failed to notice for some time that in our serious discussions we were no different from children? Above

all, is the truth such as we used to say it was, whether the majority agree or not, and whether we must still suffer worse things than we do now, or will be treated more gently, that nonetheless, wrongdoing is in every way harmful and shameful to the wrongdoer? Do we say so or not?

CRITO: We do.

SOCRATES: So one must never do wrong.

This text, and ones like it, make it much easier for one not only to discern what Socrates' philosophical beliefs are but also to recognize that their source is none other than "our serious discussions," to which Socrates has devoted his life. Although Vlastos was wrong to think that Socrates regarded his elenctic arguments as proofs, his nonconstructivist critics have also been wrong to overlook the value of the elenchos as a way to do philosophy in a constructive way, discovering and securing those doctrines and principles that it is best for one to believe and that reveal themselves as generating consistent, rather than inconsistent, sets of philosophical beliefs. The picture we have offered here for the constructive work of the elenchos is not deductive but is, instead, an inductive one. Socrates learns from the regularities of many experiences, observing many examples of arguments and making what is called an induction from his observations. We believe, moreover, that this not only provides the most adequate interpretation of the texts but also gives a fairly accurate picture of how philosophy continues to do its work even today. But that is a topic for a different book.

2.3 Self-Knowledge and Psychological Constructivism

2.3.1 Being "Out of Tune" with Ourselves

In his account, Vlastos stressed what he called the "say what you believe" requirement. We have already shown how this requirement can lead to perplexity in Socrates' interlocutors and how it can also help Socrates to discern which beliefs seem always to get people into consistency problems and which do not. But there is still more to be said about this rule and about how Socrates always insists that his interlocutors always say only what they believe.

Let us return to look again at the way Socrates mocks and challenges Callicles, in the *Gorgias,* about what Socrates perceives as inconsistencies in Callicles' position.

T2.50 *Gorgias* 482a-b (immediately precedes T2.37):

As for that son of Clinias [Alcibiades], what he says differs from one time to the next, but what philosophy says always stays the same, and she's saying things that now astound you, although you were present when they were said. So, either refute her and show that doing what's unjust without paying what is due for it is *not* the ultimate of all bad things, as I just now was saying it is, or else if you leave this unrefuted, then by the Dog, the god of the Egyptians, Callicles will not agree with you, Callicles, but will be dissonant with you all your life long.

When one first reads this passage, one might find it puzzling in several ways: (1) How does Socrates know what "philosophy" says? (2) Socrates has not yet established that Callicles has inconsistent beliefs, for Callicles at this point in the *Gorgias* has only just started talking with Socrates, so how can Socrates say that if Callicles leaves what "philosophy" says unrefuted, then Callicles will not agree with Callicles and "will be in conflict in [his] whole way of living"? (3) Why does Socrates think that a conflict in Callicles' belief system is tantamount to a conflict in Callicles' "whole way of living"?

Given what we have already said, we are in a position now to answer the first two of these questions quite easily. Socrates has devoted his life to a "mission" of testing others with the elenchos, and as a result of this, he is in an excellent position to know what "philosophy" says. Socrates knows what "philosophy" says because he is in a position to see how his elenctic arguments always seem to come out, regarding certain positions. And Socrates can claim that Callicles has an inconsistent set of beliefs, just on the basis of the one claim he has made, because—unless Callicles can refute what philosophizing has shown Socrates—the one claim Callicles has made is one of those that Socrates has come to recognize as always and only found within an inconsistent belief set. Let us turn, then, to the third of our puzzles: Why is an inconsistent belief set tantamount to a conflict in Callicles' "whole way of living"?

2.3.2 Acting for the Sake of the Good

Prior to Callicles' entry into the conversation in the *Gorgias*, Socrates showed Polus why it is that one who does whatever he thinks is best does not always do what he wants. The argument begins at *Gorgias* 466a, when Socrates challenges Polus to refute the claim that rhetoric is nothing but flattery. Polus, a great admirer of rhetoric, attempts to defend it by showing that rhetoric can win great power in the Greek cities. Socrates gets Polus to agree, however, that it is no great power one has if one does what seems best for him but does so in a way that is "without intelligence" (*Gorgias* 466e). One might think, for example, that the possession of certain weapons makes one powerful, but Socrates and Polus agree that there is no genuine power unless one has the intelligence to *use* the tools of power in such a way as to gain what one truly wants. Thus, even the possession of such weapons is not sufficient for true power, if, for example, one stupidly uses them in ways that are self-destructive or self-defeating. To put it another way, a loaded gun in the hands of a child might make the child *dangerous* but will not truly make the child *powerful*: The child might use the weapon in a way that the child *thinks* is best but not use it in a way that will achieve what the child really *wants*.

Having won this point, however, Socrates is now in a position to make the distinction that had initially confused Polus: Even if rhetoric will win one certain opportunities in the cities, it will only follow that rhetoricians can do whatever they *think* is best. They will not necessarily do what they truly *want*, because they may not have the intelligence to make the correct judgments, wherein what they *think* is best really is always the same as what they *want*. What everyone *wants*, Socrates gets Polus to agree, is whatever is best for them (*Gorgias* 468a-c). Accordingly, everyone does what they *think* is best for them. The problems come when what one *thinks* is best for one is not what is really best. In cases such as these, one is revealed as not powerful, for one does not do what one *wants*.

The importance of this argument, for our present purposes, is in the recognition that everyone does what they *think* is best for them. Here is where we find the justification for Socrates' tentative diagnosis of Callicles as having a conflict in his "whole way of living." Socrates and Polus, and then Socrates and Callicles, dispute whether it is better to do or to suffer injustice. Socrates' position is that he wants neither of these but would prefer to suffer than to do injustice. Polus and Callicles state that they would rather do than suffer injustice—indeed, both seem to think that being unimpeded in doing injustice would be best of all (even better than Socrates' highest preference, which was neither to do nor to suffer injustice). This is not some minor point, one unlikely to have any consequence in the way these men lead their lives—it is such a basic issue of preference and life goals that it is sure to have profound and perhaps even daily effects on the ways in which these men will live. But Socrates is convinced that his philosophizing has shown him that the view Polus and Callicles have endorsed is one that no one can ever fit into a consistent set of beliefs.

Everyone acts on the basis of what they believe is best for them. If Socrates is right, however, some significant part of what Polus and Callicles believe is best for them is in conflict with their belief that it is better to do than to suffer injustice. If these beliefs form the basis for how they will live, then this inconsistency in their beliefs will inevitably yield deep conflicts and confusions in the way these men will live. Accordingly,

Socrates warns Callicles that unless he can refute the view that philosophy has revealed to Socrates, Callicles will be in conflict in his "whole way of living."

2.3.3 Self-Knowledge

Socrates goes even further than this, however. Not only does he diagnose those who disagree with the positions he has discovered through philosophy as being in conflict in their lives, but he also claims that they can be exposed as *sharing* Socrates' positions even when they begin by denying that they do. Several times, in his discussion with Polus, Socrates attributes beliefs to Polus that Polus himself seems prepared quite vigorously to deny.
   T2.51 *Gorgias* 466d-e:

> SOCRATES: . . . I say, Polus, that orators and tyrants have the very least power in their cities, as I was saying just now, for they do just about nothing they want to, though they certainly do whatever they see most fit to do.
>
> POLUS: Well, isn't this having great power?
>
> SOCRATES: No; at least Polus says it isn't.
>
> POLUS: I say it isn't? I certainly say it is!
>
> SOCRATES: By . . . , you certainly don't! since you said that having great power is good for the one who has it.
>
> POLUS: Yes, I do say that.

Socrates perceives that one of the things Polus is affirming implies the opposite of one of the other things Polus is affirming, and Polus does not see this (yet). And Socrates goes even further than this: He is prepared to predict what Polus will do—which position he will abandon—when he comes to recognize the conflict in his positions. And not just Polus: Socrates is willing to make claims about what *everyone* will decide, if only they thought about these issues carefully.
   T2.52 *Gorgias* 474b:

> SOCRATES: For I do believe that you and I and everybody else consider doing what's unjust worse than suffering it, and not paying what is due worse than paying it.
>
> POLUS: And I do believe that I don't, and that no other person does, either. So you'd take suffering what's unjust over doing it, would you?

SOCRATES: Yes, and so would you and everyone else.

POLUS: Far from it! I wouldn't, you wouldn't, and nobody else would, either.

Here is a good time to remind ourselves of what we called the *Principle of Charity* in the Introduction: We must not suppose that Socrates is making the obviously false claim that Polus is *aware* of believing what Socrates says he and everyone else believes. But Socrates will use the elenchos to bring Polus to the realization that various other beliefs Polus holds entail the very position Socrates claims everyone accepts.

When we looked at the basic logical structure of elenctic arguments, we found that the interlocutor would always be free to retract or withdraw his assent to any of the premises, which led him to a position that is incompatible with the belief Socrates targeted for refutation. After a lifetime of philosophizing, however, Socrates is in a position to predict that there are certain premises his interlocutors will never retract or dissent from. When he encounters some new person willing to assert some view that Socrates recognizes is in conflict with these premises, all he needs to do is to reveal the conflict to them, and he is confident—if they will only lead what he calls "the examined life"—that they will abandon the conflicting view rather than the premises that reveal the problem with the conflicting view.

It is understandable that Polus remains extremely dubious at the end of the discussion with Socrates (see *Gorgias* 480e [**T2.47**]), despite having been brought—entirely on the basis of his own beliefs (having satisfied the "'say what you believe' requirement")—to the acknowledgment of precisely the position Socrates had attributed to him at the beginning of their discussion. Even though Polus has said only "what he believed," because the conclusion reached is so foreign to what he thought he believed, he no doubt wonders whether the reasoning was really correct or whether Socrates managed to trick him in some way. We have all had the experience of reaching a conclusion that is at odds with what we expected and thinking, "This can't be right." And we are right to go back and reexamine our reasoning again. No doubt this is at least part of the reason Socrates says in the *Apology* that moral examination is something we need to practice everyday.

T2.21 *Apology* 38a (repeated):

> I say that it is the greatest good for a human being to discuss virtue every day and those other things about which you hear me conversing and testing myself and others, for the unexamined life is not worth living for a human being . . . .

Unless Polus is prepared to live an "examined life" he is likely just to fall right back into his old bad habits of belief and not to recognize the deep conflicts in his system of beliefs or the effects of these conflicts on his "whole way of living."

Plato's Socrates is fond of quoting one of the inscriptions carved into the rock at the shrine to Apollo at Delphi: "Know Thyself" (see *Charmides* 164d; *Protagoras* 229e; *Phaedrus* 229e; *Philebus* 48c; *Laws* 11.923a; [Ps.-Plato] *Alcibiades* 124a, 129a, 132c). We now see how his fondness for this maxim is connected to his insistence on what Vlastos called the "'say what you believe' requirement" of the elenchos. By requiring his interlocutors always to say what they believe, Socrates gives them an opportunity to improve their own self-knowledge. If we lead the "examined life" and, in doing so, say always only what we believe, we will discover what we really believe and jettison those more superficial beliefs that conflict with what we find we really believe. The benefits of this are not just increased self-knowledge, however. Because we shape every activity in our lives around what we think is best for us, if we can only get straight on what we really believe, we can also straighten out our priorities and our lives.

2.3.4 Constructivism and Socrates as a Teacher

We began this chapter with questions about Socrates as a teacher and immediately confronted various things Socrates said that seemed to conflict with the widely held idea that Socrates was a teacher. We are now in a position to see how Socrates was and was not a teacher. We argued that we had strong reasons for believing that Socrates was sincere in his profession of ignorance, but we also acknowledged that a fuller examination of Socrates' conceptions of knowledge and wisdom was necessary, to which we turn in the next chapter. We also noted that Socrates readily professed to have certain views on a number of very significant issues but stipulated that his holding certain views did not make him a teacher of those views. We then turned to the question of whether Socrates' unique form of philosophizing—the elenchos—was a *constructive* form of inquiry, that is, one that discovers and justifies certain positions while refuting or offering evidence against others, and we found that it was.

But does this not, then, land us in the very place Socrates' interlocutors inevitably found themselves? That is, are we not now committed to saying, after all, that Socrates *was* a teacher and that his elenctic arguments were examples of teaching? Yes and no: According to the interpretation we have developed in this chapter, those who engaged in elenctic argument with Socrates were in a position to learn very important things in the process, especially if they were willing to lead "examined lives" and engage in philosophy. But if they did learn anything, would it be accurate to say that they had learned it from Socrates? No; now that we understand the significance of Socrates' insistence on the "'say what you believe' requirement," we can see that anyone who learned anything in conversation with Socrates would ultimately be learning it from themselves, for it would be *their own* views they would discover. If Socrates' interlocutors benefit from having been examined by Socrates, it is true that they have learned something *because* of Socrates: But for Socrates' skillful and relentless questioning, they would not have learned what they did. But they have learned nothing *from* Socrates, at least not in the sense in which we would ordinarily say that someone learned something from a teacher.

Moreover, for Socrates, it is one thing to undertake to *persuade* someone of something and quite another to *teach* them something.

T2.53 *Gorgias* 454c-d:

SOCRATES: Come then, and let's examine this point. Is there something you call "to have learned"?

GORGIAS: There is.

SOCRATES: Very well. And also something you call "to be persuaded"[26]?

GORGIAS: Yes, there is.

SOCRATES: Now, do you think that to have learned, learning, are the same as to be persuaded and persuasion, or different?

GORGIAS: I certainly suppose that they're different, Socrates.

SOCRATES: You suppose rightly. This is how you can tell: If someone asked you, "Is there such a thing as true and false persuasion, Gorgias?" you'd say yes, I'm sure.

GORGIAS: Yes.

SOCRATES: Well now, is there such a thing as true and false knowledge?

GORGIAS: Not at all.

SOCRATES: So it's clear that they're not the same.

When Socrates makes this distinction, he intends to secure Gorgias's acknowledgment that orators in courtrooms produce mere persuasion and not learning. But we can also apply this same distinction between what Socrates does—when he very obviously tries to persuade his interlocutors to accept certain positions—and what he would count as "teaching." Socrates certainly does attempt to persuade people of certain moral positions, but he also quite sincerely denies teaching anyone anything—

for Socrates supposes that he has no knowledge for others to learn from him.

Notes

1. This is the translation provided in Cooper (1997). In **T3.9**, we provide our own translation, for greater precision on an issue we discuss in Chapter 3.

2. Vlastos (1991).

3. Ibid., 22.

4. Ibid., 21.

5. Ibid., 22.

6. Ibid., 23.

7. Ibid., 29.

8. Ibid., 28.

9. Vlastos does acknowledge that some irony involves mockery, but we wish to identify a separate category of such irony here, in which the mockery is achieved through intended deception.

10. See, for examples, *Apology* 20c, 21d, 23b; *Charmides* 165b-c, 166c-d; *Euthyphro* 5a, 15c, 15e–16a; *Laches* 186b-e, 200e; *Lysis* 212a, 223b; *Greater Hippias* 286c-e, 304d-e; *Gorgias* 509a; *Meno* 71a, 80d; *Republic* 1.337e.

11. At the end of this quote, we have used the alternative translation given in Cooper (1997)—see Cooper (1997), 28, n. 4—on the ground that we do not think that the other translation offered there is grammatically tenable.

12. One of the most detailed and impressive arguments for this position can be found in Benson (1995). For a much earlier expression of this view, see Grote (1865).

13. Grote (1865), vol. 1, 292.

14. Zeller (1885), 121.

15. Robinson (1953), 28.

16. In fact, Vlastos's "solution" has gone through several versions. We focus on the one that was published in Vlastos (1994b), which notes the differences from his earlier attempts.

17. Vlastos used the Latinized form "elenchus" rather than "elenchos," which is closer to the original Greek word and which most scholars now prefer.

18. Vlastos (1994b), 11.

19. Ibid., 3–4.

20. Ibid., 7–8.

21. Ibid., 25.

22. Ibid., 28.

23. Ibid., 27.

24. Ibid., 27, n. 69.

25. Actually, Vlastos gives a list of ten theses, which he thinks Socrates counts himself as having proved using the elenchos, and says that this list is not exhaustive (ibid., 11–12). A more recent (and more exhaustive) study, by the best-known

nonconstructivist (Benson 1995), however, has shown that all the texts support the more modest claim that such theses are only what Socrates' arguments with his interlocutor have led to. This is a much more modest claim, because it may well be that an argument leads to a certain conclusion only because one or more of the premises is faulty, such that if the faulty premise were removed or fixed, the same conclusion would not be supported.

26. Here, we deviate from the translation given in Cooper (1997), which has "convinced" and "conviction." The Greek word *(pepisteukenai)* does not require as high a level of cognitive commitment as "convinced" and "conviction" seem to denote, and Socrates' distinction seems to require that the relevant results can be neither reliable nor stable. Donald J. Zeyl's translation (in Cooper 1997) no doubt uses "convinced" and "conviction" here to reserve "persuasion" for *peithein,* which the passage goes on to say is produced both in those who have learned and in those who have been "convinced." We do not mean to argue that the Zeyl's decision was inappropriate; we have modified the translation only to clarify the difference Socrates intends between the products of the two kinds of persuasion: belief versus knowledge.

Suggested Readings

On the "Socratic Method,"
the Elenchos (or Elenchus), and the
Constructivism-Nonconstructivism Debate

The standard work on what is known as "the Socratic method" for many years was Robinson (1953). But the work most often cited now is the famous article by Vlastos, originally published in 1983 but later revised and included in Vlastos (1994b, ch. 1). In Vlastos's view, the Socratic elenchos was a reliable method, by which Socrates could argue to conclusions he would know were true, using true premises he could find among his interlocutors' own belief sets. Well-known criticisms of Vlastos's view include Kraut (1983), Brickhouse and Smith (1984), Polansky (1985), and Benson (1987). Several alternatives to the account given by Vlastos have more recently been offered. Kraut (1983) expresses doubts that the elenchos is really all that different from other forms of deductive argumentation. Bolton (1993) asserts that what secures the premises of elenctic arguments is that they are what Aristotle later calls *endoxa*—opinions that are either so widely held or are held by people of such credibility as to be beyond serious doubt. Benson (1995) argues that Plato's Socrates simply never conceived the elenchos as a form of argumentation that would prove its conclusions true but viewed it, rather, as only an instrument for revealing the interlocutor's lack of wisdom. (Our own argument against Vlastos's account, in this chapter, owes much to Benson's comprehensive study.) In Brickhouse and Smith (1994, sections 1.2–1.3, revised from an earlier article, published in 1991), we argue for the account we have offered in this chapter. May (1997) argues for a special role for elenctic argument, when applied to definitions of value terms.

On Socratic Irony

As with nearly every aspect of Socratic philosophy, the most widely cited recent study is by Vlastos (1991, ch. 1). A critique of Vlastos's account of Socratic irony may be found in Brickhouse and Smith (1993), especially 397–401.

On Self-Knowledge as a Socratic Aim

Our first study of this topic was published as an article in 1992 and was revised in Brickhouse and Smith (1994, ch. 3). Rappe (1995) argues that the "self" of which Socrates seeks knowledge is ultimately impersonal and entirely intellectual.

3

Socrates on
Knowledge and Ignorance

3.1 Knowing and Not Knowing

3.1.1 Two Problems

In the Introduction, we noted that one of the most common ways in which problems for interpretation are spotted is by noticing an apparent conflict in the relevant texts. This creates an interpretive problem because the *Principle of Charity* requires interpretations that do not commit the author or speaker to foolish or inconsistent positions. Clearly, where the texts seem to present Socrates advocating inconsistent positions, the *Principle of Charity* requires us at least to consider if there might be some way out of the apparent inconsistency. However, we must always bear in mind the requirements set by the *Principle of Textual Fidelity* and the *Principle of Interpretive Plausibility,* which require us not to advance interpretations that violate the clear sense of any of the texts and to accept only those interpretations that plausibly explain what the text says. Where the text seems to commit Socrates to inconsistent positions, then, these principles tend to pull the interpreter in different directions: *Textual Fidelity* and *Interpretive Plausibility* seem to require us to accept the inconsistency, whereas *Charity* pushes us to reject the inconsistency. Plainly, satisfying all of these principles in such cases can be tricky!

In the last chapter, we considered the possibility that Socrates' famous profession of ignorance might be ironical. After reviewing several sorts of irony and what the consequences of interpreting the profession as ironical might be, we tentatively concluded that it would be best to regard Socrates' profession of ignorance as sincere and not ironical, except perhaps in the tragic sense of irony, which allows the profession to be genuine. The fact is, however, that the texts in this case present formidable challenges, which is why we said our earlier conclusions about Socrates' profession of ignorance could only be tentative. The challenges concern texts in which Socrates says things that seem to be in direct conflict with his profession of ignorance, for we sometimes find Socrates claiming to have knowledge. To make matters even more puzzling, Socrates also occasionally seems to grant that *others* have knowledge—in some cases, knowledge that he, Socrates, does not have. It is not at all obvious how we are to square these remarks with his claim to be the wisest of men, because only he recognizes that he has no knowledge or wisdom and that others are every bit as ignorant, only they do not realize it.

There are actually two different problems here. In addition to the obvious one, there are other texts that seem to commit Socrates to a philosophical position that would help to explain why he regards himself and others as ignorant. Many texts appear to commit Socrates to a principle known as the *Priority of Definitional Knowledge* (PD):

Priority of Definitional Knowledge (PD) *Only if one knows the definition of some quality (F-ness) can one know anything about F-ness or F-things, including whether any instance of F-ness is really an instance.*

Not once, however, in any of Plato's early dialogues, do we find an instance where Socrates or an interlocutor manages successfully to give the definition of any value term. For example, Euthyphro and Socrates try in vain to produce an adequate definition of "piety" in Plato's *Euthyphro*, and nowhere else do we find Socrates or an interlocutor successfully defining piety. According to (PD), therefore, since neither Socrates nor anyone else knows what piety is, no one knows whether or not any putative instance of piety is truly pious—in effect, it follows that no one knows anything at all about piety. In the *Laches*, Socrates and his interlocutors fail to define "courage," and no successful definition of "courage" can be found anywhere else in Plato's early dialogues. From principle (PD), then, it follows that no one knows anything about courage, and so on for friendship (the definition of which is sought in vain in the *Lysis*), beauty or fineness *(Greater Hippias)*, justice *(Republic 1)*, temperance *(Charmides)*, and even virtue itself *(Meno)*. If Socrates really is committed to (PD), it is easy to explain why he thinks he has no knowledge or wisdom and why he thinks no one else has them either. But the texts that seem to provide support for his being committed to (PD) raise additional questions about those texts in which Socrates seems prepared to claim, and grant others' claims, to have knowledge. If Socrates thinks that he and others have knowledge, then either Socrates must not accept (PD) after all or else he must think that he knows a great deal more than his profession of ignorance would appear to allow, including especially what the definitions of all the qualities of whatever it is that Socrates or others know about. At any rate, the texts in which Socrates claims or discusses knowledge and ignorance very clearly present us with problems to solve.

In this chapter, we consider these problems in the order in which we have just now raised them, first considering how the profession of ignorance might be reconciled with Socrates' occasional claims of knowledge and acknowledgments of others' knowledge, and then applying the results of our interpretation on this issue to the complicated problems involving principle (PD). We will begin by trying to get clear on exactly what Socrates means by knowledge, when he professes ignorance and tests others. Our survey of this issue reveals that Socrates employs two very different conceptions of knowledge, which we will show to be consistent by showing that the kind of knowledge Socrates claims to lack (and claims all other human beings lack) is not the same as the kind of knowledge he occasionally claims to have and seems willing to grant to others. We then review the texts that seem to commit Socrates to principle (PD), and assess the interpretive options open to us in reading these texts. In this section of our argument, we attempt to show that Socrates is not committed to (PD) in any way that conflicts with his occasional claims of knowledge. Given the complexities of the texts and the relevant issues, readers should bear in mind the interpretive principles that govern adequate interpretation and decide for themselves whether the interpretations we offer are satisfactory. The solutions to the problems presented here are controversial.

3.1.2 What Does Socrates Know?
What Does Anyone Know?

We have already reviewed several texts in which Socrates makes his famous profession of ignorance. Let us now look at a few texts in which he seems to make a conflicting claim. In the first of these, we find Socrates not only claiming to know "many things" but actually repeating his claim of knowledge a second time.

T3.1 *Euthydemus* 293b-c:

(Socrates speaking, recalling a conversation he had with Euthydemus) Then come answer me this, he [Euthydemus] said: Is there anything you know?

Oh, yes, I said, many things, though trivial ones.

That will serve the purpose, he said. Now do you suppose it possible for any existing thing not to be what it is?

Heavens no, not I.

And do you know something? he said.

Yes, I do.

Then you are knowing, if you really know?

Of course, as far as concerns that particular thing.

Thus, at least when it comes to "trivial things," it turns out that Socrates actually knows "many things." Moreover, it is not just Socrates who can know "trivial things"; apparently anyone can know things of this nature.

T3.2 *Ion* 532d-e:

> SOCRATES: . . . As for me, I say nothing but the truth, as you'd expect
> from an ordinary man. I mean, even this question I asked you—
> look how commonplace and ordinary a matter it is—the sort of
> thing that anyone could know.[1]

We might feel a little easier about the apparent conflict between this passage and Socrates' customary profession of ignorance if we focus on his disclaimer that the "many things" he and others might know are all "trivial" things. We have good reason to think that it was not just *any* knowledge that Socrates claims he and others lack. After all, in one of the clearest expressions of his profession of ignorance, Socrates allows that *some* people do have *some* knowledge. However, those who have such knowledge do not qualify as wiser than Socrates, for if they did, Socrates would be mistaken in his understanding of the famous oracle, referred to in the *Apology* (20e–23b) about his "wisdom." Whatever wisdom these other people have is offset by a kind of ignorance that makes them, on balance, less wise than Socrates.

T3.3 *Apology* 22c-e:

> Finally, I went to the craftsmen, for I was conscious of knowing practically
> nothing, and I thought that I would find that they had knowledge of many
> fine things. In this I was not mistaken; they knew things I did not know, and to
> that extent they were wiser than I. But, gentlemen of the jury, the good crafts-
> men seemed to me to have the same fault as the poets: each of them, because
> of his success at his craft, thought himself very wise in other most important
> pursuits, and this error of theirs overshadowed the wisdom they had, so that I
> asked myself, on behalf of the oracle, whether I should prefer to be as I am,
> with neither their wisdom nor their ignorance, or to have both. The answer I
> gave myself and the oracle was that it was to my advantage to be as I am.

Socrates' own lack of wisdom and knowledge includes those areas where he finds the craftsmen really are wise and do have knowledge: in their crafts. But it is not this lack of knowledge and wisdom that Socrates counts as the most significant, for the craftsmen share Socrates' own lack of knowledge and wisdom about what he calls "the most important things" but do not realize they do, and in this failure, they prove to be even less wise, all told, than Socrates.

As anyone who reads Plato's *Apology* can discern, by "the most important things," Socrates is referring to moral or ethical matters—the kinds of topics, that is, that we find him always discussing in Plato's early dialogues. At any rate, if it is knowledge and wisdom about *these* matters that Socrates is referring to in making his own disclaimer of knowledge and wisdom and in denying knowledge and wisdom to others, then his claim to know "many things, though trivial ones" in **T3.1** and his recognition that others may know certain "trivial things" in **T3.2** do not conflict with his disclaimers, as long as we suppose that no moral matters are included among the "trivial things" that Socrates and others know.

But even if we can escape conflict with these texts, we also find Socrates occasionally claiming and granting others claims to *morally significant* knowledge. No doubt, Socrates' most famous knowledge claim appears in his first speech in the *Apology*, where he begins with what looks like his customary declaration of ignorance but then suddenly contrasts this ignorance with something he *does* know.

T3.4 *Apology* 29b (partially overlaps with **T6.21** and **T7.20**):

> It is perhaps on this point and in this respect, gentlemen, that I differ from the majority of men, and if I were to claim that I am wiser than anyone in anything, it would be in this, that, as I have no adequate knowledge of things in the underworld, so I do not think I have. I do know, however, that it is wicked and shameful to do wrong, to disobey one's superior, be he god or man. I shall never fear or avoid things of which I do not know, whether they may not be good rather than things that I know to be bad.

Nor is this the only place where Socrates is ready to claim moral knowledge. Although it is not specific, it seems inescapable that Socrates thinks of himself as knowing that some things are bad, when he considers what sort of penalty to offer in his second speech in the *Apology*.

T3.5 *Apology* 37b (part of longer quote at **T4.22**):

> What should I fear? That I should suffer the penalty Meletus has assessed against me, of which I say I do not know whether it is good or bad? Am I then to choose in preference to this something that I know very well to be an evil and assess the penalty at that?

If Socrates had no morally significant knowledge, which he sometimes refers to as the "knowledge of good and evil," the contrast between his lack of knowledge about death with his knowledge that some things are evil in **T3.4** and **T3.5** would make no sense.

One more such passage may be found in the *Euthydemus*, the same dialogue in which we earlier found Socrates claiming to know only "trivial things" (in **T3.1**). Even though it is likely that Socrates' only point is to show how foolish his interlocutor is, there is no reason to think that he is not serious when he talks about what he knows and what he does not know.

T3.6 *Euthydemus* 296e–297a:

> (Socrates speaking) Euthydemus—how shall I say I know that good men are unjust? Come tell me, do I know this, or not?
>
> Oh yes, you know it, he said.
>
> Know what? said I.
>
> That the good are not unjust.
>
> Yes, I've known that for a long time, I said. But this isn't my question—what I'm asking is, where did I learn that the good *are* unjust?
>
> Nowhere, said Dionysodorus.
>
> Then this is something I do not know, I said.

Socrates, we see, gladly affirms that he not only does know but has known "for a long time" that the good are not unjust, and we find him arguing from that premise that it must be that he does *not* know that the good are *unjust*.

Finally, Socrates also seems to recognize that others, too, can have certain sorts of morally significant knowledge. The most famous example of this kind of concession may be found in the *Gorgias*.

T3.7 *Gorgias* 512a-b (part of longer quote at **T4.19**):

> But if a man has many incurable diseases in what is more valuable than his body, his soul, life for that man is not worth living, and he won't do him any favor if he rescues him from the sea or from prison or from anywhere else. He knows that for a corrupt person it's better not to be alive, for he necessarily lives badly.

3.1.3 Knowledge and Wisdom

We earlier found that we might escape the appearance of conflict between Socrates' profession of ignorance, on the one hand, and texts like **T3.1** and **T3.2**, on the other, just by being careful about what *kinds* of knowledge we take all of the relevant passages to refer to. Unfortunately, it has now turned out not to be adequate simply to distinguish "trivial" knowledge from moral knowledge, in order to resolve the apparent conflict in our texts. But at least our momentary success with that distinction can give us a clue as to how to resolve the further difficulty presented by texts like **T3.4**, **T3.5**, **T3.6**, and **T3.7**: Is there, perhaps, some *other* distinction we can use to distinguish between the kinds of knowledge Socrates claims to have and grants to others, on the one hand, and the kind or kinds of knowledge he always professes to lack and which he also denies to others, on the other hand?

Our search for an answer to this question should begin with a closer look at the kind of knowledge Socrates clearly professes to *lack*. One peculiar feature of Socrates' account of his own ignorance may be seen in his uses of various Greek words we translate as "knowledge" and the Greek word we translate as "wisdom." The passage in which Socrates distinguishes his own ignorance from that of the craftsmen (**T3.3**) is a good example.

T3.3 *Apology* 22c-e (partially repeated):

> Finally, I went to the craftsmen, for I was conscious of knowing practically nothing, and I thought that I would find that they had knowledge of many fine things. In this, I was not mistaken; they knew things I did not know, and to that extent they were wiser than I.

Notice how Socrates in this passage simply moves from "knowledge" to "wisdom": the kind of knowledge that Socrates lacks is (or would be) a kind of wisdom, and the kind of knowledge the craftsmen have (which Socrates lacks) is also a kind of wisdom. In fact, we often see this kind of exchange when Socrates professes to be ignorant, and we should not miss how this linkage requires us to understand Socrates' interpretation of the oracle. Whatever knowledge it is that Socrates professes to lack is a kind of knowledge that is constitutive of wisdom. Here, the possibility of a distinction is raised. Are all kinds of knowledge, for Socrates, constitutive of wisdom, or are only some? Plainly, if we can distinguish the kinds of knowledge Socrates professes to have from the kinds he professes to lack—and the kinds of knowledge he is willing to grant to others from the kinds he is unwilling to grant to others—we will be able to resolve our conflict.

3.1.4 Wisdom, Craft, and Expertise

Most contemporary philosophical analyses of knowledge—and most of the examples of knowledge we would commonly give in courses on epistemology (the philosophical study of knowledge)—conceive of knowledge as a cognitive *state* that consists in the knower standing in a certain relationship to some *proposition* or some *information*. For this reason, we call such cases of knowledge "propositional knowledge" or "informational knowledge." Examples of this knowledge might include the following: Mary knowing that two plus two equals four; John knowing that his car keys are in his right-front pants pocket; Sue knowing that her ticket won the lottery. Standard philosophical analyses of knowledge typically begin with what is called the "JTB" or "Justified True Belief" account of knowledge, which holds that some knower (S) knows some proposition or information (p) just in case:

- (i) p is true,
- (ii) S believes that p is true, and
- (iii) S is justified in believing that p is true.

In fact, few epistemologists these days accept that this traditional analysis is adequate, but many believe that all that is needed for an adequate conception of knowledge is some revision or clarification of these conditions—particularly the third one concerning justification. Most epistemologists now agree that knowledge is a species of belief (as per condition [ii]), but there is quite a bit of controversy over what is necessary in addition to true belief (now generally identified as "warrant") that will make the true belief an example of knowledge rather than mere belief.

This quick foray into epistemology serves to clarify precisely how the concept of knowledge Socrates has in mind when he disclaims knowledge is actually very different from the concept so evident in contemporary epistemological debates. For one thing, the kind of knowledge Socrates grants to the craftsmen is not (or at least is not obviously) propositional or informational knowledge. The craftsmen have a kind of knowledge and wisdom that Socrates lacks in so far as they have "success at [their] craft." Even if (as seems obvious) this kind of knowledge—"know-how," "skill," or "craft knowledge"—might not be possible without some examples of propositional knowledge (the craftsman must know *that* a certain tool is for cutting), it is not clear that "know-how" can be understood entirely in terms of the knower's possession of some specifiable bits of information, which can be put into propositional form. Know-how is exemplified, we tend to think, in the performance of certain sorts of activities and in the production of certain sorts of products. The connections between such performances and productions are so essential that without them, we would be inclined to disqualify any claim to such know-how. Of course, a very careful analysis would have to take into account that a person with such know-how might possess it even when that person was not *actually* performing such activities and not *actually* producing such products (such as when sleeping). Even with the relevant qualifications, we would expect any adequate analysis to feature some conditions that required the one with know-how to have the right sorts of abilities or capacities to *do* and to *produce* the right sorts of things. It is not clear that *any* sort of propositional knowledge would suffice to guarantee the satisfaction of such requirements. For example, just because one knows *that* a certain tool is for cutting, it does not follow that one knows *how* to cut with the tool in question; just because one knows *that* a certain kind of wood is best for making chariot wheels, it does not follow that one would know *how* to make good chariot wheels from such wood, and so on.

Moreover, it is hardly obvious that craft knowledge or know-how is a species of belief, though as we shall see, Socrates thinks that at least some propositional knowledge is required for the species of know-how he considers moral wisdom to be. We certainly do think that skills can vary in degree. The apprentice is not as skilled as the master craftsman, even if the apprentice does have some skill, and even master craftsmen may vary in the fineness or completeness of their skills. In contrast, it does not seem that propositional knowledge comes in degree. Instead, it seems to be "all-or-nothing": With respect to any given proposition or set of propositions, either one has knowledge or one lacks it. Nor do we regard differences in skill as differences between having know-how or craft knowledge, on the one hand, and having only "belief-how" or "craft belief," on the other. We may or may not be willing to say that an apprentice has know-how, or craft knowledge, depending upon how closely the apprentice approximates a master; Socrates, however, seems willing to say that people have craft knowledge only when they can prove to be error-free (*Euthydemus* 279d–280a). But regardless of whether we require standards as high as Socrates does, something that falls short of know-how or craft knowledge is not to be understood as some sort of *belief*, which is shared by both apprentice and master, where only the master has what it takes to convert this belief into knowledge. In this way, too, then, know-how or craft knowledge looks quite different than propositional knowledge.

One kind of knowledge Socrates is prepared to recognize as a form of wisdom, then, is craft knowledge. Those with such knowledge have a kind of *expertise,* and for this reason, scholars have sometimes called the sort of knowledge Socrates is interested in "expert knowledge."[2] It is not unreasonable to suppose that all experts typically have some substantial propositional knowledge applicable to their fields of expertise, and as we have noted, Socrates thinks this is true of anyone who would qualify as a moral expert. It is unreasonable, however, to suppose that anyone who has only such propositional knowledge qualifies as an expert. For example, we might suppose that an expert mechanic would know that a certain car was not running properly. The car's owner might also know this—after all, this is why the owner would take his car to the mechanic in the first place—but just knowing this does not make the owner an expert mechanic. It follows from this, however, that not every example of propositional knowledge qualifies as the sort of knowledge that Socrates says that he and all others lack.

3.1.5 Expert Knowledge and Knowing How or Why

A passage in the *Gorgias* calls attention to another feature of the sort of knowledge Socrates takes himself to lack.
T3.8 *Gorgias* 508e–509a:

> (Socrates speaking to Callicles) These conclusions, at which we arrived earlier in our previous discussions are, as I say, held down and bound by arguments of iron and adamant, even if it's rather rude to say so. So it would seem, anyhow. And if you, or someone more forceful than you won't undo them, then anyone who says anything other than I'm now saying cannot be speaking well. And yet for my part, my account is ever the same: I don't know *how these things are,* but no one I've ever met, as in this case, can say anything else without being ridiculous.

Socrates does not say whether he regards himself as knowing *that* it is better to suffer than to do injustice. He has what he calls "reasons of iron and adamant" for thinking that it is so, but he also allows that perhaps "you [Callicles], or someone more forceful than you" might "undo" the bindings of such arguments. Contemporary philosophers divide over the question of fallibility in one's reasons for believing, in order to know *that* something is true. Depending upon whether Socrates is an "infallibilist" (one who holds that the justification or warrant for a true belief must be *infallible,* for knowledge) or a "fallibilist" (one who allows a certain degree of fallibility in the justification or warrant, for knowledge), he might or might not be prepared to claim to know *that* it is better to suffer than to do injustice, given reasons of the sort he claims to have in this case. But Socrates is not focused on the issue of whether or not he knows *that* it is better to suffer than to do injustice; he attends only to the fact that he does not know *"how these things are."*

There is a significant difference here. One need not be a trained scientist to know that $E = MC^2$. One can have such knowledge without having mastered or even studied all of the physics that goes into the truth of this equation. One may not have any know-how at all with respect to physics. But lacking this know-how, one is in no position to know *why* $E = MC^2$, or in other words, *why it is* or *how it is* that $E = MC^2$. Take another example. Nearly everyone knows that the engines in cars are in front of the passenger compartment (under the hood) and not behind it (in the trunk). (A few models are exceptions to this general rule.) But only experts in automotive engineering or mechanics really know *why it is* or *how it is* that most cars have their engines in the front rather than the middle or rear. Most of us know that ivy clings to the walls of buildings but do not know *why* or *how* it does this.

The difference between knowledge *that* something is the case and knowledge *how it is* that something is the case (or *why it is*) is one feature of the difference between what we might call "ordinary" knowledge and the kind of knowledge that scholars have come to call "expert" knowledge. Many of us have ordinary knowledge about certain scientific laws and theories, but only scientists have expert knowledge of these things. Most of us have lots of ordinary knowledge about cars, but only automotive engineers and mechanics have expert knowledge about them. Most of us know lots and lots of things (in the ordinary sense of knowing that such and such is the case) about our worlds, but only experts have *know-how* and only experts know *how* (or *why*) things are the way they are, and we are suggesting that the possession of *know-how* and of knowing *how* (or *why*) something is the way it is are concepts that are (at least typically) linked. This linkage may not be an essential one, and the specifics of such a connection are a topic for a separate study, which we do not need to pursue here. For our purposes, it is enough to note that the kind of knowledge Socrates claims to lack—at least in **T3.8**—is knowing *how* his result is the way it is. Socrates claims not to be wise; in other words, he is no expert.

3.1.6 Definitional Knowledge and the Ability to Judge All Cases

In several places in our texts, Socrates explains why he thinks *this* kind of knowledge (the kind that makes its possessor wise, or expert knowledge) is so important.

T3.9 *Euthyphro* 4e–5d (includes most of **T2.9**)[3]:

EUTHYPHRO: [My relatives say that] it is impious for a son to prosecute his father for murder—since they know so little, Socrates, of how it is with the divine regarding the pious and the impious.

SOCRATES: But, by Zeus, do you think that you have such precise knowledge about divine things, how they are, and about pious and impious things, that, when those things happened as you say, you are not afraid of doing something impious yourself by prosecuting your father?

EUTHYPHRO: I would be worthless, Socrates, and Euthyphro would be no different from most people, if I were not to know precisely about all such things.

[…]

SOCRATES: So tell me now, by Zeus, what do you now claim to know clearly, about the nature of the pious and impious, with regard to murder and other things?

One problem with propositional knowledge, as opposed to expert knowledge or wisdom, is that it is so very *specific*. If one knows that some proposition, *p*, is true, then, as good as this is, the knowledge goes no further than the specific case of *p*. Determining that *p* is true may require no special judgment, no great expertise—knowing that *p* may turn out to be no great cognitive achievement. But what about difficult cases, more challenging judgments, where ordinary people may disagree or find themselves confused? Euthyphro and Socrates agree that Euthyphro would never have dared to make the decision to prosecute his father unless Euthyphro had "precise knowledge about divine things, how they are." Euthyphro's claim of superiority over other people is not just that he has *some* knowledge about divine things but the kind of knowledge that allows him to recognize truths others would miss, or at least misjudge. Euthyphro takes himself to be an expert, to be wise about piety. Just a little bit later in the dialogue, Socrates shows that the kind of knowledge he thinks would provide such wisdom is not simply specific to one or two cases of piety but would allow him to judge any and all instances of piety. **T3.10** *Euthyphro* 6d-e (= **T5.3**):

SOCRATES: Bear in mind then that I did not bid you tell me one or two of the many pious actions but that form itself that makes all pious actions pious, for you agreed that all impious actions are impious and all pious actions pious through one form, or don't you remember?

EUTHYPHRO: I do.

SOCRATES: Well, then, teach me what this form itself is, so that I may look upon it, and using it as a model, say that any action of yours or another's that is of that kind is pious, and if it is not that it is not.

Here we find what has come to be known as Socrates' "What is F-ness?" question.[4] Socrates thinks that the sort of expertise or wisdom of any moral property (F-ness) that is required to judge the difficult or unusual cases of F-ness (such as the one in which Euthyphro finds himself, regarding piety) requires definitional knowledge of F-ness: The genuine expert about piety can define piety in a way that applies to all and only pious things and not just get some few such judgments right. Socrates shows no interest at all in the kind of knowledge that gets a single, specific case right, knowledge that some specific F-thing is F. He neither accepts nor rejects the specific examples Euthyphro advances; and we find him behaving the same way in other dialogues, where he seeks definitional knowledge and an interlocutor offers only examples of the moral property in question (see, for example, *Laches* 190e–191b). Socrates does not always simply grant that the specific examples given by his interlocutors are accurate ones, nor should we simply assume that he would count his interlocutors' or his own cognitive state, regarding such examples, as cases of knowledge *that* these were examples of the relevant sort. (Surely, Socrates would deny that Euthyphro knows that it is pious for him to prosecute his father, for example! Again, one cannot have propositional knowledge of what is false—see **T3.6.**) Our point is only that Socrates seems uninterested in such specific claims of propositional knowledge; he is interested in a different sort of knowledge, one that he professes not to have.

3.1.7 A Return to What Socrates and Others Know

Now that we are clearer on what sort of knowledge it is that Socrates always searches for and never finds—what sort of knowledge it is that he claims no human beings have—it is time for us to return to the passages in which Socrates is willing to claim to have knowledge or grant knowledge claims to others. It is probably best if we review these texts one by one.

T3.4 *Apology* 29b (repeated):

> It is perhaps on this point and in this respect, gentlemen, that I differ from the majority of men, and if I were to claim that I am wiser than anyone in anything, it would be in this, that, as I have no adequate knowledge of things in the underworld, so I do not think I have. I do know, however, that it is wicked and shameful to do wrong, to disobey one's superior, be he god or man. I shall never fear or avoid things of which I do not know, whether they may not be good rather than things that I know to be bad.

In this passage, is Socrates claiming to have the sort of knowledge that would prove him to be an expert about good and evil? Hardly; Socrates is emphasizing his very inability to make the kinds of judgments an expert in such matters could make (as in **T3.10**). Instead, he is claiming knowledge of a specific example (or specific sort of example): He knows *that* it is wrong to disobey one's superior. He is not claiming to have the know-how, craft knowledge, or skill that would allow him to perform all and only good actions, for example. He is not claiming to know *how it is* that disobeying one's superior is evil. He is not claiming to have definitional knowledge of goodness or badness. This is the sort of knowledge claim, in short, that Socrates does not find especially philosophically interesting, and if it were made by one of his interlocutors, we might well expect Socrates not to respond to it one way or the other. He does not deny that people can have this sort of knowledge, nor does he show any interest in this sort of knowledge. Instead, we can imagine him saying, "Perhaps you do know this. But can you tell me what goodness or badness is? Can you tell me *how it is* that disobeying your superior is evil?" For if Socrates could only have *this* sort of knowledge, he might also be able to judge cases that are more difficult cases (which this one is *not*). After all, when he makes this claim to his jurors, he plainly does not suppose that he is revealing some great moral truth to them, which they would not also know themselves. If he did not expect them to know what he knows about this, he would not expect them to get the point he is making and would have to explain it to them. The explanation, however, is one that Socrates no doubt could not (or at least not completely or adequately) give, since, as we have seen, he lacks the expertise.

T3.5 *Apology* 37b (repeated):

> What should I fear? That I should suffer the penalty Meletus has assessed against me, of which I say I do not know whether it is good or bad? Am I then to choose in preference to this something that I know very well to be an evil and assess the penalty at that?

Here, too, we find Socrates considering examples in which he is prepared to make claims to know *that* something is an evil. But here, too, there is no trace of any suggestion that Socrates has such knowledge in virtue of knowing *how it is* that something is bad or as a result of any special expertise that he has. Again, whatever powers of judgment he might have for making these sorts of decisions are ones he seems fully prepared to grant to his jurors as well. He does not expect the kinds of cases he has in mind to count as difficult or controversial ones, but only as cases which are so obvious that, as he says to Ion in **T3.2**, "anyone could know." As "wisdom," therefore, this kind of knowledge counts for "little or nothing" (see **T2.18**).

T3.6 *Euthydemus* 296e–297a (repeated in part):

> (Socrates speaking) Euthydemus—how shall I say I know that good men are just? Come tell me, do I know this, or not?
>> Oh yes, you know it, he said.
>> Know what? said I.
>> That the good are not unjust.
>> Yes, I've known that for a long time, I said.

T3.7 *Gorgias* 512a-b (repeated in part):

(Socrates speaking) He knows that for a corrupt person it's better not to be alive, for he necessarily lives badly.

Nothing in these texts requires us to see Socrates as claiming or granting to others anything even approximating expert knowledge, craft knowledge, or definitional knowledge—wisdom, in other words. Socrates is occasionally willing to claim to know, or to grant that another might know, that some specific moral proposition is true, in a context where he makes it very clear that he regards such knowledge as only a slight and insignificant achievement. Such specific propositional knowledge claims seem to Socrates only to state such obvious moral truths as to be commonplaces. It is clear that Socrates did not become the controversial and challenging figure he became simply by celebrating or promoting moral platitudes.

Socrates only rarely makes these kinds of knowledge claims and seems uninterested when others make them. His philosophical interests do not extend to careful analyses of how such claims of knowledge might be justified or warranted—except in cases where more daring examples are advanced, as the products of a kind of knowledge that is not ordinary but extraordinary. It may not be that Socrates' interests coincide with those of contemporary epistemologists, therefore, but we have found that there is nothing inconsistent in his claiming to have specific examples of propositional knowledge, on the one hand, and denying that he has wisdom, or expertise, or definitional knowledge, on the other.

3.2 The Priority of Definitional Knowledge

3.2.1 A New Problem

In a famous article, Peter Geach argued that one principle found in Socrates' reasoning was fallacious.[5] The fallacy involved was so common in Socratic arguments that Geach dubbed it "the Socratic fallacy." Specifically, Socrates in many passages seems to affirm a commitment to what we noted earlier is known as the *Priority of Definitional Knowledge* (PD):

(PD) *Only if one knows the definition of some quality (F-ness) can one know anything about F-ness or F-things, including whether any instance of F-ness is really an instance.*

Geach was convinced that this principle is fallacious, for he argued that it would be only through knowledge of examples that one could ever achieve knowledge of a definition and so (PD) managed to get things exactly the wrong way around.

In the years following Geach's article, there has come to be an extensive scholarly literature on whether or not Socrates really commits the "Socratic fallacy." In the last section, we argued that there was no conflict between the texts in which Socrates professes ignorance or accuses others of ignorance, on the one hand, and texts in which he claims knowledge or counts others as having knowledge, on the other, by making a distinction between two kinds of knowledge: a kind that we called expert knowledge, craft knowledge, or wisdom, which includes not only know-how but also knowing *how* or *why* something is and knowledge of definitions; and a kind we called "ordinary" propositional knowledge. We claimed that there was no conceptual problem with the claim that one might very well suppose that Socrates thought he and others had the latter sort of knowledge but denied that he or others had the former sort of knowledge. But even if (PD) is not a fallacy, we face a problem in our texts anyway, for (PD) would appear to link the two sorts of knowledge we have found in the texts, making neither one possible without the other. At least on the face of it, this principle would commit Socrates to saying that without definitional knowledge there can be *no knowledge at all*—even ordinary propositional knowledge—that some specific action is pious or impious, just or unjust, good or bad, or anything else. If so, then any passage committing Socrates to (PD) will conflict with each of the passages we cited earlier (**T3.4**, **T3.5**, **T3.6**, and **T3.7**), in which Socrates claims to have or acknowledges others' claims to have moral knowledge. Moreover, (PD) would also conflict with knowledge claims that were not necessarily about moral issues (**T3.1** and **T3.2**), for it seems highly unlikely that Socrates or anyone else would know all of the definitions required by (PD) to make even specific nonmoral knowledge claims.

As a number of recent discussions of (PD) have shown, the issues surrounding Socrates' interest in knowing the definitions of moral terms are considerably more complex than was suggested by Geach's pioneering work. We need not review all of the many texts that bear on this issue to arrive at a coherent account.[6] It is worthwhile, however, at least to sample a few of the most controversial texts and see what they commit Socrates to.

3.2.2 A Few Texts

T3.11 *Greater Hippias* 304d-e:

SOCRATES: . . . [H]e asks me if I am not ashamed that I dare to discuss fine activities when I've been so plainly refuted about the fine, and it's clear that I don't even know at all what *that* is itself! "Look," he'll say. "How will you know whose speech—or any other action—is finely presented or not, when you are ignorant of the fine? And when you're in a state like that, do you think it's any better for you to live than die?"

It is easy enough to see why one might take this passage to commit Socrates to (PD). Socrates is imagining being challenged by someone to justify his making judgments about what is fine when he is not able to say what the fine is. It is certainly tempting to think that what lies behind such a challenge is a commitment to (PD), according to which Socrates *cannot* know "whose speech—or any other action—is finely presented or not" unless he knows what the fine is.

However, several things about this passage should make us just a little bit cautious about attributing too much to Socrates. To begin with, Socrates is *imagining* what someone might say in issuing a challenge to him, so Socrates himself provides the formulation of the challenge. But we should not necessarily suppose that any degree of failure to meet the challenge is tantamount to complete defeat, either. Should we attribute to Socrates, for example, the view that anyone who cannot say what fineness is would be better off dead?

Indeed, how *would* Socrates answer the challenging question, "And when you're in a state like that, do you think it's any better for you to live than die?" Presumably, he would acknowledge that, yes, he was, indeed, ignorant of what fineness is. He could then explain that even though "the unexamined life is not worth living for men" (*Apology* 38a [**T2.20**]), it is none the less true that the "examined life" *was* worth living and then explain that he was, indeed, living an "examined life." In other words, it is not only possible, it is, in fact, *very likely* that Socrates would reject what appears to be the presumption behind this challenge.

The same sort of possibility exists with the other part of the challenge Socrates imagines here. "How will you know whose speech—or any other action—is finely presented or not, when you are ignorant of the fine?" This question challenges Socrates' ability to judge fine speeches or other fine things. But we do not need to accept what might appear to be the presumption behind this challenge, that without knowing what fineness is, we could never know that *any* speech was finely presented or that *anything* was fine. Socrates might well reply that without knowing what fineness is, he could never count as an expert judge of fine things. But to concede that much is not at all to concede that he is incapable of knowing that anything at all is fine. As we argued in the last section, he might know about some fine things, as ordinary people do, without being an expert. Socrates' imaginary challenger, then, makes the challenge to warn Socrates that he has no right to act as if he is an expert about fineness. But just because one is not an expert, it does not follow that one has no knowledge at all in the relevant area.

T3.12 *Lysis* 223b:

> SOCRATES: . . . Now we've done it, Lysis and Menexenus—made fools
> of ourselves, I an old man, and you as well. These people here will
> go away saying that we're friends of one another—for I count
> myself in with you—but what a friend is we have not yet been able
> to find out.

Here again we find Socrates "reporting" someone else's reaction to his
(and in this case, also Lysis's and Menexenus's) inability to provide a definition. But again, if we read this passage in such a way as to commit
Socrates to what might appear to be the presumption behind his imaginary other's evaluation, it will follow that unless one can provide an adequate definition of friendship, one is not even entitled to *think* of oneself
as a friend of another. If so, then Socrates must be committed to the view
that no one ever has the right to think of oneself as having friends, for, as
we have seen, Socrates is convinced that no one is wiser than he, and he
certainly does not know the relevant definition. If anyone else did, that
person *would* be wiser than Socrates. Accordingly, we should not read this
passage as committing Socrates to (PD). It is very like the last example,
however, in having Socrates stress the gap between his and others' abilities to make certain morally significant judgments and their inability to
define the terms of those judgments.

T3.9 *Euthyphro* 4e–5d (repeated):

> EUTHYPHRO: [My relatives say that] it is impious for a son to
> prosecute his father for murder—since they know so little,
> Socrates, of how it is with the divine regarding the pious and the
> impious.
>
> SOCRATES: But, by Zeus, do you think that you have such precise
> knowledge about divine things, how they are, and about pious
> and impious things, that, when those things happened as you say,
> you are not afraid of doing something impious yourself by
> prosecuting your father?
>
> EUTHYPHRO: I would be worthless, Socrates, and Euthyphro would
> be no different from most people, if I were not to know precisely
> about all such things.
>
> [. . .]
>
> SOCRATES: So tell me now, by Zeus, what do you now claim to know
> clearly, about the nature of the pious and impious, with regard to
> murder and other things?

T3.13 *Euthyphro* 15d (partially repeats **T2.14**):

SOCRATES: If you had no clear knowledge of piety and impiety you would never have ventured to prosecute your father for murder on behalf of a servant.

In both of these passages, it is Socrates himself who seems to be issuing the challenge, rather than some imaginary challenger, and the challenge does seem to tie Euthyphro's daring to take action against his father with a presumption to know the definition of piety. Socrates' position does seem to be that Euthyphro's willingness to take action would only make sense if Euthyphro supposed himself to know the definition of piety, as an expert would.

But even these passages do not commit Socrates to (PD). In the first part of this chapter, we distinguished two kinds of knowledge: one that we have called ordinary propositional knowledge of some specific information and one that we have called expert knowledge or wisdom. It is plain from Euthyphro's own admission (in **T3.9**) that what he is planning to do to his father is hardly what one would ever dare to undertake on the basis of any ordinary knowledge or understanding of piety and pious action. Most Athenians would find it outrageous. As we noted above, one difference between ordinary and expert knowledge in some area is that only the latter puts one in a position to judge not just certain very specific (and ordinary) individual cases but *all* cases in that area—in particular, the more difficult or controversial ones. Euthyphro and Socrates completely agree that Euthyphro's decision to prosecute his own father is plainly one that, if Euthyphro's judgment is correct, *must* be the result of expert knowledge or wisdom, precisely because it deviates so clearly from the path of what most (ordinary) people would do in such a case.

Moreover, Socrates seems to share what we have called the "ordinary" view in this case: Like Euthyphro's relatives and father, Socrates expresses shock at Euthyphro's presumption. Because he does not find Euthyphro's decision to be one that is obviously or uncontroversially correct, he has every right to challenge the expertise by which Euthyphro made such a startling decision. And Euthyphro admits that this was not some special, individual case for him—he is fully prepared to generalize and claim that it *was* on the basis of his expert knowledge that he made his decision. Precisely because Euthyphro agrees that his decision is a reflection of expertise, Socrates' challenge is entirely appropriate. Accordingly, Socrates does not have to think that *any* judgment or knowledge about piety requires definitional knowledge—as (PD) requires—in order to make this challenge, especially when Euthyphro himself accepts that *this* judgment requires such knowledge.

3.2.3 Why Socrates Emphasizes Definition

Socrates sometimes seems to be very interested in definitions, and given the connection Socrates makes between definition and wisdom or expert knowledge, it is no wonder that we find such emphasis on definitions in the dialogues. Socrates believes that the more he can know about the definition of a moral term, the more he will be in a position to make the more difficult judgments and the closer he will be to the kind of knowledge that allows one to make such judgments.[7] For this reason, we often see Socrates attempting to divert discussions away from particular claims to definitional issues: Socrates is convinced that answers to definitional questions will also allow him to answer all questions about specific issues.

T3.14 *Meno* 100b:

> (Socrates speaking) We shall have clear knowledge of this when, before we investigate how it comes to be present in men, we first try to find out what virtue in itself is.

Even if Socrates does not accept the priority of definitional knowledge for any other sort of knowledge, as (PD) would have it, he does accept the pursuit of definitional knowledge as a priority for philosophical discussion. And when this priority is not satisfied in some discussion he finds himself in, he always expresses a kind of regret or inability at the end, sometimes framed in an imaginary criticism aimed at himself or his interlocutor and sometimes more directly stated. Moreover, there are more specific propositions that Socrates would very much like to know, which he feels certain would be available to him if only he could satisfy his desire to know definitions.

T3.15 *Republic* 1.354b-c:

> (Socrates speaking) I seem to have behaved like a glutton, snatching at every dish that passes and tasting it before properly savoring its predecessor. Before finding the answer to our first inquiry about what justice is, I let that go and turned to investigate whether it is a kind of vice and ignorance or a kind of wisdom and virtue. Then an argument came up about injustice being more profitable than justice, and I couldn't refrain from abandoning the previous one and following up on that. Hence the result of the discussion, as far as I'm concerned, is that I know nothing, for when I don't know what justice is, I'll hardly know whether it is a kind of virtue or not, or whether a person who has it is happy or unhappy.

Recall (from **T3.6**) that Socrates does claim to know that good people are not unjust. Socrates therefore does know *something* about justice and goodness. But he does not have the *kind* of knowledge that he wants, and without that kind of knowledge there will remain many, many things he would like to know about justice and virtue and happiness that he does not know. And he is sure that if he can ever come to have knowledge of definitions, all the rest he would like to know will follow.

3.2.4 Summary and Conclusion

In this chapter, we have identified two very different sorts of knowledge that apply to different claims Socrates makes. We called one kind of knowledge ordinary knowledge and said that this kind of knowledge is of very specific (and ordinary) information. Socrates sometimes claims to have such knowledge and also seems ready to admit that others have such knowledge, and it is clear that he would not regard such knowledge as giving its possessor any expertise or wisdom worth mentioning.

It is an interesting question whether Socrates believes that his philosophizing can generate this kind of knowledge. Certainly, several scholars have claimed that the elenchos might generate this kind of nonexpert knowledge, but it is certainly a problem for such a view that not once in our texts does Socrates claim to have such knowledge as a result of his elenchos or as a result of philosophizing in general. He makes several such knowledge claims, as we have seen, and grants some to others, but not once does he explain where such knowledge comes from or how one might come to possess it. We might find it interesting and challenging to speculate as to how such knowledge might be gained, but our speculation will have to proceed without any clear assistance from our texts. Perhaps the safest conclusion to make about this kind of knowledge, then, is that Socrates would not share any enthusiasm we might have for explaining and evaluating it.

Instead, we find that Socrates is almost exclusively interested in another kind of knowledge, a kind that can supply the definitions of its central terms and that makes its possessor wise. We have surveyed a few texts that are sometimes supposed to reveal Socrates' commitment to (PD) and have argued that they do not, in fact, commit him to this thesis. If he *were* committed to this thesis, we would have very serious difficulty explaining how and why Socrates could claim to know what he does claim to know and how and why he would count others as knowing what he counts others as knowing. But as we have seen, even if Socrates thinks that *some* knowledge is possible without definitional knowledge, he seems to have little interest in such knowledge and regards what knowledge we can have, apart from wisdom, as no great achievement and no worthy goal for philosophy. Precisely because such knowledge seems to provide no more than the most ordinary sort of insight, one cannot rely on it to make any very significant judgment on any very significant moral issue. As such, it is fair for Socrates to describe anyone with such knowledge as wise only in so far as he "understands that his wisdom is worthless" (*Apology* 23b [**T2.19**]).

Notes

1. Here, we modify the translation given in Cooper (1997) because we believe the translation given there modifies the specific claim that Socrates is making, namely, that anyone could know what he was asking about.

2. An excellent discussion of this can be found in Woodruff (1990).

3. Here, we provide our own translation of the passage rather than use the one in Cooper (1997), for we find that one too imprecise on exactly what sort of knowledge is at issue. Our own translation may be more awkward, but it does, we believe, better capture the actual sense of this passage. In **T2.9**, we used the translation in Cooper (1997), for the unclarities of that translation for our argument in Chapter 2 made no difference.

4. A particularly clear discussion on what exactly Socrates is asking for in such questions may be found in Benson (1990a).

5. Geach (1966).

6. Those who do wish to make a more comprehensive study of this issue can find all of the texts cited and discussed in Benson (1990b) and in Brickhouse and Smith (1994), ch. 2. Benson makes the case in favor of the claim that Socrates is committed to (PD), and Brickhouse and Smith make the case against it.

7. An interesting account of how this works can be found in May (1997).

Suggested Readings

On Socrates' Profession of Ignorance and What He Means to Disclaim in It

Gulley (1968) argues that Socrates' profession of ignorance is insincere, a ploy to seduce interlocutors into expressing their own opinions. Vlastos (1994, ch. 2; revised from an article published in 1985) disputes this and argues for a distinction between certain knowledge and what he calls "elenctic knowledge." In Vlastos's view, Socrates disclaims possessing the former and claims only to have the latter. A thoughtful criticism of Vlastos's argument can be found in Lesher (1987). The idea that the kind of knowledge Socrates professes not to have is "expert knowledge" (as opposed to ordinary propositional knowledge) is explained in Woodruff (1987) and (1990). An argument very similar to Woodruff's is set forth in Reeve (1989, 33–62). The connection between the kind of knowledge Socrates claims not to have and wisdom is explored in Brickhouse and Smith (1994, ch. 2).

On Socrates' Interest in Definitions and Problems Involving (PD)

In this chapter, we noted the importance of Geach's article (1966). Beversluis first affirms (1974) and then denies (1987) that Socrates was committed to (PD). Others offering arguments against attributing (PD) to Socrates include Brickhouse and Smith (1989, 100–108; revised from an article published in 1984); Vlastos (1994b, ch. 2; revised from an article published in 1985); Nehamas (1986), and Lesher (1987). But a very thorough and powerful defense of attributing (PD) to Socrates has more recently been made in Benson (1990b). We respond to Benson's interpretations of the relevant passages and come to an opposing conclusion about Socrates and (PD) in Brickhouse and Smith (1994, ch. 2). A novel explanation of why Socrates was so interested in definitions is offered in May (1997).

Socratic Values

4.1 What Is Valuable?

4.1.1 Virtue and Other Good Things

Modern philosophers see the study of ethics primarily as a search for the basic criteria by which we can identify right action. Socrates conceived of ethics rather differently. Socrates thought he should spend his life searching for what he calls *aretē*, which is usually translated as "virtue" or "excellence." In attaching great weight to *aretē*, Socrates was no different than other Greeks of his time. Virtually everyone in fifth-century B.C. Athens would have agreed that one should make oneself and those one cares about as excellent as possible. As Socrates reminds us in the *Apology* (20a-c), small fortunes were spent by the rich on those Sophists who claimed to be able to teach virtue. But as we also learn in the *Apology*, Socrates has been unable to find anyone who actually *is* virtuous or who even possesses a clear idea of what virtue consists in. It is in recognizing that he knows that he does not know what virtue is that Socrates differs from other people.

As we saw in Chapter 2, although Socrates claims not to be wise, he nevertheless holds a number of beliefs about what virtue is. For example, he was convinced that virtue is a kind of wisdom (*Apology* 29e) and that it is the best condition of the human soul (*Apology* 30a-b; *Gorgias* 467e-ff.). What is controversial is why he thinks that this condition of the soul is valuable and how he ranks virtue in relation to the other things he values and why.

4.1.2 Why Do We Do What We Do?

Let us begin by trying to see how the value Socrates places on virtue fits into his overall theory of desire. One of the hallmarks of Socratic ethics is

Socrates' view that whenever we do anything, we do it because we think that some good will result.

T4.1 *Gorgias* 467d–468b (immediately precedes **T4.4**):

> SOCRATES: With seafarers, too, and those who make money in other ways, the thing they're doing at the time is not the thing they want—for who wants to make dangerous and troublesome sea voyages? What they want is their being wealthy, the thing for the sake of which, I suppose, they make their voyages. It's for the sake of wealth that they make them.

> POLUS: Yes, that's right.

> SOCRATES: Isn't it just the same in all cases, in fact? If a person does anything for the sake of something, he doesn't want this thing that he's doing, but the thing for the sake of which he's doing it?

> Polus: Yes.

> SOCRATES: Now is there anything that isn't either *good* nor *bad*, or, what's in between them, *neither good nor bad?*

> POLUS: There can't be, Socrates.

> SOCRATES: Do you say that wisdom, health, wealth, and the like are good, and their opposites bad?

> POLUS: Yes, I do.

> SOCRATES: And by things which are neither good nor bad you mean things which sometimes partake of what's good, sometimes of what's bad, and sometimes of neither, such as sitting or walking, running or making sea voyages, or stones and sticks and the like? Aren't these the ones you mean? Or are there any others that you can call neither good nor bad?

> POLUS: No, these are the ones.

> SOCRATES: Now whenever people do things, do they do these intermediate things for the sake of good ones or the good ones for the sake of the intermediate ones?

> POLUS: The intermediate ones for the sake of the good ones, surely.

Socrates is not claiming that either wealth or health or even wisdom is always good.[1] What he wants to establish is that we explain what we do by pointing out the good that we believe will be achieved by it. It is the assumption that wealth, for example, is a good that explains why one would make a sea voyage, which is itself neither good nor bad. We do not try to explain why we pursue what we assume is good by citing that it will achieve what is neither good nor bad.

Of course, the good that is the immediate aim of some particular desire might itself be desired not for what it is but for its usefulness in achieving some other good. For instance, we might seek to help a stranger in trouble in order to be well thought of by others, and we might wish to be well thought of by others in order to make our parents happy. In this case, we regard the immediate goal of our action as a means to some further end, which is in turn valued as a means to some yet further end. But as Socrates points out in the *Lysis*, if this way of explaining action is to make sense, there must be at least one thing that we desire for its own sake and not merely for the sake of something else. There, Socrates uses the expression "being friend to something for the sake of something" to express the idea of wanting something as a good for the sake of some further good.

T4.2 *Lysis* 219c-d:

(Socrates speaking to Menexenus) . . . Medicine, we say, is a friend for the sake of health?

Yes.

Health, then, is also a friend.

Very much a friend.

If, therefore, it is a friend, it is for the sake of something.

Yes.

And that something is a friend, if it is going to accord with our previous agreement.

Very much so.

Will that too, then, also be a friend for the sake of a friend?

Yes.

Aren't we going to have to give up going on like this? Don't we have to arrive at some first principle which will no longer bring us back to another friend, something that goes back to the first friend, something for the sake of which we say that all the rest are friends too?

Socrates stops short of saying that there is a *single* "first friend," that is, a single first principle for the sake of which we do everything.[2] To this point, all Socrates establishes is that whenever we desire something for the sake of something else, there must be something that we desire for its own sake. Were there not something that we desire for its own sake, the "something elses" we were pursuing would be an infinite regress, so the idea that we desire for the sake of something else would be unintelligible. But as Socrates goes on, it appears that he thinks there must be a *single* first principle.

T4.3 *Lysis* 220a-b:

> (Socrates speaking) When we talk about all the things that are our friends for the sake of another friend, it is clear that we are merely using the word "friend." The real friend is surely that in which all these so-called friendships terminate.

Nowhere in the *Lysis* does Socrates tell us what this single friend is "in which all other friends terminate," but as we shall see, Socrates has an opinion about the matter.

4.1.3 Socrates on Goods and Happiness

It is perhaps tempting to think that for Socrates, the ultimate good is being just to other people or in some way helping others independently of how we ourselves are benefited thereby. But Socrates tells us that the ultimate good at which we aim is what philosophers call a "self-regarding" good. It is something that we at least think is good *for us*.

    T4.4 *Gorgias* 468b (immediately follows **T4.1**):

> SOCRATES: So, it's because we pursue what's good that we walk whenever we walk; we suppose that it's better that we walk; we suppose that it's better to walk. And conversely, whenever we stand still, we stand still for the sake of the same thing, what's good. Isn't that so?
>
> POLUS: Yes.
>
> SOCRATES: And don't we also put a person to death, if we do, or banish him and confiscate his property because we suppose that doing these things is better for us than not doing them?
>
> POLUS: That's right.
>
> SOCRATES: Hence, it's for the sake of what's good that those who do all these things do them.
>
> POLUS: I agree.

Even if Socrates thinks that what is good *for us* is only being just to or helping others, it is clear that he thinks that the reason we are just to others can only be that doing whatever it is we are doing is good *for us*.

    We can perhaps see more clearly that this is Socrates' view of rational motivation by turning to a famous passage in the *Meno*. Here, we see

Socrates explaining to Meno why he, Meno, does not really believe that anyone ever pursues what they perceive as an evil.[3]

T4.5 *Meno* 77e–78b (= **T5.17**):

(Socrates speaking first, with Meno responding) Well then, those who you say desire bad things, believing that bad things harm their possessor, know that they'll be harmed by them?

Necessarily.

And do they not think that those who are harmed are miserable to the extent that they are harmed?

That too is inevitable.

And that those who are miserable are unhappy?

I think so.

Does anyone wish to be miserable and unhappy?

I don't think so, Socrates.

No one then wants what is bad, Meno, unless he wants to be such. For what else is being miserable but to desire bad things and secure them?

You are probably right, Socrates, and no one wants what is bad.

Socrates' explanation of why no one wants what is bad once the person recognizes that it is bad is really very straightforward. Bad things harm their possessor and no one wants to be harmed because being harmed makes one (to that extent) miserable and no one wants to be miserable. But if Socrates thinks, as the context suggests he does, that happiness and misery, good and evil, and benefit and harm are exclusive pairs, we can infer that Socrates thinks that just as people do not desire what they believe to be evil because evils move them in the direction of misery, so all people desire what they believe to be good because they will be made happier thereby and everyone wants to be made happier. We can now see why Socrates values virtue. He values it because its possession will make the possessor happier. Socrates, then, thinks that virtue *pays* and that being immoral *never pays*.

4.1.4 Socratic Eudaimonism

Thus far, we have seen that the "first friend" Socrates discusses in the *Lysis*, the goal at which Socrates thinks all actions aim, is our own happiness and that any account of the desirability of virtue Socrates is prepared to give must be cast in terms of the contribution virtue makes to one's own happiness. Socrates, of course, was not the only Greek to believe that our own happiness is always our ultimate goal in everything we do, nor was he the first to believe that being moral is always in our interest and that being immoral is never in our interest. But Socrates was the first thinker to offer an explanation of why and how being moral always makes one better off. The influence his theory had on his Greek-speaking philosophical successors was enormous, for although they differed with Socrates about what happiness itself is and exactly how it is related to being moral, each of them, in one way or another, accepted his twin claims that our own happiness is always everyone's ultimate goal and that moral excellence always makes us better off with respect to that ultimate goal.

The Greek word ordinarily translated as "happiness" is *eudaimonia*, which is why scholars ordinarily call Socrates' approach to ethics an example of "eudaimonism." One is committed to eudaimonism by accepting what we might call the *Principle of Eudaimonism:*

Principle of Eudaimonism: *Happiness is everyone's ultimate goal, and anything that is good is good only insofar as it contributes to this goal.*

Socrates' conviction that people desire happiness (and its equivalents, living well and doing well) as their ultimate goal and desire everything else that they desire because they think it will contribute to their happiness is, therefore, plainly an example of the eudaimonistic approach to ethics. It is interesting that in saying that happiness—one's own happiness—is our ultimate goal, Socrates does not take himself to be making a deep or controversial philosophical claim. Not only does the principle seem to Socrates to be obviously true, but it seems obviously true to others when he brings it up. As a result, nowhere do we find him arguing for the *Principle of Eudaimonism.*

T4.6 *Euthydemus* 278e:

> (Socrates speaking) Do all men wish to do well? Or is this question one of the ridiculous ones that I was afraid of just now? I suppose it is stupid even to raise such a question, since there could hardly be a man who would not wish to do well.
>
> No, there is no such person, said Clinias.
>
> Well, then, I said, the next question is, since we wish to do well, how are we to do so? Would it not be through having many good things? Or is this question still more simple-minded than the other, since this must obviously be the case too?

Although Socrates thinks that virtue pays by always being good "for us," it is not clear at this point in precisely what way it is good for us. Socrates may think that it benefits its possessor by actually being a *part* of happiness. If so, we would say that Socrates thinks of virtue as a *component* or a *constituent good*. On the other hand, Socrates might think that virtue is beneficial because, and only because, it somehow causes its possessor to be better off with respect to happiness. In this case, though virtue is always a good, its goodness resides in its causal power to produce something else that makes its possessor happy. If it is its power to cause happiness that makes virtue a good, then he regards it as what philosophers call an *instrumental good*.

4.2 Socratic Conceptions of Happiness

4.2.1 The First View: Socrates the Hedonist

To help us understand which of these two sorts of goods Socrates takes virtue to be, it will be helpful at this point if we ask what Socrates thinks that happiness itself consists in. We start by examining the view that Socrates thinks that happiness is really nothing more than pleasure. According to this view, virtue can only be an instrumental good, for its value can only be its power to produce pleasure. We shall then consider the view that Socrates considers virtue to be of intrinsic value and so is actually a part of happiness. As we shall see, according to the second view, Socrates believes that there can be other components of happiness in addition to virtue but that nothing else can be a part of happiness unless one first possesses virtue. Finally, we shall consider the view that for Socrates, happiness consists not simply in the possession of virtue but in *actions* that manifest virtue, or what we might call "right actions."

The view that Socrates is a hedonist trades on his belief that virtue is a kind of wisdom and then argues that moral wisdom must consist in the power to produce the maximal benefit, whatever that turns out to be.[4] To justify the claim that for Socrates, the maximal benefit is the greatest balance of pleasure over pain for the agent, proponents of this view point us to a single, extended passage in the *Protagoras*. Socrates and the famous Sophist, Protagoras, have been pursuing the question of whether it is possible to have any single virtue without the others or whether anyone who possesses one of the virtues must possess all of them. When Protagoras balks at the notion that those who possess moral knowledge must be courageous, Socrates suddenly takes a different tack.

T4.7 *Protagoras* 351b-e:

(Socrates speaking) Would you say, Protagoras, that some people live well and others live badly?

Yes.

But does it seem to you that a person lives well, if he is distressed and in pain?

No, indeed.

Now, if he completed his life, having lived pleasantly, does he not seem to you to have lived well?

It seems that way to me.

So, then, to live pleasantly is good, and unpleasantly, bad.

Yes, so long as he lived having taken pleasure in honorable things.

What, Protagoras? Surely you don't, like most people, call some pleasant things bad and some painful things good? I mean isn't a pleasant thing good just insofar as it is pleasant, that is, if it results in nothing other than pleasure; and, on the other hand, aren't painful things bad in the same way, just insofar as they are painful?

I don't know, Socrates, if I should answer as simply as you put the question—that everything pleasant is good and everything painful is bad. It seems to me safer to respond not merely with my present answer in mind but from the point of view of my life overall, that on the one hand there are pleasurable things which are not good, and on the other hand, there are painful things which are not bad but some of which are, and a third class which is neutral—neither bad or good.

You call pleasant things those which partake of pleasure or produce pleasure?

Certainly.

So my question is this. Just insofar as things are pleasurable, are they good? I am asking whether pleasure itself is not a good.

Just as you always say, Socrates, let us inquire into this matter, and if your claim seems reasonable and it is established that pleasure and the good are the same, then we will come to an agreement; otherwise we will disagree.

Later, toward the end of this part of the dialogue, Socrates sums up what they have found.

T4.8 *Protagoras* 356e–357b (immediately follows T5.22):

(Socrates speaking) What if our salvation in life depended on our choices of odd and even, when the greater and the lesser had to be counted correctly, either the same kind against itself or one kind against another, whether it be near or remote? What then would save our life? Surely nothing other than knowledge, specifically some kind of measurement, since that is the art of the greater and the lesser? In fact, nothing other than arithmetic, since it's a question of odd and even? Would these men agree with us or not?

Protagoras thought they would agree.

Well, then, my good people: Since it has turned out that our salvation in life depends on the right choice of pleasures and pains, be they more or fewer, greater or lesser, farther or nearer, doesn't our salvation seem, first of all, to be measurement, which is the study of relative excess and deficiency and equality?

It must be.

What is perhaps most surprising about **T4.7** is that it is Protagoras the Sophist who doubts the identity of pleasure and the good, just as Socrates himself had done in the *Gorgias* (498d–499e). Those who think that Socrates is a hedonist might, of course, concede the inconsistency, but then argue that the *Gorgias* is really a "transitional dialogue" in which Plato remains faithful to some but not all of the basic doctrines of Socratic philosophy.[5] In this view, hedonism was one of the doctrines Plato decided to jettison as he began to develop his own views and to depart from the philosophical positions endorsed by the historical Socrates. At the time he wrote the *Gorgias*, Plato became convinced of the point he had earlier put into the mouth of Socrates' antagonist, Protagoras: that only some pleasures are good, namely, the pleasures experienced in temperate actions performed by good people.

The attribution of hedonism to Socrates in the *Protagoras*, however, requires that we pay a very high price, for it implies that by the time he wrote the *Gorgias*, Plato came to realize that it was, in fact, Protagoras the Sophist who had the right understanding of the relationship between pleasure and happiness and that it was Socrates who had been mistaken. This seems quite implausible given Plato's unqualified scorn for the Sophists and their philosophical views in general. Nowhere does Plato ever suggest that he (Plato) shared an important view with one of the great Sophists—in this case, Protagoras—in opposition to a contrasting Socratic position. Before we accept that this is precisely what we find in the *Protagoras*—which obviously has serious implications on how we are to understand the *Gorgias*, as well—perhaps we should consider more carefully whether Socrates' remarks in the *Protagoras* really do commit Socrates to some version of hedonism.

We note, first, that Socrates never actually says that *he* accepts hedonism. Hedonism, Socrates says, is what "most people" *(hoi polloi)* believe happiness to be (355a). The closest Socrates comes to an endorsement of hedonism is his remark in **T4.7**, where he says that being able to distinguish correctly pleasure from pain "appears to be our savior." But even here, all that Socrates has committed himself to is the hypothetical statement that *if* one accepts hedonism *then* one has to conclude that the knowledge of how to get the most pleasure and avoid the most pain is the best way to acquire happiness. But this is compatible with Socrates not revealing in these passages his own view of the good at all. Rather, Socrates' discussion with Protagoras can be viewed as just a typical Socratic elenchos. In this particular case, it is an elenchos in which Socrates is testing the view held by most people that one can know what course of action will lead to happiness but yet not follow that course because one is overcome by a desire to do what is pleasant.[6] A crucial premise of that elenchos is the view most people hold that hedonism is true (351c,

355a-b). If the argument is just an elenchos directed at most people, we need not think that Socrates is revealing his own views. He is showing what the many would have to think about the power of knowledge if *they* remain loyal to *their* hedonism. Finally, we should note that toward the end of the argument, Protagoras, who earlier, in **T4.7**, was trying to be cagey about his own view of happiness, concedes that in fact he agrees with most people that pleasure is the good (358a). Thus, in showing that most people, who are hedonists, are also committed to the view that knowledge can never be overcome by pleasure, Socrates is showing Protagoras that Protagoras is committed to the same view of the power of knowledge that has just been demonstrated. Knowledge of what is good cannot be overcome. Since Socrates seems to assume that Protagoras believes that all of the other virtues are goods, he is thereby closing off from Protagoras the possibility that one could know that one of the other virtues is a good but fail to acquire it. But if this is right, the use of hedonism in the argument against what most people think about knowledge tells us something important about what Protagoras thinks about what happiness is but it tells us nothing about how Socrates views happiness.[7]

4.2.2 *The Second View:*
The Sovereignty of Virtue Thesis

Perhaps the most influential view of the relationship between virtue and happiness is the one articulated by Gregory Vlastos.[8] According to Vlastos, Socrates believes that virtue is not an external cause of one's being happy; virtue is actually a *part* of one's happiness. It is a *component* of happiness. But, of course, for Socrates, virtue is a very special component of happiness, special in at least three ways. To begin with, the possession of virtue is always sufficient for happiness: Regardless of the circumstances of the virtuous person, the mere possession of virtue is enough to make the virtuous person happy.

4.2.2.1 The Sufficiency Thesis.
Let us look first at the evidence cited in support of the claim that virtue actually guarantees happiness. Consider Socrates' claim made to the jury in the *Apology* that neither Meletus nor Anytus can harm him.
    T4.9 *Apology* 30c-d:

> (Socrates speaking) Be sure that if you kill the sort of man I say I am, you will not harm me more than yourselves. Neither Meletus nor Anytus can harm me in any way; he could not harm me, for I do not think it is permitted that a better man be harmed by a worse.

Although it is always cited by those who endorse the idea that virtue is sufficient for happiness, this passage is less helpful than it is typically claimed to be, for Socrates leaves open the possibility that the virtuous could be the victim of all sorts of devastating evils caused by nonmoral sources.

A second passage in the *Apology*, however, is typically read as closing off just this possibility. Here, Socrates is trying to encourage those jurors who voted for his acquittal that good people need not fear death.

T4.10 *Apology* 41c-d (= **T7.4**):

(Socrates speaking) You too must be of good hope as regards death, gentlemen of the jury, and keep this one truth in mind, that a good man cannot be harmed either in life or in death and that his affairs are not neglected by the gods.

But this passage also falls short of endorsing the sufficiency of virtue for happiness, however. Even if we simply assume that the good person Socrates refers to is the virtuous person[9] and also that Socrates means to claim that the virtuous person can never suffer any evils at all, all that follows from what he says is that the virtuous person will never be miserable. But, of course, from the fact that the virtuous cannot be miserable, it does not follow that they are always happy. Moreover, we cannot simply assume that Socrates thinks that someone who possesses one good, namely, virtue, and who suffers no evils is happy, without begging the question regarding whether virtue really is sufficient for happiness.

Two other passages seem to offer even more explicit support for the claim that the possession of virtue is always, by itself, enough to guarantee the happiness of its possessor. Consider the following exchange between Socrates and the Sophist Thrasymachus in Book 1 of the *Republic*. Socrates has just gained the admission from Thrasymachus that the function of the soul is "taking care of things, ruling, deliberating, and the like" (353d). Socrates then proceeds to draw the following inference regarding virtue and happiness.

T4.11 *Republic* 1.353d–354a:

(Socrates speaking) And don't we also say that there is a virtue of a soul?
(Thrasymachus speaking) We do.
Then, will a soul ever perform its function well, Thrasymachus, if it is deprived of its peculiar virtue, or is that impossible?
It's impossible.
Doesn't it follow, then, that a bad soul rules and takes care of things badly and that a good soul does all these things well?
It does.

Now, we agreed that justice is a soul's virtue, and injustice its vice?
We did.
Then, it follows that a just soul and a just man will live well, and an unjust
one badly.
Apparently so, according to your argument.
And surely anyone who lives well is blessed and happy, and anyone who
doesn't is the opposite.
Of course.
Therefore, a just person is happy, and an unjust one wretched.

Socrates seems to be saying the same thing again in the *Gorgias*. He
summarizes for the benefit of his interlocutor Callicles what he takes the
argument to have shown.

T4.12 *Gorgias* 507a-c (= **T5.13**, immediately follows **T5.12**):

(Socrates speaking first, with Callicles responding) And surely a self-controlled person would do what's appropriate with respect to both gods and
human beings. For if he does what's inappropriate, he wouldn't be self-controlled.
That's necessarily how it is.
And of course if he did what's appropriate with respect to human beings,
he would be doing what's just, and with respect to gods he would be doing
what's pious, and one who does what's just and pious must necessarily be
just and pious.
That's so.
Yes, and he would also necessarily be brave, for it's not like a self-controlled man to either pursue or avoid what isn't appropriate, but to avoid
and pursue what he should, whether these are things to do, or people, or
pleasures and pains, and to stand fast and endure them where he should. So,
it's necessarily very much the case, Callicles, that the self-controlled man, because he's just and brave and pious, as we've recounted, is a completely
good man, that the good man does well and admirably whatever he does,
and that the man who does well is blessed and happy, while the corrupt
man, the one who does badly, is miserable.

Here, Socrates certainly seems to be claiming that the possession of virtue
is *always* enough to *guarantee* the virtuous person's happiness.

4.2.2.2 The Necessity Thesis.
The second way in which virtue is a special component of happiness, according to the sovereignty of virtue thesis, is that virtue is necessary for
happiness. No one, in other words, can be happy without virtue. Two
passages—both from the *Gorgias*—are often cited in support of the neces-

sity thesis. In the first, Socrates has been verbally sparring with young Polus, who thinks he can refute Socrates' claim that being just is always better than being unjust merely by pointing to the life of the king of Persia, who was widely envied for the enormous pleasures he enjoyed.

T4.13 *Gorgias* 470e:

> POLUS: It's obvious, Socrates, that you won't even claim to know that the Great King is happy.
>
> SOCRATES: Yes, and that would be true, for I don't know how he stands in regard to education and justice.
>
> POLUS: Really? Does all happiness depend on that?
>
> SOCRATES: Yes, Polus, so I say anyway. I say that the admirable and good person, man or woman, is happy, but that one who's unjust and wicked is miserable.

If "all happiness depends on justice," then no one is happy who lacks justice.

The second passage occurs later in the same dialogue, after Socrates has shown that the best life cannot be one of enjoying limitless pleasures, as Socrates' new opponent, Callicles, had been urging.

T4.14 *Gorgias* 507c-e:

> (Socrates speaking) . . . So this is how I set down the matter, and I say that this is true. And if it is true, then a person who wants to be happy must evidently pursue and practice self-control. Each of us must flee away from lack of discipline as quickly as his feet will carry him, and must above all make sure that he has no need of being disciplined, but if he does have that need, either he himself or anyone else in his house, either a private citizen or a whole city, he must pay his due and must be disciplined, if he's to be happy. This is the target which I think one should look to in living, and in his actions he should direct all of his own affairs and those of his city to the end that justice and self-control will be present in one who is to be blessed.

Since, for reasons we give in the next chapter, Socrates believes that anyone who possesses justice and self-control must also possess the other virtues (piety, courage, and wisdom) as well, and so be completely virtuous, Socrates seems to be committing himself to the view that virtue is required for happiness. No one can be happy without possessing virtue.

Let us now turn to the third way in which virtue seems to be a unique component of happiness. According to the sovereignty of virtue thesis, Socrates holds the commonsense view that happiness can have more than one component good and that the more component goods one has, the happier one is—provided of course that one is virtuous. Thus, although virtue is sufficient for happiness according to the sovereignty of virtue thesis, someone who possesses virtue and some other component good is happier than someone who possesses only virtue without the other good. Moreover, virtue is the power by which something that would otherwise not be a good at all is transformed into a good. Consider the following reason Socrates gives his jurors for making the acquisition of virtue their first concern.

T4.15 *Apology* 30a-b (part of longer quote at **T2.25**):

(Socrates speaking) For I go around doing nothing but persuading both young and old among you not to care for your body or your wealth in preference to or as strongly as for the best possible state of your soul, as I say to you: "Wealth does not bring about excellence,[10] but excellence brings about wealth and all other public and private blessings for men, both individually and collectively."

Thus, wealth is something that can be good—but Socrates seems to be saying here that it is excellence or virtue that *makes* wealth good for those to whom it is a good.[11]

The same point is made in the *Euthydemus*. In that dialogue, Socrates calls virtue by one of its other names—"wisdom"—and points out that, as such, it has the power to transform various things into actual goods.

T4.16 *Euthydemus* 279a-c:

(Socrates speaking) Well then, what kinds of existing things are good for us? Or, perhaps this isn't a difficult question and we don't need an important personage to supply the answer because everyone would say that to be rich is good—isn't that so?

Very much so, he [Clinias] said.

And so with being healthy, and handsome, and having a sufficient supply of the other things the body needs?

He agreed.

And again, is it clear that noble birth, and power, and honor in one's country are goods.

He agreed.

Then which goods do we have left? I said. What about being self-controlled and just and brave? For heaven's sake tell me, Clinias, whether you think we will be putting these in the right place if we class them as goods or if we refuse to do so? Perhaps someone might quarrel with us on this point—how does it seem to you?

They are goods, said Clinias.

Very well, said I. And where in the company shall we station wisdom? Among the goods, or what shall we do with it?

Among the goods.

Now be sure we do not leave out any goods worth mentioning.

I don't think we are leaving out any, said Clinias.

But I remembered one and said, Good heavens, Clinias, we are in danger of leaving out the greatest good of all!

Which one is that? He said.

Good fortune, Clinias, which everybody, even quite worthless people, says is the greatest of the goods.

As the argument unfolds, Socrates shows that, in fact, wisdom is the basis of all good fortune, for it is wisdom that transforms all the other items mentioned as goods into things that are advantageous to their possessors.

T4.17 *Euthydemus* 281a-e:

(Socrates speaking) And also, I said, with regard to using the goods we mentioned first—wealth and health and beauty—was it knowledge that ruled and directed our conduct in relation to the right use of all such things as these, or some other thing?

It was knowledge, he [Clinias] said.

Then knowledge seems to provide men not only with good fortune but also with well-doing, in every case of possession or action.

He agreed.

Then in heaven's name, I said, is there any advantage in other possessions without good sense and wisdom? Would a man with no sense profit more if he possessed and did much or if he possessed and did little? Look at it this way: if he did less, would he not make fewer mistakes; and if he made fewer mistakes, would he not do less badly, and if he did less badly, would he not be less miserable?

Yes, indeed, he said.

And in which case would one do less, if one were poor or if one were rich?

Poor, he said.

And if one were weak or strong?

Weak.

And if one were held in honor or dishonor?

In dishonor.

And if one were brave and self-controlled would one do less, or if one were a coward?

A coward.

Then the same would be true if one were lazy rather than industrious?

He agreed.

And slow rather than quick, and dull of sight and hearing rather than keen?

We agreed with each other on all points of this sort.

So, to sum up, Clinias, I said, it seems likely that with regard to all of the things we called good in the beginning, the correct account is not that in themselves they are good by nature, but rather as follows: if ignorance controls them, they are greater evils than their opposites, to the extent that they are capable of complying with a bad master; but if good sense and wisdom are in control, they are greater goods. In themselves, however, neither sort is of any value.

It seems, he said, to be just as you say.

Then what is the result of our conversation? Isn't it that, of the other things, no one of them is either good or bad, but of these two, wisdom is good and ignorance bad?

He agreed.

According to **T4.17**, Socrates thinks that the items other than wisdom that can be good are, in themselves, neither good nor bad. They are bad things for their possessor if their possessor is ignorant. But if their possessor is wise, those same items are goods because wisdom ensures that they will be advantageous to their possessor. Thus, when Socrates says at the end of **T4.17** that only "wisdom is good and ignorance bad," he means that only wisdom is always good just because of what it is and only ignorance is always bad just because of what it is. Everything else that is good or bad is so depending on whether it is used through wisdom or ignorance. In short, anything other than wisdom that is good has its goodness *dependent* on the agent's wisdom. Beauty, power, and the other items mentioned by Socrates in **T4.16** and **T4.17** *can* be good. But they can also be bad. Whether they are beneficial or damaging to the well-being of their possessor depends entirely upon whether their possessor is wise or ignorant.

We are now in a position to see why Vlastos thinks that this should be called Socrates' sovereignty of virtue thesis. Vlastos takes the various items that have been transformed into goods by wisdom to be *components* of happiness. Moreover, they augment the happiness that wisdom or virtue secures just by itself, but only because virtue ensures that they actually benefit their possessor. But virtue differs from the various items that *can* become goods in another way as well. Riches and power can always be taken away by others. Beauty can turn to ugliness by accident or disease. The respect of others depends on what others believe about you, so even the most respected people can quickly become objects of derision. The sufficiency of virtue thesis, however, ensures that even if these other goods are lost, owing to the vicissitudes of human life, virtue by itself ensures that the virtuous person will be happy. Moreover, the necessity of virtue thesis ensures that no amount of other things could ever be worth more than virtue by itself.

4.2.3 A Problem:
Is Virtue Really Sufficient for Happiness?

As we have seen, there are a number of passages that can be plausibly cited in support of the sufficiency of virtue thesis, according to which nothing can make individuals less than minimally happy as long as they possess virtue. But there are two texts in which Socrates seems to be saying the opposite. In the first, Socrates is discussing with his friend Crito whether we should concern ourselves with what most people say about how to take care of the body or whether we should listen, instead, only to the person with the relevant expertise, the physician.

T4.18 *Crito* 47d–48a (immediately precedes **T6.6**):

SOCRATES: Come now, if we ruin that which is improved by health and corrupted by disease by not following the opinions of those who know, is life worth living for us when that is ruined? And that is the body, is it not?

CRITO: Yes.

SOCRATES: And is life worth living with a body that is corrupted and in bad condition?

CRITO: In no way.

Socrates: And is life worth living for us with that part of us corrupted that unjust action harms and just action benefits? Or do we think that part of us, whatever it is, that is concerned with justice and injustice, is inferior to the body?

CRITO: Not at all.

SOCRATES: It is more valuable?

CRITO: Much more.

It is the first part of this passage that presents the problem for the sufficiency of virtue thesis. Although wisdom guarantees that the virtuous person will never do what is wrong, it cannot protect the person from ever falling victim to a debilitating and painful disease so terrible that it would make the virtuous person prefer to be dead. But there is no reason to think that such a disease would necessarily destroy the virtuous person's virtue.[12] After all, bearing in mind that Socrates thinks of virtue as a kind of knowledge, there is no reason to think that Socrates believes that the possession of a diseased body somehow necessarily makes the soul ignorant in the relevant way. But since having a life that is not worth living is incompatible with happiness and yet is compatible with virtue, this passage would appear to show that Socrates does not think virtue by itself is enough to make its possessor happy.

Socrates makes the same point toward the end of the *Gorgias* when he points out to Callicles that a ship captain who saves someone from death may or may not have done a good thing, for the ship captain never knows which of his passengers he has benefited when he conducts them safely across the sea. That is why the thoughtful ship captain does not demand a great reward for the safe passage.

T4.19 *Gorgias* 511e–512b:

> (Socrates speaking) . . . And the man who possesses this craft [of sailing] and who has accomplished these feats, disembarks and goes for a stroll along the seaside and beside his ship with a modest air. For he's enough of an expert, I suppose, to conclude that it isn't clear which ones of his fellow voyagers he has benefited by not letting them drown in the deep, and which ones he has harmed, knowing that they were no better either in body or soul when he set them ashore than they were when they embarked. So he concludes that if a man afflicted with serious incurable physical diseases did not drown, this man is miserable for not dying, and has gotten no benefit from him. But if a man has many incurable diseases in what is more valuable than his body, his soul, life for that man is not worth living, and he won't do him any favor if he rescues him from the sea or from prison or from anywhere else. He knows that for a corrupt person it's better not to be alive, for he necessarily lives badly.

The implication is that anyone with "serious incurable physical diseases" would be better off dead. But once again, there is no reason to think that virtue can always protect one from contracting such diseases or that such terrible disease would, of necessity, cause virtuous people to lose their virtue. The inescapable conclusion is that virtue does not always make one's life a happy one. Sometimes, Socrates seems to think, even the virtuous would be better off dead.

4.2.4 Virtue Is a Technē

As we saw in Chapter 2, Socrates thinks that the sort of wisdom about which he questions those who profess to be wise and which he himself is seeking is in many respects like the wisdom, or *technē*, a craftsman possesses, which enables the craftsman to produce or perform some characteristic *ergon* (product or task). But one might argue that we value a craft *because* we value its product or performance. We seek out the physician's wisdom when we are ill and want the physician to employ medical skill to restore us to health, the characteristic product of the craft of medicine. We seek out the shoemaker when we need shoes, the characteristic product of the craft of shoemaking. In other words, a craft derives its worth from what it *produces* or *performs*. This is a problem for the sovereignty of virtue thesis because the thesis maintains that Socrates thinks of virtue as a sufficient *part* of happiness and as such it must be something that is valuable for what it is.

Although the objection makes the important point that as a craft, virtue can only be of instrumental value, it is not a point the proponent of the sovereignty of virtue thesis has to deny. Recall that according to **T4.17**, Socrates believes that virtue is the sort of wisdom that transforms things such as money, power, health, and good looks into real goods—goods that augment the happiness already secured by the possession of virtue itself. A proponent of the sovereignty of virtue thesis might argue that this is the characteristic product of virtue conceived as a craft. This is what gives the craft of virtue its worth. However, virtue, nonetheless, has intrinsic value that makes it a component of happiness, and of course it is for this reason that Socrates believes that the mere possession of virtue always makes one better off.

4.3 Is Virtue Really a Component of Happiness?

4.3.1 A Third Possibility

Let us return to Socrates' discussion of the relationship between wisdom and the items it transforms into goods in the *Euthydemus*. In the following passage, Socrates is questioning Clinias about the way the various items mentioned in **T4.1**, **T4.16**, and **T4.17** make us happy.

T4.20 *Euthydemus* 280b-e:

(Socrates speaking) . . . We decided [earlier], I said, that if we had many good things, we should be happy and do well.

He [Clinias] agreed.

And would the possession of good things make us happy if they were of no advantage to us, or if they were of some?

If they were of some advantage, he said.

And would they be advantageous to us if we simply had them and did not use them? For instance, if we had a great deal of food but didn't eat any, or plenty to drink but didn't drink any, would we derive any advantage from these things?

Certainly not, he said.

Well then, if every workman had all the materials necessary for his particular job but never used them, would he do well by reason of possessing all of the things a workman requires? For instance, if a carpenter were provided with all his tools and plenty of wood but never did any carpentry, could he be said to benefit from their possession?

Not at all, he said.

Well then, if a man had money and all of the good things we were mentioning just now but made no use of them, would he be happy as the result of having these good things?

Clearly not, Socrates.

So it seems, I said, that a man who means to be happy must not only have such goods but must use them too, or else there is no advantage in having them.

You are right.

Then are these two things, the possession of good things and the use of them, enough to make a man happy, Clinias?

They seem so to me, at any rate.

If, I said, he uses them rightly, or if he does not?

If he uses them rightly.

In this passage, we learn that it is not the mere possession of goods that makes one happy; it is the right employment of those goods. If so, the sovereignty of virtue thesis is guilty of what philosophers call a "category mistake," for it claims that happiness, as Socrates conceives it, consists of various component goods, whereas in **T4.20**, we learn that Socrates thinks of happiness as the right employment of the right possessions. But if so, it is also a mistake to think that for Socrates, virtue is valuable just for what it is. Its value resides *solely* in its power as a craft after all. The value of virtue is its power to produce the right sorts of action, which presumably is the characteristic product of virtue.

It is important to notice that if we understand the Socratic conception of happiness as consisting of right activity we can avoid saddling Socrates with a morally questionable view of how the various items he lists in **T4.16** as potential goods contribute to happiness. It follows from that sovereignty of virtue thesis that not only are we happier, according to Socrates, when we possess more things such as money and honor when they are accompanied by wisdom but we are even happier still when we possess more of those things. Provided that one is morally wise, the richer one is the better off one is; the more powerful one is, the better off one is, and so forth. We are left, however, with utterly no explanation of why more money is *always* better. But if happiness is right activity, as we are now proposing, Socrates thinks that we should want such things as power, honor, and even good looks *only* insofar as they support the performance of right action. To the questions "Why is *more* money always better than less and why is *more* honor always better than less?" we can answer that neither is always better, unless more money or more honor is necessary to support more of the right activities that express moral virtue. The *Principle of Charity* in interpretation, then, should lead us to prefer this understanding of Socrates' views rather than the one proposed by those who endorse the interpretation that attributes the sovereignty of virtue thesis to Socrates—even if our texts (and hence, the *Principle of Interpretive Plausibility* and the *Principle of Textual Fidelity*) were not by themselves sufficient to decide the case—as we would argue they are in this case.

4.3.2 What Virtue Protects Against

According to the view we are considering, Socrates thinks that virtue cannot protect its possessor from every evil. Some evils that a virtuous person can suffer would render even the virtuous person incapable of right action and would therefore destroy even the virtuous person's happiness. But it would be a mistake to infer that according to the third view we are promoting, Socrates must think that an evil could ever render virtuous people unhappy or miserable as opposed to merely reaching the point where they would judge their lives to be no longer worth living. For Socrates, there are in fact two things that are worse than being enslaved or suffering the most painful diseases: The first is living a life of *wicked activity*, for which the wicked person undergoes the healing effect of punishment and is cured. The second, however, is even worse—far worse—in Socrates' eyes than the first: living a life of wicked activity that goes *unpunished*. This is how Socrates makes the point to Polus in the *Gorgias* after Polus has arrogantly claimed that it is always better to do injustice than to suffer it.

T4.21 *Gorgias* 478c-e:

SOCRATES: Now, would a man be happiest, as far as his body goes, if he's under treatment, or if he weren't even sick to begin with?

POLUS: If he weren't even sick, obviously.

SOCRATES: Because happiness evidently isn't a matter of getting rid of something bad; it's rather a matter of not even contracting it to begin with.

POLUS: That's so.

SOCRATES: Very well. Of two people, each of whom has something bad in either body or soul, which is the more miserable one, the one who is treated and gets rid of the bad thing or the one who doesn't but keeps it?

POLUS: The one who isn't treated, it seems to me.

SOCRATES: Now, wasn't paying what's due getting rid of the worst thing there is, corruption?

POLUS: It was.

SOCRATES: Yes, because such justice makes people self-controlled, I take it, and more just. It proves to be a treatment against corruption.

POLUS: Yes.

SOCRATES: The happiest man, then, is the one who doesn't have any badness in his soul, now that this has been shown to be the most serious kind of badness.

POLUS: That's clear.

SOCRATES: And, second, I suppose is the man who gets rid of it.

POLUS: Evidently.

SOCRATES: This is the man who gets lectured and lashed, the one who pays what is due.

POLUS: Yes.

SOCRATES: The man who keeps it, then, and who doesn't get rid of it, is the one whose life is the worst.

The reason that the unjust person who escapes punishment has the worst life of all, as Socrates later tells Callicles in the *Gorgias* (507c), is that such a person is bound to "*do badly* and so be miserable." Because *living* unjustly *is* misery and since virtue ensures that one will never live unjustly, virtue guarantees that one will never be miserable.

4.3.3 Does Socrates Have a Coherent View of Virtue and Happiness?

At this point, someone might well argue that Socrates simply fails to have a coherent position about the relationship between virtue and happiness. After all, the argument might go, **T4.9** clearly states that a good man cannot be harmed by a worse man and **T4.10** clearly states that *no* harm can come to a good man. If losing one's happiness is a kind of harm, as it surely is, then, at least sometimes, Socrates says that virtue indemnifies its possessor against the loss of happiness, in which case, Socrates *is* committed, at least sometimes, to the thesis that virtue is sufficient for happiness. Moreover, one might argue that **T4.11** and **T4.12** could not be plainer: Both claim that the virtuous person will always live well.

But before we convict Socrates of inconsistency on such an important matter, let us look more carefully at the passages that seem to favor the sufficiency thesis. Notice that both **T4.9** and **T4.10** appear in the *Apology*. Let us consider, then, yet another passage that also appears in the same work. When it becomes time for Socrates to tell the jury what sort of counterpenalty he thinks he deserves, he states that there are some things he cannot propose because they would be evils.

T4.22 *Apology* 37b-c:

> Since I am convinced that I wrong no one, I am not likely to wrong myself, to say that I deserve some evil and to make some such assessment against myself. What should I fear? That I should suffer the penalty Meletus has assessed against me, of which I say that I do not know whether it is a good or bad? Am I to choose in preference to this something that I know very well to be an evil and assess the penalty at that?

Socrates then goes on to list a number of things—imprisonment, imprisonment until a fine can be paid, and exile—that would be evils. Of course, Meletus actually proposed death as Socrates' punishment upon conviction. But Meletus could have proposed any of the things Socrates says would be evils for him, and had he done so and had the jury accepted any of them as Socrates' punishment, Socrates would have suffered an evil. Harm would, therefore, have come to him, according to his own view of what counts as an evil, and it would have been visited on him by a worse man!

Because this contradiction is so obvious, we think that it is unlikely that Socrates means in **T4.9** and **T4.10** that no harm *of any kind* could ever befall anyone who possesses virtue. We think that at least in these two passages Socrates is referring to a particular kind of harm that can never be visited on a good person. The particular harm he has in mind is harm to the *soul*. In other words, in **T4.9** Socrates is claiming that no inferior person can ever harm the soul of a good person, and in **T4.10** that the soul that is good can never be harmed. If so, the two passages in the *Apology* are not at all at odds with his view that devastating evils can indeed make the lives of even the best people not worth living.

We must be careful not to infer from the claim that no harm comes to the soul of a good person, that a soul that has once attained virtue can never be harmed. Clearly, if virtue is a kind of wisdom, as Socrates thinks it is, even virtue can be lost through disease or accident that has a catastrophic effect on one's abilities to know, think, or reason. Even the most virtuous person might have a devastating stroke, or get Alzheimer's disease, or be the victim of a horrible accident. Such events would obviously be evils, for if wisdom is lost, virtue itself is lost. Thus, when Socrates says in **T4.10** that "a good man cannot be harmed either in life or in death," he can mean only that no evil comes to one's soul as long as one remains morally upright (as Socrates himself did). Socrates' message to the jurors who voted for his acquittal, then, seems to be this: Although even virtuous people are always in danger of losing their virtue through some form of misfortune, they can be sure that as long as they *are* virtuous, no one and nothing can harm their most precious possession, which is their soul.

But even if the reading of **T4.9** and **T4.10** we are suggesting is correct, we have not yet shown that Socrates has a coherent conception of the relationship between virtue and happiness. Are not **T4.11** and **T4.12**, one might ask, clear and unequivocal endorsements of the sufficiency of virtue thesis? We think not. Before we concede that Socrates' position on the value of virtue is just hopelessly confused, perhaps we should ask whether in saying that the virtuous person will always live well, Socrates is saying (1) those who possess virtue are bound to be happy regardless of what circumstances they find themselves in, or (2) that virtuous people are bound to be happy provided they have at least the minimal number of nonmoral items of the sort mentioned in **T4.16** that are necessary for virtuous action. If Socrates means (1), then his remarks about the relationship between virtue and happiness are simply contradictory after all. Plainly, there can be no clearer violation of the *Principle of Charity* in interpretation than this! However, if Socrates really intends (2), his remarks are not inconsistent, but one might begin to wonder if (2) really satisfies the *Principle of Interpretive Plausibility* and the *Principle of Textual Fidelity*. But in the dialogues in which **T4.11** and **T4.12** appear, the *Gorgias* and the *Republic,* respectively, the issue between Socrates and his opponents is whether justice is more valuable than injustice, *not* whether justice is sufficient for happiness. Thus, relieving his interlocutors of their false view of the value of injustice does not require that Socrates hold (1), as opposed to (2). Moreover, since **T4.19**, which also appears in the *Gorgias,* implies that virtuous people can suffer evils that would make their lives not worth living, we should attribute (2) to Socrates rather than convicting him of an obvious contradiction about such an important matter within a single dialogue. Finally, if (2) is the preferred interpretation of **T4.11**, we should assume that (2) also gives us the proper interpretation of **T4.12**, the passage in *Republic* 1, since there seems to be no good reason to think that Socrates is making different points in the two passages. Since (2) is, then, a plausible understanding of what Socrates has to say in all of these texts, it satisfies, we contend, all of our interpretive principles in a way that (1) does not.

4.4 Does Socrates Think that
Virtue Is Necessary for Happiness?

4.4.1 Is Anyone Happy?

According to the third view of Socrates' conception of happiness, Socrates thinks that happiness consists in right actions, undertaken over a lifetime, or at least a long period in one's life. Virtue, then, is the craft that produces happiness. Thus, virtue is a cause of happiness, but it is not actually a *part* of happiness. Virtue causes its possessor always to engage in right activity, provided that its possessor also possesses what else is required for right activity. But even if virtue is not by itself sufficient for right activity, do not **T4.13** and **T4.14** show that Socrates thinks that virtue is a necessary condition of right activity? That is, does not Socrates believe that no one can be happy without virtue?

Before we attribute the necessity of virtue for happiness thesis to Socrates, we should first consider one *very* paradoxical consequence of this claim. Socrates, as we have seen, thinks that virtue is a kind of moral wisdom. But we have also seen that he thinks that neither he nor anyone he has ever encountered has actually attained this wisdom. In fact, it is not at all clear that he thinks any mortal can, as a matter of fact, ever attain moral wisdom. If, therefore, we accept that Socrates identifies moral wisdom and virtue and then also accept that he thinks that no one is happy without possessing virtue, we have to believe that Socrates also thinks that it is unlikely that anyone in Athens, including himself, is actually happy. If so, because he believes that the god is really wise (*Apology* 23a), Socrates thinks that only the Delphic god or perhaps all of the gods are really happy.

4.4.2 Philosophizing as a Right Activity That
Brings Happiness Without Virtue

It is possible, of course, that this is precisely what Plato wants us to believe about Socrates. But there is at least one text that appears to conflict with this conclusion. At the end of the *Apology*, Plato tells us that Socrates, before being led away to the prison to await his execution, had an opportunity to speak briefly with those jurors who voted for his acquittal. The main point he wants to emphasize is that good people should be optimistic about death, for, he says, death is one of two things: a dreamless and undisturbed sleep from which we never awaken or the soul's migration to Hades once we are dead, where only good judges "sit in judgment."[13] The idea seems to be that good people have nothing whatever to fear from good judges. But migration to Hades, Socrates goes on, will be especially wonderful for him because good judges will never prevent him from questioning and testing those who are there.

T4.23 *Apology* 41a-c (partially repeats, then continues **T7.23**):

> Again, what would one of you give to keep company with Orpheus and Musaeus, Hesiod and Homer? I am willing to die many times if that is true. It would be a wonderful way for me to spend my time whenever I met Palamedes and Ajax, the son of Telemon, and any other of the men of old who died through an unjust conviction, to compare my experience with theirs. I think it would be pleasant. Most important, I could spend my time testing and examining people there, as I do here, as to who among them is wise, and who thinks he is and is not. What would one not give, gentlemen of the jury, to examine the man who led the great expedition against Troy, or Odysseus, or Sisyphus, and innumerable other men and women one could mention. It would be an extraordinary happiness to talk with them, to keep company with them, and to examine them.

If those in Hades can be extraordinarily happy because they engage unhindered in philosophical activity and Socrates has engaged in that same activity throughout his life on earth, we have to conclude that Socrates judges his own life to have been a happy one, in spite of the fact that it has not been guided by virtue. But if so, Socrates does not accept the necessity of virtue for happiness thesis after all, since he thinks his life has been happy but he also thinks that he lacks virtue.

Still, one might reasonably ask, if Socrates rejects the idea that virtue is strictly necessary for happiness, why does he imply, as he does in **T4.11** and **T4.12**, that it is? If we reflect for a minute on the dramatic setting in which Socrates makes these claims, we can see that, given the point in his life at which Plato portrays him as making these claims, Socrates may think that there are some virtuous people, though he has not yet discovered them and that his own life, by the time it is over, is not likely to be assessed as a happy one, for it is very likely that he will make significant moral errors during its course, just as all other people do. We must recall that at the time he is speaking to Callicles in the *Gorgias*, however, Socrates would never have had reason to think that either of these would turn out to be the case. Were he asked by Callicles, "Have you engaged in nothing but the right activities throughout your life?" Socrates could have answered, "Indeed, I have, though only up to this point. Because I lack wisdom, however, it is unlikely that I, or any one else for that matter, will be able to live a long life that is not marred in some way by disastrous wrong. Regardless of how careful I am and even though I am fortunate enough to have a *daimonion* that turns me away from many wrongs that I would do, it is unlikely that I will not make some important mistakes. To live well over a complete lifetime one needs virtue to engage consistently in the right actions that constitute the best life for human beings." If we think that **T4.11** and **T4.12** only express Socrates' view that it is unlikely—highly unlikely—that anyone can be happy without virtue, there is no reason that he cannot go to his death confident that in spite of his own lack of virtue, he has beaten the odds. It is *only at the end of his life* that Socrates can say, as far as he has been able to tell, that no one in Athens has acquired virtue and that he has consistently performed the right activities and, thus, that his life has been a happy one. We believe, then, that Socrates agrees with Solon, the great Athenian statesman of an earlier generation, who is reported by Herodotus to have said that we should count no one happy until he is dead.[14] Like Solon, Socrates believes that misfortune can strip even the best of people of their happiness and so the fact that one appears to be happy at some point in life does not tell us how that person's life is to be judged when it comes to an end.

4.5 Goodness and Virtue

4.5.1 Is There a Distinction?

At this point, one might object that somewhere in our discussion we have taken a wrong turn. We have argued that

(1) Socrates does not possess virtue,

because

(2) Socrates does not possess moral wisdom.

But we have also argued that **T4.10** implies that

(3) No harm can come to the soul of the good person.

Yet surely Socrates says what he does in **T4.10** to reassure those jurors in the audience that no harm can come to his soul. If so, Socrates believes that

(4) Socrates is a good person,

in which case Socrates must also believe

(5) Socrates possesses virtue.

But (5) obviously contradicts (1). Somewhere, then, one might argue, our thinking about Socrates' view of the value of virtue has gone wrong.

We believe that this attempt to find a contradiction in the view we are attributing to Socrates rests on a non sequitur. Specifically, we think that the mistake is in inferring (5) from (4). We think the inference does not follow because we think that Socrates draws a sharp distinction between being a good person, on the one hand (that is, a person who possesses many right beliefs both about what sorts of policies to follow in one's life and many right beliefs about what actions are the right ones to perform in particular circumstances), and a virtuous person, on the other hand (a person with the moral qualities Socrates is convinced that he lacks). Our reasons for thinking that Socrates is prepared to accept (1) and so deny (5) are precisely those we examined in Chapter 2, where we argued that Socrates sincerely believes that he lacks moral wisdom and that he believes that virtue is a form of moral wisdom. What we must now show is that there is good reason to think that Socrates recognizes moral goodness as a moral category distinct from virtue.

To begin with, in spite of the fact that he lacks wisdom, Socrates' speech to the jury makes it clear that he considers himself vastly superior to most of his fellow Athenians. He claims, for example, to be the only Athenian alive to have always acted in such a way as to aim at what is best (*Gorgias* 521d—**T6.2**). In one respect, his moral superiority derives from the fact that unlike so many others in Athens, he is convinced that the best thing one can do to improve one's life is to engage in philosophical examination.

T4.24 *Apology* 38a (part of longer quote at **T2.21**):

. . . the unexamined life is not worth living . . . .

To the extent that most of his fellow Athenians fail to live by this precept, they are at risk—a very substantial risk—of pursuing goals that will turn out disastrously for them. Because Socrates thinks that engaging in philosophical examination, as he has done so scrupulously throughout so much of his life, is the best way to root out false moral views, he has reason to think that he is morally superior at least to most people. Even though he lacks virtue just as they do, he is dedicated to living a moral life as none of them are.

Not only does Socrates think that he is trying to lead a morally faultless life, but according to the *Apology*, he believes that he has actually suc-

ceeded! Before actually making his offer to pay a counterpenalty following his conviction, Socrates explains what he deserves to suffer or to pay.
T4.25 *Apology* 37b (repeats **T4.22** in part):

> Since I am convinced that I wrong no one, I am not likely to wrong myself, to
> say that I deserve some evil and to make some such assessment against my-
> self.

Socrates plainly sees himself has someone who has done the city enormous good and who has done no one any harm. If so, he has good reason
to think he is a good person, morally superior to all others he has encountered even though he lacks virtue.

4.5.2 What Is the Value of Virtue?

We have argued that Socrates' seemingly conflicting remarks can be un-
tangled if we think that at the end of his life, Socrates judges his own life
to have been happy, even though he has only managed to sustain a kind
of moral goodness that falls short of virtue. But if virtue is not strictly necessary for happiness, why would Socrates, even at the very end of his life,
continue to exhort others to become virtuous? Why would Socrates not
have encouraged those who hear his words to develop the kind of goodness he has acquired if wisdom is so hard to acquire and turns out not to
be necessary anyway?

First, let us not forget that he *does* actually exhort his jurors to do as he
has done. He tells them that "the unexamined life is not worth living"
(**T4.24**) and leaves it not at all unclear what they should do to become
good in the way Socrates has managed to be. But second, even if Socrates
thinks that his own life has been happy, it does not follow that he thinks it
is the best life anyone could lead. He may think that even if happiness
consists in right activity (and the absence of wrong activity), some sets of
right activity are better than others, so some people are happier than others. For example, Socrates may well be right in thinking that using the
elenchos to achieve some benefit is an example of right action. But lacking
wisdom, he may not have seen that he could have performed an even better action had he used his elenctic powers in some other way, to help
some other person avoid some moral disaster. The morally wise person
would have recognized the better course of action and would have taken
it. Socrates always ends up doing a right thing, but only the possession of
wisdom would allow him to know that what he does is the best of the options available to him. If we think that some right actions are none the less
better than others and that how happy one is depends upon the activities
making up one's life, then even though Socrates' life is a happy one, his

life would have been *happier* had he succeeded in his search for virtue. Moreover, if, as seems likely, Socrates thinks that the gods do possess moral wisdom and since they do not need the sorts of things such as mortals need to engage in virtuous activity, then he also thinks that the lives of the gods are supremely happy. If this is right, even though he sees himself as a good person, Socrates has good reason to prize and to seek virtue, and to think that one who had virtue would be vastly better off than he has managed to be.

Third, Socrates is well aware that he is not like other people in that he has a divine voice, a *daimonion,* that frequently steers him away from evils, large and small.[15] For this reason, the fact that he has led a life that is free of injustice is the result of guidance that is simply not available to others. Where Socrates is turned away from evil by his divine sign, others can only rely on their ability to reason, and the best sort of reasoning about moral matters is that done by virtuous people. Thus, Socrates has good reason to do what he says in the *Apology* he has always done—exhort others to make themselves "as wise as possible," for if and only if they attain virtue can they be assured of acting rightly.

It is important to remember that the divine assistance Socrates receives does not provide him with an absolute safeguard against wrongful action. Although the *daimonion* has come to him ever since he was a child, Socrates is careful not to say that it always warns him away whenever he is about to do something evil. Thus, Socrates cannot infer from the silence of the *daimonion* that whatever it is that he is thinking about doing is actually permissible. Whenever the *daimonion* fails to interfere and warn him, Socrates must rely on his own power to discover whether he is acting rightly. On those occasions when he lacks divine assistance and so must reason for himself about what he ought to do, Socrates can never be entirely confident that he has reached the right conclusion. Even though Socrates' *daimonion* allows him to avoid moral errors that others who lack virtue would likely fall into and even though his own powers to reason about how he ought to act are doubtless considerably more powerful than those of others who lack virtue, Socrates is still vulnerable to moral mistakes of the sort the virtuous person would not make. In an important sense, then, Socrates has been lucky when he reaches the end of his life and realizes that he has managed to have harmed no one. We can say that "as it turns out," Socrates' life has been happy. Even with the assistance of his divine warning and even with his commitment to reasoning about how he ought to act, Socrates could have had no rational expectation that his life would be free from error. In this respect, his life stands in sharp contrast to the virtuous person's, whose wisdom would allow such a person unerringly to discern right from wrong and so live a life of right activity. Once again, then, Socrates has reason to exhort others, who lack his divine guidance, to pursue virtue and to pursue it himself until the Athenians take his life away.

4.6 A Preliminary Assessment of the Plausibility of Socrates' View

In this chapter, we have tried to explain how, according to Socrates, virtue and virtuous action fit into his scheme of values. We believe that the texts are best understood as not attributing to Socrates either that virtue is sufficient or that it is necessary for happiness. Our conclusion in both regards is controversial, and many scholars would take issue with us. If we are right, Socrates thinks that we are always better off pursuing virtue. Because he thinks that virtue is a kind of wisdom that assures its possessor never to go wrong in choosing the best action to perform, those who do attain virtue will have good lives.

At this point, however, one might well wonder just how plausible Socrates' view of the power of virtue really is. After all, because of the emphasis Socrates places on the pursuit of moral wisdom, as opposed to the training of desire for what is right, he seems to be assuming that knowledge of what is best for one to do is always, by itself, sufficient to cause one to do what one recognizes to be best. In other words, he seems to be assuming that whatever motivates our actions will always follow the recognition that something is the best course of action for us. In fact, this very paradoxical view of motivation seems to be precisely what is behind the claims Socrates makes in **T4.5**. As we shall see in the next chapter, Socrates is fully committed to just this assumption about the relationship between a belief about what is good and desire to do what is good. To see why he thinks it is plausible, let us turn to his more general views about moral psychology.

Notes

1. In fact, as we shall see below, Socrates denies that wealth and health are always good. He does, however, think that wisdom is always good, though he is not trying to make that point in this passage in the *Gorgias*.

2. Aristotle is making the same point, it appears, in bk. 1, ch. 2 (1094a18–22) of the *Nicomachean Ethics*.

3. We discuss the full implications of this passage for Socrates' moral psychology in Chapter 5.

4. The most influential recent defense of this position can be found in Irwin (1977), 102–114, and (1995), 78–94.

5. This is the position Irwin takes regarding the *Gorgias* in Irwin (1977), 115–131, and (1995), 111–117.

6. The phenomenon of knowing what one ought to do and failing to do it because one is overcome by a stronger desire for something other than the good is what is called *akrasia*. As we shall see in Chapter 5, Socrates denies that *akrasia* ever really occurs.

7. For an excellent response to the attribution of hedonism to Socrates based on the *Protagoras*, see Zeyl (1980), 250–269.

8. Vlastos (1991), 200–235.

9. We argue below that there is good reason not to make this assumption and that Socrates thinks we can distinguish between the virtuous person and someone who is morally good but not virtuous.

10. The Greek word here is *aretē*, which, as we have said, is normally translated as "virtue."

11. Most translators simply make the text state this, but we think the text actually reads as we have rendered it—even if we do not really doubt that this gives the sense of Socrates' odd claim. See Chapter 2, n. 11 about this translation.

12. We must remember that sometimes Socrates uses "justice" as a synonym for virtue. This passage is one of those instances.

13. We discuss Socrates' beliefs about death and the possibility of an afterlife in Chapter 7.

14. Herodotus, *Historiae*, bk. 1, 32. See also Aristotle, *Nicomachean Ethics*, bk. 1, ch. 10.

15. We discuss Socrates' belief in this, as a religious belief, in Chapter 7.

Suggested Readings

On the Claim that Socrates Was a Hedonist

Most scholars have not accepted the claim that Socrates' arguments in the *Protagoras* commit him to hedonism. But several important scholars have argued for this controversial thesis nonetheless. As we have noted in this chapter, the most influential arguments for this position have been made in Irwin (1977) and (1995). Gosling and Taylor (1982) also argue for this position. Weiss (1989) argues against Gosling's and Taylor's interpretation. A very original argument for attributing hedonism to Socrates is made in Rudebusch (forthcoming), who claims that Socrates was indeed a hedonist but that his conception of pleasure was itself radically different from that of ordinary hedonists. The most frequently cited argument against the thesis that Socrates was a hedonist may be found in Zeyl (1980).

The Relationships Between Virtue and Happiness

As we have noted in this chapter, Irwin (1977) and (1995) argues for the view that Socrates thought virtue was purely instrumental for happiness. The most spirited opposition to Irwin's argument can be found in Vlastos (1991, ch. 8; revised from an article published in 1984). Vlastos argues, instead, for the sovereignty of virtue thesis. A position similar to the one offered by Vlastos (and published before Vlastos's) can be found in Zeyl (1982). We argued that Socrates thought that virtue was necessary but not sufficient for virtue, in Brickhouse and Smith (1987). We later changed our minds about the necessity of virtue for happiness, arguing that good activity was both necessary and sufficient for happiness but that virtue was neither necessary nor sufficient, in Brickhouse and Smith (1994, ch. 4).

Socrates on Wisdom and Motivation

5.1 The Socratic Paradoxes

Students of Socratic philosophy are immediately struck by just how hard it is to believe some of the things Socrates says. In this they are not alone, for the people Socrates converses with often express the same reluctance to agree with him. In this chapter, we focus primarily on two of the most important and most controversial parts of Socratic philosophy. We devote a whole chapter to them, in part, because they are interesting in themselves but also because the doctrines we consider rest on Socrates' views about cognition and motivation and the relationship between the two. Thus, as we explore Socrates' reasons for holding such seemingly strange views, we get a better insight into the psychological underpinnings of his moral theory.

The first doctrine we consider is what is usually called the "unity of the virtues." Like most of his fellow fifth-century B.C. Greeks, Socrates believed that there are five cardinal moral virtues—wisdom, justice, piety, courage, and temperance. But unlike most of his fellow Greeks and, no doubt, unlike most of us, Socrates is convinced that these five virtues are intimately connected to each other. In fact, Socrates seems to think that it is conceptually necessary that anyone who has any one of these virtues will have *all* of the others as well. Thus, Socrates thinks that it is simply not possible for someone to be courageous and not just, for example, or pious and not wise. Scholars agree about this much. But as we shall see, there has been, and continues to be, considerable disagreement about exactly how Socrates' commitment to the "unity of the virtues" is to be understood.

The second doctrine we explore is Socrates' notorious conviction that there is no such thing as weakness of will, or what the Greeks called *akra-*

sia. Socrates thinks we are simply misdescribing what occurred whenever we say that we did something that we thought we knew or believed we should not do but did anyway because some desire or emotion simply overcame our better judgment. Socrates thinks that this never happens— we always do what we think will be best for us at the time. Not only does Socrates think that *akrasia* is just an illusion, but because he is equally convinced that acting morally is always good for us, he believes that all evildoing is the result of ignorance! Thieves know that they are stealing, all right. But if Socrates is right, thieves do not see that they are also harming themselves, something they would never do if they but understood that fact.

5.2 The Unity of the Virtues

5.2.1 Parts and Wholes

In the *Protagoras*, Plato has Socrates confronting the great Sophist for whom the dialogue is named. After Protagoras offers a long explanation of how virtue is teachable, Socrates raises the question of how the various virtues are related to each other.

T5.1 *Protagoras* 329c-d (immediately precedes **T5.2**):

> (Socrates speaking to Protagoras) You also said, at many points in your speech, that justice and temperance and piety and all of these things were somehow collectively one thing: virtue. Could you go through this again and be more precise? Is virtue a single thing, with justice and temperance and piety its parts, or are the things I have just listed all names for a single entity? This is what still intrigues me.

Protagoras is quick to respond, saying that the individual virtues are really just parts of a single thing, virtue. Socrates immediately points out that Protagoras's answer is ambiguous, since it is not clear in what sense the various virtues are parts. Once the problem is pointed out, Protagoras leaves no doubt about how he thinks it is to be resolved.

T5.2 *Protagoras* 329d–330b (immediately follows **T5.1**):

> (Socrates speaking first and Protagoras responding) Parts as in the parts of a face: mouth, nose, eyes, and ears? Or parts as in the parts of gold, where there is no difference, except for size, between parts or between the parts and the whole?
>
> In the former sense, I would think, Socrates: as the parts of the face are to the whole face.
>
> Then tell me this. Do some people have one part and some another, or do you necessarily have all the parts if you have any one of them?

By no means, since many are courageous but unjust, and many again are just but not wise.

[. . .] And does each have its own unique power or function? In the analogy to the parts of the face, the eye is not like the ear, nor is its power or function the same, and this applies to the other parts as well: They are not like each other in power or function or in any other way. Is this how it is with the parts of virtue? Are they unlike each other, both in themselves and in their powers or functions? Is it not clear that this must be the case, if our analogy is valid?

Yes, it must be the case, Socrates.

Protagoras's position, then, is clear. He thinks what most people think. First, Protagoras believes that the individual virtue names—"courage," "justice," "piety," "temperance," and "wisdom"—refer to *different* powers or functions of the soul, and second, he believes that it is entirely possible to have one of these powers without having any of the others. Protagoras, in other words, begins the conversation convinced that the individual virtues do not in any sense form a unity.

As the dialogue unfolds, it becomes clear where Socrates stands on the second point. He disagrees with Protagoras about whether it is possible to have one of the individual virtues without possessing the others. Socrates believes that the individual virtues do form a unity, that—paradoxical as it seems—it is impossible to possess one of the individual virtues without possessing all of the others. What is not immediately clear, though, is where Socrates stands on the first point. Does Socrates think that the individual virtues refer to different powers or functions, or does he think that they refer to one and the same power and function? We will use the terminology that is now standard in the secondary literature on this topic and call the first option the "equivalence thesis" and the second option the "identity thesis."[1]

5.2.2 The Equivalence Thesis

The most influential proponent of the equivalence thesis is Gregory Vlastos. According to Vlastos, each of the individual virtue names refers to an individual power. Each individual virtue name refers to a different piece of moral knowledge, and each individual virtue has its own definition. Thus, the knowledge that is justice and that makes its possessor a just person, for example, is not the same knowledge that is piety and that makes its possessor pious. Vlastos agrees, of course, that Socrates differs with Protagoras about whether the individual virtues nonetheless form a unity. To grasp how the unity of the virtues is possible, we must see that one of the individual virtues, wisdom, enjoys a special status. Although wisdom is not the same thing as the other virtues—remember, according to the equivalence thesis, *all* of the individual virtues are different pieces of knowledge—wisdom makes the unity of the virtues possible, first, because wisdom is a necessary condition for the possession of any of the other virtues, and second, because wisdom is sufficient for the possession of each of the others as well. Thus, on Vlastos's understanding of Socrates' position, one cannot be courageous or temperate, for example, unless one is also wise, *and* if one is wise, one will be courageous and temperate as well. Still, wisdom, courage, temperance, and the other individual virtues are each separate and distinct powers of the soul.

Perhaps the strongest part of Vlastos's defense of the equivalence thesis is its indictment of its principal rival, the identity thesis. First, Vlastos bids us to consider Socrates' response to Euthyphro's attempt to teach Socrates the definition of piety by citing a single example.[2]

T5.3 *Euthyphro* 6d-e (= **T3.10**):

> SOCRATES: Bear in mind then that I did not bid you tell me one or two of the many pious actions but that form itself that makes all pious actions pious, for you agreed that all impious actions are impious and all pious actions pious through one form, or don't you remember?
>
> EUTHYPHRO: I do.
>
> SOCRATES: Tell me then what this form itself is, that I may look upon it, and using it as a model, say that any action of yours or another's that is of that kind is pious, and if it is not that it is not.

Here Socrates is making two points: (1) that all pious acts are pious through their possession of the same property—or what Socrates calls a "form"—and (2) that the proper account of what that property is would enable Socrates to identify correctly any and all instances of piety. Presumably, Socrates would say that the same two points apply to all of the other individual virtues as well. Vlastos cites this passage because he thinks that it would be absurd for Socrates to assert these two points *and* to maintain the identity thesis, for that would entail that merely by learning the proper account of what piety is, Socrates would also be able *thereby* to identify correctly *all* instances of *all* of the other virtues. It would follow that from knowing what it is that makes pious acts pious, one would able to say whether Socrates' behavior at the Battle of Delium, for example, constituted an act of courage!

A second problem with the identity thesis, according to Vlastos, has to do with the implication of the identity thesis that all of the individual virtue names have the same definition.[3] Vlastos thinks we should take seriously Socrates' suggestion to Euthyphro that the definition of justice is broader than the definition of piety.

T5.4 *Euthyphro* 12c-d (immediately follows **T5.8**):

> This is the kind of thing I was asking before, whether where there is piety there is also justice but where there is justice there is not always piety, for the pious is a part of the just. Shall we say that, or do you think otherwise?

Were Socrates to think that all of the individual virtues have the same definition, then one should be able to substitute any one virtue name for any other virtue name without changing the meaning of a sentence. For example, one would have to say that the sentences "Socrates is courageous" and "Socrates is just" have the same meaning, on the hypothesis that courage and justice are synonyms. But as Vlastos points out, we can see that the hypothesis is absurd if we try to make the substitution of "justice" for "piety" in **T5.4**. The substitution would be nonsense, for justice cannot be both a part of itself and distinct from the rest of justice, which is precisely what Socrates says holds between piety and justice.

If Vlastos is right, the final argument of the *Laches* (197e ff.) presents yet another problem for the identity thesis.[4] Up to this point, Socrates has been engaged with Laches and Nicias in an unsuccessful search for an account of what courage is. The argument, too long to quote in its entirety, can be summarized as follows.[5] It begins with Socrates reminding Nicias of his earlier assertion that

(1) Courage is a part of virtue (198a).

Moreover, Nicias thinks that

(2) Courage is knowledge of what is to be feared and hoped for (199b),

which Socrates immediately points out is equivalent to

(3) Courage is the knowledge of future goods and evils (198b-c).

Socrates, however, is quick to point out that there is no special knowledge of future goods and evils. Anyone who has knowledge of future goods and evils necessarily has the knowledge of all goods and evils, past, present, and future. Hence,

(4) The knowledge of past evils, the knowledge of present evils, and the knowledge of future evils is the same knowledge (198d–199a).

If so, it follows that

> (5) Courage is the knowledge of past, present, and future goods and evils (199b-c).

But since

> (6) Anyone who has knowledge of all goods and evils—past, present, and future—has complete virtue (199d),

we can infer from (5) and (6) that

> (7) Courage is not a part of virtue but the whole of virtue (199e), which directly contradicts (1).

Once the problem is out in the open, Socrates concludes that Nicias and he have not discovered what courage is.

Vlastos is right in thinking that the argument itself only shows that we cannot accept both (1) and (7) if the sense in which courage is said to be a part in (1) contradicts the sense in which courage is said to be the whole of virtue in (7). Nonetheless, we should not be persuaded by Vlastos's claim that (7) is what Vlastos terms an "outrage to common sense" and that Socrates expects us to see that (7) is outrageous.[6] After all, *many* of Socrates' most basic views are thoroughly at odds with what most people think is plainly true. What we do find telling in favor of Socrates' acceptance of (1) is the fact that Plato has Socrates explicitly state that he, Socrates, *agrees* with Nicias that courage is one of several parts of the whole of virtue.

T5.5 *Laches* 198a-b:

> SOCRATES: And you, Nicias, tell me again from the beginning—you know that when we were investigating courage at the beginning of the argument, we were investigating it as a part of virtue?
>
> NICIAS: Yes, we were.
>
> SOCRATES: And didn't you give your answer supposing that it was a part, and, as such, one among a number of other parts, all of which taken together are called virtue?
>
> NICIAS: Yes, why not?
>
> SOCRATES: And do you also speak of the same parts that I do? In addition to courage, I call temperance and justice and everything else of this kind parts of virtue, don't you?

NICIAS: Yes, indeed.

SOCRATES: Stop there. We are in agreement on these points, but let us investigate the grounds of fear and confidence to make sure that you don't regard them in one way and we in another . . . .

Clearly, up to this point at least, Socrates endorses the notion that courage is a part of virtue, though he is less confident that Nicias and he share the same understanding of what constitutes courage. That this is the right reading of the passage and that Socrates does think that individual virtues such as courage should be thought of as parts of the whole of virtue seem to be strongly confirmed by a remark Socrates makes in yet another dialogue, this time in the *Meno,* immediately after Meno has attempted to define virtue in terms of acquiring what are commonly regarded as good things.

T5.6 *Meno* 78d-e:

SOCRATES: Very well. According to Meno . . . virtue is the acquisition of gold and silver. Do you add to this acquiring, Meno, the words justly and piously, or does it make no difference to you but even if one secures these things unjustly, you call it virtue none the less?

MENO: Certainly not, Socrates. [. . .]

SOCRATES: It seems then that the acquisition must be accompanied by justice or moderation or piety or some other part of virtue; if it is not, it will not be virtue, even though it provides good things.

What is significant, we think, is Socrates' reference to justice, temperance, moderation, and piety as "parts of virtue," for Socrates could have made his point to Meno—that the acquisition of such things as gold and silver is virtuous only if it is morally acquired—without referring to the individual virtues as parts of a whole. That Socrates did choose to describe them in this way strongly suggests that he thinks they are indeed parts. **T5.6**, then, gives us some evidence external to the *Laches* for thinking either that Socrates rejects (7), not (1), or that he thinks that (1) and (7) rely on different senses of part and whole and so are not really contradictory after all. We shall return below to which of the two options Socrates, in our judgment, accepts.

So far, we have seen that **T5.4**, **T5.5**, and **T5.6** give us good reason to think that the individual virtues are, *in some sense,* distinguishable from the whole of virtue, though the specific sense in which they are distinguishable is, at this point, far from clear. And since it is not clear in just what sense Socrates thinks that the individual virtues are parts of the whole of virtue, we cannot immediately infer that Vlastos is also right about the equivalence thesis. In fact, we think there are good reasons for not accepting the equivalence thesis. To begin with, if the equivalence view were correct, why would Socrates think that wisdom is a necessary condition of the possession of any of the other individual virtues? After all, according to the equivalence thesis, each of the other individual virtues—piety, justice, courage, and self-control—is itself a distinct piece of moral knowledge. As we have seen, according to Vlastos, the necessity and sufficiency of wisdom for each of the other individual virtues explains the sense in which all of the individual virtues form a unity. But this should make us wonder why a special virtue—wisdom—is needed at all. Since each of the other individual virtues are themselves pieces of moral knowledge, each governing some aspect of morality, why must they be accompanied by an additional virtue, namely, wisdom? The other virtues seem sufficient unto themselves for their "parts" of the moral world.

There is a second problem with the equivalence thesis. Before Socrates completes questioning Protagoras, he asks the Sophist to clarify once again where he stands on the question of how the virtues are related to each other. Socrates once again poses the parts of gold–parts of the face analogy.

T5.7 *Protagoras* 349a-d:

(Socrates speaking): So right now I want you to remind me of some of the questions I first asked, starting from the beginning . . . I believe the first question was this: Wisdom, temperance, justice, courage, and piety—are these five names for the same thing, or is there underlying each of the names a unique thing, a thing with its own power or function, each one unlike any of the others? You said that they are not names for the same thing, that each of these names refers to a unique thing, and that all these are parts of virtue, not like the parts of gold, which are similar to each other and to the whole of which they are parts, but like the parts of the face, dissimilar to the whole of which they are parts and to each other, and each one having its own unique power or function. If this is still your view, say so; if it's changed in any way, make your new position clear, for I am certainly not going to hold you accountable for what you said before if you want to say something at all different now.

The equivalence thesis, recall, maintains that Socrates is only committed to the denial of Protagoras's claim that it is possible to have one of the individual virtues without the others. Socrates is not denying that the individual virtues are essentially different powers. But **T5.7** is clearly a warning to Protagoras that he is on the wrong path and that if he continues down it he will be shown to be wrong. In **T5.7**, then, Socrates is warning Protagoras away not only from the claim that one can have one individual virtue without the others but *also* from the claim that the individual virtues are different powers—the very position that, according to the equivalence thesis, Socrates himself supposedly shares with Protagoras! Since Socrates, obviously, is not arguing against a view he thinks is true, we must infer that he thinks the individual virtues are, in some sense, the same power.

5.2.3 The Identity Thesis

There can be little doubt that in **T5.7** Socrates is committed to some version of the identity thesis. But Socrates also seems to be committed to the "parts of gold" analogy and is not just trying to find out what Protagoras's view amounts to. To see why Socrates accepts the "parts of gold" analogy we need only consider the fact that Socrates' subsequent arguments are developed against the "parts of the face" analogy—Protagoras's conception of what it means to say that virtue has parts, according to which one could possess one virtue and not the others. Because the disjunction presented to Protagoras is either the "parts of gold" analogy or the "parts of the face" analogy and Socrates argues against the latter, Socrates must think that what the various arguments in the dialogue demonstrate is that the "parts of gold" analogy is the appropriate way to think about the various virtues. The various individual virtues, according to this analogy, are distinguishable and yet are also parts of *the same thing*, moral knowledge. Were this not the case, Socrates' subsequent arguments would show only that Protagoras had the wrong idea of how the parts of virtue are related to each other, but Socrates would have done nothing to show that the identity thesis is correct.

How, then, are we to square Socrates' apparent endorsement of the "parts of gold" analogy in the *Protagoras* with **T5.4, T5.5,** and **T5.6,** the three passages taken from other early dialogues? One way of attempting such a reconciliation would be to argue that when Socrates refers to the "parts" of virtue in **T5.4, T5.5,** and **T5.6,** he is referring to the fact that each of the individual virtue terms—"piety," "justice," "courage," and so forth—have different *meanings* or different *definitions*, though the terms always *refer to* or *pick out* the same things. Only the latter, that the individual virtue terms always *refer* to the same things, is essential to the identity thesis, for that thesis claims only that for Socrates, all of the individual virtues are really constituted by one and the same thing, moral knowledge. Thus, the proponent of the identity thesis might argue, when Socrates suggests in **T5.4,** for example, that "the pious is a part of the just," that he is asserting that the *meaning* of "piety" includes the meaning of "justice" but the *meaning* of "justice" does not include the meaning of "piety" and thus that when it is true to describe someone as a "just person," we are not thereby describing that individual *as* a "pious person," though, as a matter of fact, the just person will always turn out to be a pious person and vice versa, because what makes someone a just person and what makes someone a pious person, according to the identity thesis, is in fact the same thing, namely, moral knowledge.

But there is good reason to think that when Socrates refers to the "parts of virtue" he does not simply mean that the individual virtue terms have different definitions. In the *Euthyphro*, Socrates tried to bring Euthyphro to an understanding of the notion of what it is to be "a part of" with the following examples.

T5.8 *Euthyphro* 12c (immediately precedes T5.4):

> SOCRATES: It is not right, then, to say that "where there is fear there is also shame," but that where there is shame there is also fear, for fear covers a larger area than shame. Shame is a part of fear, just as odd is a part of number, with the result that it is not true that where there is number there is also oddness, but that where there is oddness there is also number.

Socrates' point is that we are to understand the relationship between piety and justice in the way that we understand the relationship between the pair, shame and fear, and the pair, odd numbers and numbers. The examples he chooses to illustrate the relationship between piety and justice would be quite misleading if Socrates means only that "piety" and "justice" have different definitions, since "numbers" refers to a more extensive set of entities than does "odd numbers." Some numbers, obviously, are not odd numbers. Thus, presumably, some just acts are not pious acts (though of course they are not impious acts, either). Unless Socrates has been inept in his choice of examples, we must conclude that justice "covers a larger area" than piety. If Socrates means that the knowledge that is piety is somehow distinguishable from and less extensive than the knowledge that is justice, then the identity thesis is simply incompatible with T5.8.

5.2.4 Is There a Single Account of the Virtues in the Early Dialogues?

We have seen that the *Protagoras* appears to provide very strong support for the identity thesis. However, Socrates' references to the "parts of virtue" appear to tell against the identity thesis. At this point, then, it is tempting to think either that Plato, in trying to develop a coherent, Socratic

view, simply had not thought through how the individual virtues are related to each other and to the whole of virtue or that he had some reason to
represent the views of the character "Socrates" in one way in the *Protagoras*
and in a different way in other early dialogues in which "Socrates" endorses the notion that each of the individual virtues are "parts."[7] The former option is clearly the less attractive since it violates what in the introduction to this book we called the *Principle of Charity*, for it implies that
Plato simply missed an obvious and important inconsistency.

Concerning the second option, as we argued in Chapter 1, we believe
that compelling evidence can be drawn from the corpus for the hypothesis
that Plato's philosophical views did not simply change as he matured but
actually underwent a number of radical transformations. These changes in
Plato's philosophical outlook can be seen most clearly in the differences in
philosophical doctrine between the early- and middle-period dialogues.
But as we also pointed out in Chapter 1, the developmentalist reading of
the Platonic corpus rests on two important claims: First, there are a *number*
of apparent doctrinal developments between the early- and middle-period
works and, second, Aristotle, who was in an excellent position to know,
consistently refers to the doctrines we find in the middle and late periods as
Plato's. The problem with trying to solve apparent inconsistencies in doctrine *within* the early-period writings by trying to distinguish developments within the early period itself is the absence of supporting evidence.
At the very least, we would want some additional evidence—drawn from
passages other than those that bear on the unity of the virtues—that Plato
began actually to modify what he recognized as Socratic viewpoints in the
early dialogues. Without such additional evidence, we believe that we
should look further for a way to reconcile Socrates' apparent commitment
to the identity thesis in the *Protagoras* with those passages in which he
seems equally committed to the nonidentity of the individual virtues either
with each other or with the whole of virtue.

5.2.5 The Parts of Gold Analogy

At the end of the *Protagoras*, Socrates leaves no doubt that he believes that
virtue is not a mere collection of essentially different powers. Virtue is *one
thing:* it is moral knowledge. There, he imagines how the argument Protagoras and he have developed would make fun of both of them if it
could for having reached positions at the end of the discussion that contradict the positions each took at the beginning of the conversation.

T5.9 *Protagoras* 361a-c:

(Socrates speaking): It seems to me that our discussion has turned on us, and
if it had a voice of its own, it would say, mockingly, "Socrates and Protago-

ras, how ridiculous you are, both of you. Socrates, you said earlier that virtue cannot be taught, but now you are arguing the very opposite and have attempted to show that everything is knowledge—justice, temperance, courage—in which case, virtue would appear to be eminently teachable. On the other hand, if virtue is anything other than knowledge, as Protagoras has been trying to say, then it would clearly be unteachable. But, if it turns out to be wholly knowledge, as you now urge, Socrates, it would be very surprising indeed if virtue could not be taught."

Even though it is clear that Socrates has been "attempting to show that everything is knowledge," his position still leaves room for the individual virtues to be distinguished from each other and from the whole of virtue. To see why, let us return for a minute to the two analogies—the parts of the face analogy and the pieces of gold analogy—which we see Socrates presenting to Protagoras as different ways of understanding the relationship between the individual virtues and the whole of virtue. It is significant that Socrates presents the two analogies as if he thinks they are the only reasonable candidates. Although Socrates does not actually say that he believes that the parts of gold analogy is apt, it is reasonable to infer that is precisely what he does believe. Otherwise, Socrates would be open to the charge that he was being disingenuous—by offering Protagoras a false alternative, which actually hides some *other* option that Socrates himself finds more apt. Thus, it is reasonable to conclude that at the end of the dialogue, after it has been shown that Protagoras made a mistake in defending the parts of the face analogy, Socrates believes that the parts of gold analogy is instructive.

It is also significant that the parts of gold to which Socrates refers can be distinguished from each other in terms of their "greatness and smallness" (*Protagoras* 329d). Socrates does not say, "Isn't it true that what people call the individual virtues are really just one thing—like a single lump of gold?" Our point here is that the analogy Socrates' himself apparently endorses leaves some room for distinguishing individual virtues. How, then, might they be distinguished?

5.2.6 Disciplines and Subdisciplines

As we saw in Chapter 2, Socrates believes that moral knowledge is very much like the knowledge that a craftsman has. It is what the Greeks called a *technē*. Because a *technē*, or craft, involves possessing a body of knowledge, it is not unlike what we would call a discipline today. It is tempting to think that the relationship between the knowledge that is the whole of virtue and the knowledge that constitutes each of the individual virtues can be understood in terms of the relationship between a discipline and subdiscipline. We might think, in other words, that for Socrates, an individual virtue, such as justice, stands to the whole of virtue in the way that microeconomics stands to economics.[8] We believe that this way of understanding the relationship, however, is a mistake. As we have argued previously,[9] we believe that this analogy fails to fit the parts of gold analogy. Our concern is that there is no guarantee that mastery of one subdiscipline, such as microeconomics, ensures mastery of any of the other subdisciplines, such as welfare economics, managerial economics, or macroeconomics. Although there is no doubt considerable overlap among the various subdisciplines of economics, we believe that expert practitioners in one subdiscipline frequently (and accurately) claim to have little or no expertise in any of the other subdisciplines, much less about every one of the other subdisciplines. But expertise in each of the different moral areas with which the individual virtues are concerned is precisely what is required by Socrates' commitment to the parts of gold analogy.

5.2.7 Can the Same Knowledge Yield Different Results?

When Socrates says that virtue is like a *technē*, he commits himself to the idea not only that virtue is a form of knowledge but also that there is something that knowledge enables its possessor to do or accomplish. What is accomplished by the *technē* is what the Greeks called the *ergon* of the *technē*. We might think of the *ergon* of a craft as what the craft produces or accomplishes. One way of thinking about what constitutes a particular craft is to think about what the characteristic *ergon* of that craft is. Moreover, Socrates thinks that a satisfactory account of a *technē* must state what *ergon* results from its use or application. This is why Socrates is so disappointed when Euthyphro is unable to tell him what the *ergon* is of the *technē* that, as Euthyphro claims and to which Socrates agrees, constitutes piety.

T5.10 *Euthyphro* 14b-c (immediately precedes **T2.39**):

> You could tell me in far fewer words, if you were willing, the sum of what I asked, Euthyphro, but you are not keen to teach me, that's clear. You were on the point of doing so, but you turned away. If you had given that answer, I should now have acquired from you sufficient knowledge of the nature of piety.

Finally, Socrates thinks that the *ergon* of a craft allows us to distinguish it from every other craft. (In the following translation, *ergon* is translated as "function.")

T5.11 *Republic* 1.345e–346a:

(Socrates speaking first, and Thrasymachus responding) Tell me, doesn't every craft differ from every other in having a different function? Please don't answer contrary to what you believe, so that we can come to a definite conclusion.

Yes, that's what differentiates them.

And each craft benefits us in its own peculiar way, different from the others. For example, medicine gives us health, navigation gives us safety while sailing, and so on with the others.

Certainly.

And wage-earning gives us wages, for this is its function? Or would you call medicine the same as navigation? Indeed, if you want to define matters precisely, as you proposed, even if someone who is a ship's captain becomes healthy because sailing is advantageous to his health, you wouldn't for that reason call his craft medicine?

Certainly not.

Here we see that different products imply different crafts. But might not the same knowledge have different applications and so result in different products?[10] If so, what it is to be a craft, for Socrates, is not simply to be a certain sort of knowledge but to be a certain sort of knowledge of the production of some specific result, which is consistent with the same body of knowledge being constitutive of two or more different crafts. To use an example that we have used before,[11] consider the way coastal navigation and surveying stand to each other and to that body of knowledge called triangulation.[12] Notice first that coastal navigation and surveying are not subdisciplines of triangulation. Yet each differs from triangulation and from each other. The difference, however, is only in the different problems they are employed to solve: Coastal navigation locates a point at sea relative to a point on land and surveying takes the measurements of plots of land. But notice also that although the problems the two are designed to solve are sufficiently different to warrant our calling them by different names, they are *essentially the same problems*, which is why we say of both that they are really just examples of triangulation at work. In order to do coastal navigation, one does not need any additional and special expertise over and above what is required for surveying, and vice versa.

It should be clear at this point why we think Socrates can claim, on the one hand, that all of the virtues are really the same thing and that the individual virtues are distinct parts of virtue as a whole, on the other. In saying that all of the virtues are the same thing, Socrates does not mean that they cannot be distinguished in any sense from each other. Like coastal navigation and surveying, which are distinguished only by the different work they do, so piety, justice, courage, and temperance are each moral wisdom, distinguished by the different work they do. We can now also see how one individual virtue, piety, might be counted by Socrates as a *part* of another individual virtue, justice (see **T5.4** and **T5.8**). Just as coastal navigation and surveying are both (individual) examples of triangulation, we might distinguish different sorts of coastal navigation (harbor navigation from seacoast or river navigation, for example) or different sorts of surveying (border identification as opposed to the measurement of plots of land), such that one sort would turn out to be a "part" of the more generic discipline. Just as we would not say that a surveyor (one who always worked only on surveying problems) is a coastal navigator, we would also not say that one who only navigated rivers was a seacoast navigator—even though in each of the above cases, the discipline employed would only be triangulation. And so, too, might "justice" be the name of a more generic virtue of acting in appropriate ways toward others, whereas "piety" would be the name of the specific version of this generic virtue that identified acting in appropriate ways toward the gods. But Socrates could also insist, if we are right, that the same knowledge was at work in each of the two virtues—indeed, the same knowledge was at work in all of the virtues—even though we are able to distinguish each one from all of the others.

Toward the end of the *Gorgias*, Socrates tells us, roughly, how the different work of the individual virtues is to be marked off. In the first passage, Socrates is explaining to Callicles that the result of the argument shows that one of the virtues, temperance, is what makes the soul good and that it does so by creating order within the soul.

T5.12 *Gorgias* 506e–507a (immediately precedes **T5.13**):

(Socrates speaking first, with Callicles replying) So, it's when a certain order, the proper one for each thing, comes to be present in it that it makes each of the things that are, good?

Yes, I think so.

So, also a soul which has its own order is better than a disordered one?

Necessarily so.

But surely one that has order is an orderly one.

Of course it is.

And an orderly soul is a self-controlled one.

Absolutely.

So a self-controlled soul is a good one. I for one can't say anything beyond that, Callicles, my friend.

Temperance, or what is here translated as self-control, is concerned with establishing an orderly soul. But notice that Socrates goes on to distinguish the work temperance does from that of the other virtues.

T5.13 *Gorgias* 507a-c (= T4.12, immediately follows T5.12):

> (Socrates speaking first, with Callicles responding) And surely a self-controlled person would do what's appropriate with respect to both gods and human beings. For if he does what's inappropriate, he wouldn't be self-controlled.
>
> That's necessarily how it is.
>
> And of course if he did what's appropriate with respect to human beings, he would be doing what's just, and with respect to gods he would be doing what's pious, and one who does what's just and pious must necessarily be just and pious.
>
> That's so.
>
> Yes, and he would also necessarily be brave, for it's not like a self-controlled man to either pursue or avoid what isn't appropriate, but to avoid and pursue what he should, whether these are things to do, or people, or pleasures and pains, and to stand fast and endure them where he should. So, it's necessarily very much the case, Callicles, that the self-controlled man, because he's just and brave and pious, as we've recounted, is a completely good man, that the good man does well and admirably whatever he does, and that the man who does well is blessed and happy, while the corrupt man, the one who does badly, is miserable.

We are not suggesting that Socrates thinks he is offering definitions of the individual virtues here. What he is suggesting is that each of the moral virtues has different domains: Each does different moral work. The point Socrates wishes to make with Callicles is that one is always better off leading the moral life rather than pursuing the sort of excessive pleasures Callicles had been recommending. Although Socrates stops short of explaining just how it is that one who has self-control will have the other virtues as well, there is nothing about what he says that indicates that he does not continue to believe what he implies is his position with respect to the unity of the virtues in T5.9: They are all really just moral knowledge.

We are now, at last, in a position to see what goes wrong in the final argument in the *Laches*, discussed in section 5.2.2, above. If we are right, Socrates thinks that—in different ways—both (1), courage is a distinct part of virtue, *and* (7), courage is the whole of virtue, are true. They are not contradictory because (1) makes a claim about the criterion of courage: Courage is wisdom when it is applied to a specific range of moral problems, namely, what is to be hoped for and to be feared. And (7) tells us that what constitutes courage is the same thing that constitutes all of the virtues, the knowledge of good and evil.

If what we have said here is correct, Socrates' view of how the virtues are related to each other and to the whole of virtue will continue to strike many as paradoxical. Our goal has not been to remove the air of paradox from what he says. Instead, we have tried to show that what is attributed to Socrates throughout the early dialogues forms a consistent account. His view preserves what common sense demands, namely, that the individual virtues be seen as distinct from each other, and what he thinks philosophical reflection also demands, namely, that each of the virtues is really constituted by the same thing, moral wisdom. That he chooses to express what he thinks in such a paradoxical way is exactly what we would expect. Socrates was never one to make matters easy. On the contrary, what Socrates says about the unity of the virtues is an excellent example of how he intentionally brings out the confusions he finds in the minds of those who converse with him in order to draw them into serious reflection about what he sees as the most important of all matters, virtue.

5.3 Socrates' Denial of *Akrasia*

5.3.1 Doing What We Think Is Best for Us

Let us turn now to the second paradoxical doctrine we find Socrates promoting in the early dialogues: his denial that people ever act contrary to their belief or knowledge of what is best for them. Just what Socrates is denying is perhaps most clearly expressed in a famous passage in the *Protagoras*. Socrates asks the famous Sophist where he stands on the power of knowledge to guide us.

T5.14 *Protagoras* 352a-c:

Come now, Protagoras, and reveal this about your mind: What do you think about knowledge? Do you go along with the majority or not? Most people think this way about it, that it is not a powerful thing, neither a leader or a ruler. They do not think of it in that way at all; but rather in this way: while knowledge is often present in a man, what rules him is not knowledge but rather something else—sometimes desire, sometimes pleasure, sometimes pain, at other times love, often fear; they think of his knowledge as being utterly dragged around by all these other things as if it were a slave. Now, does the matter seem like that to you, or does it seem to you that knowledge is a fine thing capable of ruling a person, and if someone were to know what is good and bad, then he would not be forced by anything to act otherwise than as knowledge dictates, and intelligence would be sufficient to save a person? [. . .] You realize that most people aren't going to be convinced by us. They maintain that most people are unwilling to do what is best, even though they know what it is and are able to do it. And when I have asked them the reason for this, they say that those who act that way do so because they are overcome by pleasure or pain or are being ruled by one of the things I referred to just now.

Let us imagine some college roommates who know they have a philosophy quiz the next day and who say that they *know* that studying tonight would be the best thing for them to do and that even if they heard that there was to be a party tonight they would not go. But later, when they actually hear that there is a party, they put down their books and attend it, saying that their desire to go to the party just "got the better of them." Their knowledge of what they should have done, most people will say, is just no match for the strength of their desire for the enjoyment they think the party will provide. Their knowledge, most people will say, is being "dragged about as if it were a slave."

Socrates thinks that most people are misdescribing what takes place when they fail to do what they have said they recognize to be best for them, for he thinks that knowledge is a "lordly thing" that can never be overcome by a stronger passion or desire. As we consider why Socrates would think this, it is important to keep in mind that in denying that people ever act contrary to their knowledge of what is best, Socrates is denying that they ever act contrary to their knowledge of what is best *for themselves*. This is called Socrates' "prudential paradox." It follows from the prudential paradox that those who know what is good for themselves will do it, assuming that they have the requisite opportunity to act. This doctrine is sometimes stated as the aphorism often attributed to Socrates: "To know the good is to do the good." But Socrates also believes that those who know what is just, that is, what is morally right, and who know that doing what is morally right is always better for the one doing it, will always do what is morally right. This is called Socrates' "moral paradox." Like the prudential paradox, many people would initially be inclined to dismiss what Socrates says on the ground that it is perfectly obvious that people frequently know what morality requires of them and that they would be better off doing what morality requires, but they fail to do it even though they had ample opportunity to do so because some competing desire not to do it was just too strong.

5.3.2 The Prudential Paradox

Let us begin by examining an often discussed passage that appears at *Protagoras* 351b–358e. Socrates is imagining a conversation with "most people." According to Socrates, most people not only think that desire can overcome knowledge but also think that pleasure is the good and pain is the evil, a view usually referred to as hedonism. Being overcome by a stronger desire for pleasure, Socrates thinks, is what most people would say is the most common cause of *akrasia*.

T5.15 *Protagoras* 355b–d:

(Socrates speaking) Just how absurd this is [knowledge of what is better being overcome by a desire for pleasure] will become very clear, if we do not use so many names at the same time, "pleasant" and "painful," "good" and "bad"; but since these turned out to be only two things, let us call them by two names, first "good" and "bad," then later, "pleasant" and "painful." On that basis, then, let us say that a man knowing bad things to be bad, does them all the same. If then someone asks us: "Why?" "Having been overcome," we shall reply. "By what? By what?" he will ask us. We are no longer able to say "by pleasure," for that has taken on its other name, "the good" instead of "pleasure"—so we will say and reply that "he is overcome . . . ." "By what," he will ask. "By the good," we will say, "for heaven's sake!" If by chance the questioner is rude he might burst out laughing and say: "What you are saying is ridiculous—someone does what is bad, knowing that it is bad, when it is not necessary to do it, having been overcome by the good. "So" he will say, "within yourself, does not the good outweigh the bad or not?" We will clearly say in reply that it does not; for if it did, the person whom we say is overcome by pleasure would not have made any mistake. "In virtue of what," he might say, "does the good *outweigh* the bad or the bad the good? Only in that one is greater and one is smaller, or more and less." We could not help but agree. "So clearly then," he will say, "by 'being overcome' you mean getting more bad things for the sake of fewer good things." That settles that, then.

Most people, then, think that in doing what they know is contrary to their interest, people *want* to do what is evil. But when one examines the explanation of weakness that most people give—that those who are weak-willed are "overcome by pleasure"—the substitution of "good" for "pleasure," which follows from most people's acceptance of hedonism, allows us to say that "people sometimes do what they know to be evil and so act from a desire for evil because they are acting from a desire for what is good." But as Socrates points out, this is sheer nonsense. One cannot be motivated to do something by a desire to do what one takes to be evil and *also* be motivated to do that same thing by a desire for what one takes to be good. Since most people, in Socrates' view, are not likely to give up their commitment to hedonism, he concludes that it is their belief in the possibility of *akrasia* that they must give up.

The *Protagoras*'s discussion of moral weakness, summarized in **T5.15**, has an important limitation. Socrates has not shown that moral weakness can never occur. He has only shown that the explanation most people are prepared to give of its occurrence does not make sense.[13] Socrates has not shown why someone who rejected hedonism might not be right in thinking that sometimes people do what they know not to be good because their knowledge is overcome by the strength of their desire for pleasure. If this is right, though the *Protagoras* provides us with an admirably clear statement of what most people believe occurs, we must look elsewhere for Socrates' account of why most people are simply mistaken in that belief.

Recall that in Chapter 4, we argued that Socrates is a eudaimonist. He thinks that whenever we act, we act for the sake of what we at least take to be good.

T5.16 *Gorgias* 468b (part of a longer quote given as **T4.4**):

(Socrates speaking and Polus responding) And don't we also put a person to death, if we do, or banish him and confiscate his property because we suppose that doing these things is better for us than not doing them?

That's right.

Hence, it is for the sake of what's good that those who do all these things do them?

I agree.

Because he is so sure that we always act for the sake of what we take to be good for us, Socrates is confident that Meno is mistaken when Meno says, in a passage we looked at in Chapter 4, that there are people who do what they recognize to be bad for them.

T5.17 *Meno* 77e–78b (= **T4.5**):

(Socrates speaking first, with Meno responding) Well then, those who you say desire bad things, believing that bad things harm their possessor, know that they'll be harmed by them?

Necessarily.

And do they not think that those who are harmed are miserable to the extent that they are harmed?

That too is inevitable.

And that those who are miserable are unhappy?

I think so.

Does anyone wish to be miserable and unhappy?

I don't think so, Socrates.

No one then wants what is bad, Meno, unless he wants to be such. For what else is being miserable but to desire bad things and secure them?

You are probably right, Socrates, and no one wants what is bad.

If no one wants to be miserable, then no one will pursue what will make a person miserable. If a person does pursue what is in fact an evil, the explanation can only be that at the time the action is taken, the person takes what is in fact an evil to be a good. As Socrates says, in the *Protagoras*, it is just not in human nature to do otherwise.

T5.18 *Protagoras* 358d:

> Now, no one goes willingly toward the bad or what he believes to be bad; neither is it in human nature, so it seems, to want to go toward what one believes to be bad instead of to the good. And when he is forced to choose between one of two bad things, no one will choose the greater if he is able to choose the lesser.

5.3.3 The Moral Paradox

We are now in a position to see why Socrates thinks that people act immorally. They believe, mistakenly, that what they are doing is actually good for them. Evil, in other words, is the result of ignorance—ignorance of the harm moral evil does to the agent. In his discussion with Polus in the *Gorgias* about the value of justice and injustice, Socrates makes it clear that although he would never want to be treated unjustly, if he had to choose, he would always want to suffer injustice rather than do what is unjust.

T5.19 *Gorgias* 469b-c:

> POLUS: Surely the one who's put to death unjustly is the one who's both to be pitied and miserable.
>
> SOCRATES: Less so than the one putting him to death, Polus, and less than the one who's justly put to death.
>
> POLUS: How can that be, Socrates?
>
> SOCRATES: It's because doing what's unjust is actually the worst thing there is.
>
> POLUS: Really? Is *that* the worst? Isn't suffering what's unjust still worse?
>
> SOCRATES: No, not in the least.
>
> POLUS: So you'd rather want to suffer what's unjust than do it?
>
> SOCRATES: For my part, I wouldn't want either, but if it had to be one or the other, I would choose suffering over doing what's unjust.

Because the prudential paradox guarantees that anyone who does what is bad for him fails to recognize that it is bad for him and because, as we see in **T5.19**, Socrates thinks that doing injustice is the worst of all evils, Socrates must think that those who do what is unjust do not understand that what they are doing is really harming themselves. If they did, they would not have done it. As we learned in **T5.17**, no one wants to be miserable.

5.3.4 But Are Most People Really Wrong?

T5.17 and **T5.18** tell us only that people never act contrary to what they think is best. But this does not show that most people are wrong about the power of strong desire to overcome knowledge. Most people would surely say that even if Socrates is right that our party-going students *believe at the time* they put their books away and go to the party that going to the party instead of studying for the philosophy quiz is really the better thing for them, it is none the less true that they really did *know* that they should stay in and study. The problem with the students, they would say, is that their knowledge was nullified, overcome, "dragged about as if it were a slave." Their knowledge that they should study, most people will say, is not really a "lordly thing" after all. In fact, it was simply too weak to stand up to their desire to attend the party and got replaced by a belief that going to the party would be better than staying in to study.

Socrates' response would be that even prior to their having heard that there was going to be a party, our students did not really *know* that going to a party instead of studying would be bad for them. They might *claim*, prior to hearing that there was going to be a party, that they know that studying is the better thing to do. But their claim to *know* this is simply false. What in fact happened to them, according to Socrates, is that before they heard that there was to be party, our students *believed* that not studying would be bad for them. When they heard that there was a party, they changed their assessment of the relative value of the party and studying, now deciding that going to be party is the better course. Had they really known prior to hearing that there would be a party, they would not have changed their minds.

In the *Meno*, Socrates distinguishes knowledge from true belief, or true opinion, on the ground that the former is stable and the latter is alterable. In the text below, Meno has just asked Socrates why anyone should prize knowledge over true opinion, since the latter will guide an agent just as well as the former.

T5.20 *Meno* 97d–98a:

(Socrates speaking and Meno responding) Do you know why you wonder, or shall I tell you?

By all means tell me.

It is because you have paid no attention to the statues of Daedalus, but perhaps there are none in Thessaly.

What do you have in mind when you say this?

That they too run away and escape if one does not tie them down, but remain in place if tied down.

So what?

To acquire an untied work of Daedalus is not worth much, like acquiring a runaway slave, for it does not remain, but is worth much if tied down, for his works are very beautiful. What am I thinking of when I say this? True opinions. For true opinions, as long as they remain, are a fine thing and all they do is good, but they are not willing to remain long, and they escape from a man's mind, so that they are not worth much until one ties them down by (giving) an account of the reason why .... After they are tied down, in the first place they become knowledge and then they remain in place. That is why knowledge is prized higher than correct opinion, and knowledge differs from correct opinion in being tied down.

If one really knows something, Socrates thinks, nothing can persuade one to change one's mind so that one thinks that one had previously been mistaken and did not know. This is why Socrates thinks that knowledge is a "lordly thing" and cannot be "dragged about as if it were a slave." Because our students changed their minds about whether going to the party would be a good thing, they did not—in spite of what they said—really *know* that they would be better off staying in to study. They merely believed that they should. They held what Socrates calls in **T5.20** a "true opinion." What they believed prior to hearing about the party, however, could not have been knowledge, for had it been, it would have guided their action accordingly.

5.3.5 Socrates on Reason and Desire

Socrates thinks that it is "not in human nature" to do what we think is bad for us. But we have also seen that mere belief, or opinion, is inherently unstable. Of course, sometimes perception causes one to change one's mind and reject a formerly held belief. This is what happens when we say, for example, "I thought Jane was in her room but now I see that she is in the library." Sometimes reason itself causes us to change our minds and reject a formerly held belief. For example, we might say, "I thought that the square root of thirty-six was greater than seven but now I see that I am mistaken." As we have seen (**T5.14**), Socrates thinks that everyone always *acts* on the basis of one sort of desire, what is usually called a rational desire, or a desire for what one takes to be one's own good. Indeed, many commentators have assumed that this is the only sort of desire that Socrates recognizes,[14] and the authors of this book also used to think this was so.[15] But we now think that Socrates is committed to the existence of a second sort of desire—a nonrational sort of desire—namely, the desire for pleasure and the aversion to pain. After all, something made our students change their minds about whether they should stay in or go to the party, and it was not something they reasoned about, nor was it merely finding out that there was a party. What makes someone who sincerely believes smoking is bad for health go ahead and light up a cigarette? That Socrates does think there are such desires is evident from the following passage in the *Laches*. Here, Socrates is requesting that Laches give him a definition of courage that will explain the various instances of courage.

T5.21 *Laches* 191d-e:

(Socrates speaking) And I wanted to include not only those who are courageous in warfare but also those who are brave in dangers at sea, and the ones who show courage in illness and poverty and affairs of state; and then again I wanted to include not only those who are brave in the face of pain and fear but also those who are clever at fighting desire and pleasure, whether by standing their ground or running away—because there are some men, aren't there, Laches, who are brave in matters like these?

It is clear that Socrates thinks that the desires to avoid pain and to pursue pleasure exert motivational influences on us that are independent of what we think is good; otherwise, he would not think that the courageous have been successful in their "fight" to act courageously. Socrates' language here suggests that he thinks that a nonrational desire has the power to overcome us. But since we always act for the sake of what we take to be good, nonrational desire must be a causal power to make us believe that the pleasurable object to which we are attracted (or the painful object from which we are repelled) is good. Like perception and reason, appetite itself can make our beliefs "move around like the statues of Daedalus."

In Chapter 2, we explained why Socrates thinks the elenchos will not generate moral knowledge, for it cannot completely certify the correctness of any of the practitioner's beliefs. But now we see that Socrates has an additional reason for exhorting the pursuit of virtue. Belief, as we see in **T5.20**, is not "tied down" and so is always apt to "move around." Virtue, by contrast, is stable. Its possessor can be confident that what is known will not appear to be true at some times and false at others. Virtue allows its possessor to see pleasure and pain for what they are. When a particular pleasurable object is good, the virtuous person recognizes it as such and pursues it. But when a particular pleasurable object is *merely* pleasurable, the virtuous person recognizes it as such, too, and does not pursue it. Given the causal power of pleasure and pain to alter beliefs about the good, we can see why Socrates would think that there is nothing more valuable to us than virtue, the power always to recognize what is *really* good and really evil. In the following passage taken from the *Protagoras*, Socrates has just pointed out how often perception can lead to mistaken beliefs about what is large and small.

T5.22 *Protagoras* 356d-e (immediately precedes T4.8):

(Socrates speaking) If then our well-being depended upon this, doing and choosing large things, avoiding and not doing the small ones, what would we see as our salvation in life? Would it be the art of measurement or the power of appearance? While the power of appearance often makes us wander all over the place in confusion, often changing our minds about the same things and regretting our actions and choices with respect to things large and small, the art of measurement in contrast, would make the appearances lose their power by showing us the truth, would give us peace of mind firmly rooted in the truth and would save our life.

Those who lack the "art of measurement" are vulnerable to the power of appearance, for (in Socrates' analogy) they sometimes take what *appears* to be large to *be* large when it is not. Of course, Socrates thinks that our well-being depends upon choosing not the large instead of the small but the good instead of the bad. Thus, he thinks that those who lack what is really our "salvation in life"—moral virtue—will sometimes mistake what *appears* to be good for what *is* good. If we are right, their mistake owes to the fact that what satisfies our appetite for pleasure and our aversion to pain appears good to us unless that appearance is corrected by knowledge. Thus it is that Socrates can say that those who lack our "salvation in life" "wander around," "change their minds," and "regret" what they do. Lacking knowledge of what is best, they succumb to the power of what appears good. After their appetite has been satisfied and they no longer see what they have pursued as pleasurable, they "change their minds" about whether it was really good after all and regret what they have done. Those who possess the knowledge of good and evil—"our salvation in life"—are never fooled by what merely appears good, for it "makes the appearances lose their power by showing us the truth." Consequently, virtuous people pursue in their actions and choices what is really good and find that they do not subsequently change their minds. They have nothing to regret.

Notes

1. Vlastos (1981), 221–269, 418–423. Others who have defended versions of the equivalence thesis include O'Brien (1967), 129, n. 16; Kraut (1984), 258–262; and Santas (1964). The most influential version of the identity thesis is advanced by Penner (1973), 35–68. Others include Irwin (1977), 86–90, and Woodruff (1976), 101–116, whose versions of this general view feature some differences from Penner's. This is plainly not the place for us to attempt a very specific review of the subtleties of each of the many scholarly arguments on this issue.

2. Vlastos (1981), 226–227.

3. Ibid., 227–228.

4. Ibid., 266–269.

5. The argument outlined here follows roughly Vlastos's way of construing the argument. See ibid., 266.

6. Vlastos (1981), 267. Vlastos goes on to give other reasons for thinking that Socrates actually rejects (7); see 267–268.

7. This suggestion has been made by Devereux (1992), 788–789.

8. This is the example used by Richard Kraut to illustrate the relationship between the whole and the parts of virtue. See Kraut (1984), 261–262.

9. Brickhouse and Smith (1994), 70, and Brickhouse and Smith (1997a), 320.

10. A very similar strategy was adopted by Ferejohn (1982), 1–21, who points out that "the powers to perform different actions can be grounded in a single property"(18). We wish to acknowledge that Ferejohn reached what we think is the right view well before we did and we regret that we did not recognize that fact until it was recently pointed out to us, after we had published essentially the same view much later, in Brickhouse and Smith (1997). See also Ferejohn (1983–1984), 377–388.

11. See Brickhouse and Smith (1994), 70–71, and (1997a), 321–323.

12. As we have noted in our earlier works, the example was suggested to us by H. B. Miller, who may not agree that we are correctly applying the example to the whole of virtue–parts of virtue relationship. Ferejohn uses the example of "the power to ride motorcycles" and the "power to ride snowmobiles" to show how two things can be "contingently identical."

13. On this point, we are in agreement with Santas (1971), 269.

14. For example, Irwin (1977), 78, and (1995), 52–53, 116; Vlastos (1991), 148–154.

15. See Brickhouse and Smith (1994), chap. 3, and (1997b). Our views about Socrates' theory of motivation and, especially, Socrates' recognition that there are both rational and nonrational desires have changed, largely because of an important recent argument by Daniel Devereux (1995).

Suggested Readings

Socrates on the Unity of the Virtues

Of those who argue that Socrates held the equivalence thesis, the most influential position is that of Vlastos (1981). The most influential version of the identity thesis is Penner (1973). An excellent account of the reasoning behind both positions can be found in Devereux (1992), which also provides an interesting argument that the view of the unity of the virtues in the *Protagoras* and in the *Laches* cannot be reconciled and that the former may express what was essentially Socrates' position and the latter Plato's own view of the unity of the virtues. Ferejohn (1982) defends a way of reconciling the strong support for the identity thesis provided by the *Protagoras* with the strong support for the equivalence view found in other early dialogues. A similar account can be found in Brickhouse and Smith (1994) and (1997a).

Socrates' Denial of Akrasia

An excellent discussion of the argument in the *Protagoras* against the possibility of *akrasia* and of the limitations of that argument can be found in Santas (1971). Further discussion can be found in Taylor (1992) and Vlastos (1994a). An excellent, novel account can be found in Devereux (1995).

Socrates on Motivation

The standard view, that Socrates believes that adult human beings have only rational desires, is defended in Irwin (1977) and (1995). Brickhouse and Smith (1994) recognize the possibility of nonrational impulses in Socratic philosophy. The best challenge to the standard view is Devereux (1995), which provides an argument that has influenced our presentation in this chapter.

6

Socrates' Politics and Political Philosophy

6.1 Historical and Textual Problems

Socrates lived during a time of almost ceaseless turmoil in Athens. As we saw in Chapter 1, from the time Socrates was nearly forty years old until five years before his execution (431–404 B.C.), Athens was involved in the ruinous Peloponnesian War, which ended in its surrender to its enemies, Sparta and its allies. Approximately seven years before the end of this war, Athens's democracy suffered a violent overthrow (in 411 B.C.) by factions wishing to install an oligarchy (the "Four Hundred"). About a year after the end of the war, the democracy was again overthrown by an even more violent oligarchic faction (called the "Thirty Tyrants"). Both times, the democracy was restored in less than a year, but only after violent civil conflict.

Many of those loyal to the democracy left Athens during the periods of oligarchic control, but Socrates did not. This fact, when put together with many texts in which Socrates seems quite critical of prominent democratic politicians and democratic political dogmas, has led some scholars to believe that Socrates was either in favor of, or perhaps even actively involved in, the oligarchic revolutions. Other scholars, however, have found what they regard as powerful evidence against such conceptions, and some have even suggested that Socrates' own politics favored democracy.

We begin this chapter with a discussion of the evidence concerning Socrates' political ideology and activity. As we said in Chapter 1, however, debates about the historical Socrates (as opposed to the Socrates portrayed in Plato's dialogues) face profound and probably insoluble difficulties in sorting through scant and significantly conflicting evidence, most or all of which is of at least dubitable, if not outright dubious, reliability. We do not propose to revisit this controversy in this chapter, however, and will continue to focus almost exclusively upon what we find in Plato's dialogues, leaving it to those who enjoy historical speculation to judge how accurate Plato's account is regarding the historical Socrates. Our argument will be that Plato's Socrates, at least, cannot be counted either as an oligarchic extremist or as a democrat but rather as one who maintained a certain critical distance from any of Athens's political factions.

We begin with a problem in the texts: In one text, Socrates describes himself in a way that strongly suggests that he was *apolitical*, but in another text, he appears to describe himself as *more* political than any other Athenian—a remarkable claim, given that the Athenians are known to be as political as any people in any culture have ever been. We believe that once we find our way out of this conflict, we will be in a better position to assess Socrates' position on the politics and the politicians of his day. We test the results of our solution to the first textual problem against several of the other texts, which are often cited as evidence of his allegiance to certain political factions. We conclude this chapter with a discussion of two more important issues in Socrates' political philosophy, one of which has received perhaps more attention from scholars than any other issue in Socratic scholarship and one of which has received almost no serious attention.

6.2 Socrates and Political Activity

6.2.1 What Did Socrates Do?
What Did Socrates Not Do?

In his defense before the jury, in Plato's *Apology*, after characterizing himself as a gift from the god, sent to sting the Athenians into a greater concern for virtue and a greater awareness of their ignorance, Socrates considers a doubt he imagines his jurors might have.

T6.1 *Apology* 31c–32a:

> It may seem strange that while I go around and give advice privately and interfere in private affairs, I do not venture to go to the assembly and there advise the city. You have heard me give the reason for this in many places. I have a divine or spiritual sign which Meletus has ridiculed in his deposition. This began when I was a child. It is a voice, and whenever it speaks it turns me away from something I am about to do, but it never encourages me to do anything. This is what has prevented me from taking part in public affairs, and I think it was quite right to prevent me. Be sure, gentlemen of the jury,

that if I had long ago attempted to take part in politics, I should have died long ago, and benefited neither you nor myself. Do not be angry with me for speaking the truth; no man will survive who genuinely opposes you or any other crowd and prevents the occurrence of many unjust and illegal happenings in the city. A man who really fights for justice must lead a private, not a public, life if he is to survive for even a short time.

These are not the words of a man dedicated to engaging in political "affairs." We will return to Socrates' strange reference to his "divine or spiritual sign" (his so-called *daimonion*) in the next chapter, but for now it is enough to see that he has two reasons not to engage in political "affairs": His *daimonion* opposes it, and such activity would actually be ill suited to his pursuing his moral mission in Athens.

Given such a ringing condemnation of the moral prospects of politics, it is astonishing to find Socrates, in another passage, apparently claiming to be *more* political than his fellow Athenians.

T6.2 *Gorgias* 521d:

I believe that I'm one of a few Athenians—so as not to say I'm the only one, but the only one among our contemporaries—to take up the true political craft and practice the true politics.

It does not take subtle analysis to see how and why **T6.1** and **T6.2** appear to conflict. But the appearance of conflict, in this case, is easily removed, once we look more closely at the context of Socrates' remarks in the two passages. There is genuine conflict here, notice, only if what Socrates takes to be "truly the political craft" and "the true politics," in the *Gorgias* passage, is the same as what he means by "public affairs," in the *Apology* passage, and what he takes as the practitioner of "the true political craft," in the *Gorgias*, to be the same as the one who leads a "public life," in the *Apology*. It is quite plain, however, that these identifications should *not* be made.

6.2.2 *"The Public Man" and the Political Craftsman*

When Socrates says, in the *Apology*, that he has not lived a "public life," it is clear that he is saying that he has not made it his business to pursue a career in Athens's established political arenas. When he says that he has not engaged in "public affairs," he means, as he said, that he did not dare "to go to the assembly and there advise the city." Plato's texts do tell us that Socrates actually did hold political office at least once during his lifetime, or perhaps twice: in the *Apology* (32b), he acknowledges that he served on the presiding committee of the Council (in 406 B.C.), and in the *Gorgias*, he mentions a time when he actually served as the Council president.[1] But these positions were part of an Athenian's actual responsibilities as a citizen, and Socrates would have been assigned to the Council itself by a random selection (many of Athens's most important political positions were assigned by lot, including this one), and he would have been put on the presiding committee and made president as a part of the normal rotation of duties, to which all Council members were subject.

When Socrates says that he has not pursued "public affairs," therefore, he is not claiming not to have taken on the ordinary allotment of civic duties, as was legally required of all Athenian citizens. He means, instead, that he has not stood for election (for example, as a general—oddly, one of the few elected positions in Athens's democracy), has not volunteered his opinions in formal addresses to the Athenian populace (for example, and mainly, in the Assembly, where most of Athens's "political affairs" were carried out and where all laws and official policies and other state decisions were enacted).

In the *Gorgias*, Socrates is attacking the claim made by his sophistical interlocutors that rhetoric, as practiced by politicians—that is, by those leading the very kind of life he proclaims himself *not* to have led, in the *Apology*—is a kind of craft knowledge (see Chapter 3, for discussion). At 464b–465e in that dialogue, Socrates distinguishes two branches of the political craft (the judicial and the legislative, which deal with correction and prevention of wrong, respectively) and contrasts these to what he regards as mere imitations of these: rhetoric and sophistry, respectively. Accordingly, rhetoric and sophistry are not craft knowledge, after all, but mere pretenders, impostors that mimic but have none of the actual merits of the crafts they ape.

This claim, however, is shocking to Socrates' interlocutors in the *Gorgias*, for these men, like most Athenians, simply identify the rhetorical life with the political life. Socrates makes this clear when he distinguishes this sort of life with one like his own, spent in the pursuit of philosophy.

T6.3 *Gorgias* 500c:

> (Socrates speaking) For you see don't you, that our discussion's about this (and what would even a man of little intelligence take more seriously than this?), about the way we're supposed to live. Is it the way you urge me toward, to engage in these manly activities, to make speeches among the people, to practice oratory, and to be active in the sort of politics you people engage in these days? Or is it a life spent in philosophy?

The political life, in the context of this contrast, is a life, Socrates says, that substitutes pleasure for any genuine good. Philosophy seeks to know—and to pursue—only what is a genuine good, and the Socratic elenchos (see Chapter 2, for discussion) is one philosophical way to avoid being seduced or duped by things that only pretend to be, or mimic, and that might therefore be confused for, the genuine good. In Chapter 5, we discussed Socrates' conception of human psychology—a subject to which we will soon return when we talk about his conception of punishment—but it should be clear from that discussion at least that pleasure, as a substitute for the genuine good, is particularly dangerous and disruptive to human happiness, actually damaging one's ability to reason adequately about one's own best interests, perhaps eventually resulting in the actual and incurable *ruin* of one's soul. As we discuss in the next chapter, moreover, this catastrophe is completed in the afterlife, for it is in the next life, Socrates believes, that the souls of those ruined in this way are punished for all eternity.

At any rate, Socrates makes clear, in his discussion with Callicles in the *Gorgias,* that he regards the political craft itself—as opposed to its flattering imitators—as always performing its function, whatever that function turns out to be, "with regard to what is best," seeking to make the citizens "as good as possible" (*Gorgias* 502e) rather than simply seeking popularity through flattery and by doling out pleasures as if they were goods. Socrates does not actually possess this craft—if he did, he would be wise in the way he always claims not to be (see Chapter 3, for discussion). But because he has been relentlessly and indefatigably living the philosophical life, Socrates can truthfully claim, as he does in **T6.2**, to have taken up "the true political craft and [to] practice the true politics." It is an ironic—a tragically ironic—consequence of his view that the one who is closest to "the political craft" and to engaging in what is "the true politics" must "lead a private, not a public, life," just as he claims always to have done, in the *Apology*.

6.3 Socrates' Political Affiliation?

6.3.1 Socrates the Antidemocrat?

Given his claim not to have led a public life, it would be strange to find out that Socrates had none the less engaged in political action of a particularly partisan sort, in Athens. But as we noted, this is exactly what some interpreters have supposed Socrates actually did do. In particular, they have linked Socrates' disdain for what he characterizes as "the sort of politics you people engage in these days" with a disdain for *democratic* politics of any kind, for the very institutions of the democracy in Athens, such as the Assembly he apparently did not bother to attend. Instead, it has often been argued, Socrates was sympathetic to (one or more of) the oligarchic factions² in time and in some way or ways was (rightly) perceived as supporting the violent overthrow of Athens's democracy.³

Four kinds of evidence are usually cited by those who see Socrates as an opponent of democracy: (1) Socrates openly criticizes several of the most basic tenets of Athens's democratic ideology; (2) Socrates is also openly scornful of prominent Athenian democratic leaders, past and present; (3) Socrates' own friends and associates, as we find them identified in Plato's dialogues, include several of the most notorious figures in Athens's troubled political landscape, and finally (4) there is ancient evidence for supposing that Socrates' trial was not, as the formal charges might suggest, about a religious issue but was actually politically motivated. In this section, we consider these four issues, in order.

6.3.2 Socrates Versus Democratic Ideology

It is plainly a feature of a direct democracy, such as Athens had (as opposed to a representative democracy, such as our own), that important political or moral decisions are made by many rather than just a few. Athens's democracy, thus, was the most inclusive of any ancient political system we know of.⁴ But we often find Socrates disparaging the views of "the many," and he always insists that we should attend, instead, only to the one or ones who are experts.

T6.4 *Apology* 24e–25c:

(Socrates speaking) Tell me, my good sir, who improves our young men?

(Meletus) The laws.

That is not what I am asking, but what person who has knowledge of the laws to begin with?

These jurymen, Socrates.

How do you mean, Meletus? Are these able to educate the young and improve them?

Certainly.

All of them, or some but not others?

All of them.

Very good, by Hera. You mention a great abundance of benefactors. But what about the audience? Do they improve the young or not?

They do, too.

What about the members of the Council?

The Council-members, too.

But Meletus, what about the assembly? Do members of the assembly corrupt the young, or do they all improve them?

They improve them.

All the Athenians, it seems, make the young into fine good men, except me, and I alone corrupt them. Is that what you mean?

That is most definitely what I mean.

You condemn me to a great misfortune. Tell me: does this also apply with horses do you think? That all men improve them and one individual corrupts them? Or is quite the contrary true, one individual is able to improve them, or very few, namely, the horse-trainers, whereas the majority, if they have horses and use them, corrupt them? Is that not the case, Meletus, both with horses and all other animals? Of course it is, whether you and Anytus say so or not. It would be a very happy state of affairs if only one person corrupted our youth, while the others improved them.

T6.5 *Laches* 184d-e:

SOCRATES: What's that, Lysimachus? Do you intend to cast your vote for whatever position is approved by the majority of us?

LYSIMACHUS: Why, what else could a person do, Socrates?

SOCRATES: And do you, Melesias, plan to act in the same way? Suppose there should be a council to decide whether your son ought to practice a particular kind of gymnastic exercise, would you be persuaded by the greater number or by whoever has been educated and exercised under a good trainer?

MELESIAS: Probably by the latter, Socrates.

SOCRATES: And would you be persuaded by him rather than by the four of us?

MELESIAS: Probably.

SOCRATES: So I think it is by knowledge that one ought to make decisions, if one is to make them well, and not by majority rule.

T6.6 *Crito* 48a (immediately follows **T4.18**):

SOCRATES: We should not then think so much of what the majority will say about us, but what he will say who understands justice and injustice, the one, that is and the truth itself. So that, in the first place, you were wrong to believe that we should care for the opinion of the many about what is just, beautiful, good, and their opposites.

In these passages, and others like them (see also *Protagoras* 319a–328d, *Meno* 92d–94e), Socrates shows that he finds no credibility in the idea that the majority can teach anything of value to the youth and no special value in majority rule or in the opinions of the many who would make the rules in a democracy. He often characterizes the majority of people as morally whimsical (see, for example, *Crito* 48c) and thoughtlessly ignorant on even the most basic moral issues (see, for example, *Crito* 49c), disparaging even the mode of discourse one would use to garner majority support for some opinion, which, Socrates says, is "worthless, as far as the truth is concerned" (*Gorgias* 471e, see **T6.7**, below).

Given Socrates' contrasts of the ignorant "many" with the expert "few," it is understandably tempting to see, in Socrates' words, the ideology of the oligarchic revolutionaries, who sought to overthrow Athens's democracy and replace it with a government by a "few" (our word, "oligarchy" comes from the Greek words *oligos*, "few," and *archē*, "rule"). It is a temptation, however, that we should resist. Notice how Socrates characterizes the "few" to whom we should defer on important issues: He contrasts the ignorance of the many with the knowledge of the few. To whom was Socrates referring, when he refers to these "few"—Athens's oligarchic revolutionaries? If so, then the oracle that proclaimed Socrates the wisest of men (see *Apology* 21a–23b) was lying—for now it seems there are at least some "few" who are wiser than Socrates! Either that, or Socrates regards himself as one of these "few" who have the knowledge the many lack, in which case *he* is lying when he explains the meaning of the oracle in this way: "This man among you, mortals, is wisest who, like Socrates, understands that his wisdom is worthless" (see **T2.19**).

In Chapter 2, we considered and rejected the claim that Socrates' own profession of ignorance was insincere, and in Chapter 3, we showed how Socrates might allow that people might have some kinds of knowledge without contradicting the oracle about Socrates, for the only kind of knowledge he recognizes in himself or anyone else falls far short of wisdom. This being so, however, it follows that there are, in fact, no specific living "few" to whom Socrates could advocate giving political power, in preference to the ignorant majority—for any few he might select would be no less ignorant than the majority. It is one thing to say that majority rule is no way to get at the truth of an issue and quite another to say that there is some minority in Athens who *can* give us such truth. It is one thing to say that the majority of people corrupt the youth and quite another to say that some specific minority in Athens do *not* corrupt them and instead have the expertise to improve them. It is one thing to say that the opinions of the majority of people are morally worthless and quite another to say that there is some minority in Athens whose opinions are morally wise. Socrates most certainly makes the first claims in each of these pairs; but he would have to make the second claims in each pair to count as being a supporter of the oligarchic faction in Athens. Instead, he denies the second claims in the pairs with no less vehemence than that with which he affirms the first claims. It is one thing to be a critic of democratic ideology and quite another to be an advocate for an oligarchic overthrow of Athens's democracy. Socrates' views about the majority and majority rule make him the former but not the latter.

We have also seen how Socrates does not count wealth as in any way making its possessor any better than those who lack it, unless, of course, its possessor also has virtue (see our discussion in Chapter 4, and *Apology* 30b—**T2.25**). His scorn for the very superiority claimed by the oligarchs, then, shows that Socrates would have no respect for the oligarchic ideology, which held that political power should be reserved for those who are "better" than others in virtue of their wealth and property. The entire basis of the oligarchic factions' claims to power, then, was for Socrates no basis at all.

6.3.3 Socrates and Prominent Democratic Leaders

Socrates often says very negative things about highly regarded democratic leaders, accusing them of several varieties of political and moral failure.

T6.7 *Gorgias* 471e–472b:

> (Socrates speaking) This "refutation" is worthless, as far as the truth is concerned, for it might happen sometimes that an individual is brought down by the false testimony of many reputable people. Now too, nearly every Athenian and alien will take your side on the things that you're saying, if it's witnesses you want to produce against me to show that what I say isn't true. Nicias, the son of Niceratus will testify for you, if you like, and his brothers along with him, the ones whose tripods are standing in a row in the precinct of Dionysus. [. . .] And so will the whole house of Pericles, if you like, or any other local family you care to choose.

Nicias was the famous Athenian general (generals, recall, were *elected* officials); Pericles was the quintessential democratic leader in Athens (also elected general many times) in the fifth century B.C. These men, and their families, Socrates says, would be willing to provide the sort of perjury that "many reputable people" are prepared to give in court battles (especially when these are against political enemies).

T6.8 *Gorgias* 516c-d (immediately precedes **T6.9**):

> Socrates: Now as Homer says, the just are gentle. What do you say? Don't you say the same?
>
> Callicles: Yes.

SOCRATES: But Pericles certainly showed them to be wilder than they were when he took them over, and that toward himself, the person he'd least want this to happen to.[5] [...] And if wilder, then both more unjust and worse?

CALLICLES: So be it.

SOCRATES: So on this reasoning Pericles wasn't good at politics.

Elsewhere, Socrates also singles Pericles out as one who failed to teach his sons to be virtuous (*Meno* 92d–94e). In the same passage, Socrates also singles out Pericles' democratic rival, Thucydides (son of Melesias—not the historian), for failing to teach his sons virtue, as is the earlier democratic leader, Aristeides. It seems that Socrates has nothing good to say about Athens's most famous democratic leaders.

But, as we found with his criticisms of both democratic and oligarchic ideologies in Athenian politics, it is one thing to be critical of a given public official and another thing to be an advocate for some existing rival leader. The fact is that just as Socrates is plainly critical of certain democratic leaders, he also holds the favorites of the oligarchic movement up for the exact same sorts of criticism. Here is what he says about several other famous Athenian political leaders, just after showing his scorn for Pericles:

T6.9 *Gorgias* 515d–e (immediately follows **T6.8**):

SOCRATES: Let's go back to Cimon. Tell me: didn't the people he was serving ostracize him so that they wouldn't hear his voice for ten years? And didn't they do the same thing for Themistocles, punishing him with exile besides? And didn't they vote to throw Miltiades, of Marathon fame, into the pit, and if it hadn't been for the prytanis[6] he would have been thrown in? And yet these things would not have happened to these men if they were good men, as you say they were.

Cimon, we see, comes in for the exact same criticism as Pericles. But Cimon's hostility to the development of Athenian democracy was notorious.[7] Miltiades was Cimon's father. Themistocles, however, was aligned with the democrats.

Socrates' criticisms of political leaders betray no bias toward any known faction of that time. Indeed, he seems actually to be careful to hold well-known political rivals up for the same criticisms each time. When he says that past leaders only made the Athenians wilder and less controlled (**T6.8** and **T6.9**), he includes two famous democrats and two famous antidemocrats. When he says that such leaders cannot teach their own sons, he mentions the famous political rivals Pericles and Thucydides in the same breath, as well as the earlier rivals, Aristeides and Themistocles (*Meno* 92d–94e). Socrates' criticisms are not gentle, but neither are they biased by partisan politics.

6.3.4 Socrates' Nasty Friends

There is rather better evidence for thinking that Socrates' friends and associates provided grounds for hostility of a political nature, and this evidence usually supports the claim that Socrates' trial was politically motivated as well. Several ancient sources make such claims, and where there is direct ancient evidence, it is prudent to pay special attention. Perhaps the most noteworthy of these is Polycrates, whose *Accusation of Socrates* was written some time after 394 B.C., perhaps as few as five years after Socrates' trial. Unfortunately, Polycrates' speech has been lost, but several other ancient sources make reference to it, and on the basis of these later references, one scholar has attempted to reconstruct Polycrates' work.[8] Regardless of what we think of the plausibility of this reconstruction, there are enough ancient references to Polycrates' speech for us to recognize that many of its specific accusations against Socrates were political in nature.

We know that Polycrates' speech was not actually given at Socrates' trial but was composed afterward. The speech itself was a rhetorical display, intended to demonstrate the author's persuasive abilities. Speeches of this sort were not at all intended—and were not accepted by their audience—as accurate representations of fact, though this is not to say that everything included in them was untrue. Indeed, perhaps the most effective speeches of this sort would be ones that appeared very persuasive even though they argued for positions the speaker or his audience could *not* be presumed to believe. Nonetheless, Polycrates' speech received many defensive responses from Socrates' supporters. One of the first of these was Plato's contemporary, Xenophon, who goes to great lengths in his *Memorabilia* to defend the memory of Socrates against the attacks of someone Xenophon refers to only as "the accuser," whom most scholars now believe was Polycrates (and not any of Socrates' actual accusers at the trial itself).[9]

T6.10 Xenophon, *Memorabilia* 1.2.9:

> The accuser said that he taught his companions to despise the established laws by insisting on the folly of appointing public officials by lot, when none would choose a pilot or a builder or a flutist by lot, nor any other craftsman for work in which mistakes are far less dangerous than mistakes made in statecraft. Such sayings, he argued, led the young to despise the established constitution and made them violent.

Some of those whom Socrates supposedly corrupted this way are later named by "the accuser."
T6.11 Xenophon, *Memorabilia* 1.2.12:

> His accuser argued thus: Having become associates of Socrates, Critias and Alcibiades did great evils to the city.

These same, supposedly damaging associations are repeated by later authors.
T6.12 Isocrates, *Busiris* 5:

> (Addressed to Polycrates) And when your purpose was to accuse Socrates, as if you wished to praise him, you gave Alcibiades to him as a pupil.

Isocrates probably wrote this speech soon after Polycrates' own appeared. Even some fifty years after the trial, however, Polycrates' charges were being repeated.
T6.13 Aeschines Rhetor, *Against Timarchus* 173:

> (Addressed to an Athenian jury) You put Socrates, the sophist, to death because he was shown to have educated Critias.

As we saw in Chapter 1, Alcibiades was, perhaps, Athens's most notorious traitor;[10] Critias was one of the so-called Thirty Tyrants who overthrew the democracy in 404 B.C.—perhaps their leader.[11]

In his dialogues, Plato actually appears to confirm at least Socrates' associations with these men. In several dialogues, Socrates is actually portrayed as Alcibiades' elder lover (*Protagoras* 309a-b; *Gorgias* 481d; *Symposium* 213c ff.). Critias appears as a longtime acquaintance of Socrates in Plato's *Charmides* (156a), and Critias also makes an appearance in Plato's *Protagoras* (316a, 336d-e) and is Socrates' principal interlocutor in the later *Timaeus* (19d ff.) and *Critias* (106b ff.).

To these notorious men, in fact, we can add several others who appear in Plato's dialogues on friendly terms with Socrates. Critias's cousin, Charmides, who was also later one of the Thirty, is Socrates' main interlocutor in the dialogue of the same name, and Plato lets us know at least that Socrates felt some attraction to the young Charmides (*Charmides* 155c-e; *Symposium* 222b). Plato's *Laches* puts Socrates on friendly terms with Laches and Nicias. The former disgraced himself with dishonesty and corruption (in the early 420s B.C.), whereas the latter (at least in Thucydides' account) was responsible for the catastrophic loss of the Athenian fleet at Sicily in 413 B.C. One scholar, going through Plato's works, claims that "about a half" of those who speak with Socrates are "criminals and traitors."[12]

Several questions need to be sorted out at this point. The first one is easy: Does the evidence we get from Plato associate Socrates with notorious men? Certainly, it does. But what follows from this? Answers to questions about the implications of Socrates' associations are much more difficult to give decisively, even if scholarship has not always recognized much difficulty in coming to all sorts of conclusions about Socrates.

So far, we have considered whether Plato's texts gave support to the claim that Socrates was implicated in Athens's partisan political upheavals and have found such a mix of evidence that it seems impossible to place Socrates in any specific faction. His notorious associations, moreover, do not provide any clearer evidence of partisan bias. As "the accuser" of Xenophon's *Memorabilia* so clearly recognizes in **T6.11**, even the most notorious of Socrates' associates were aligned with different factions in Athenian politics, and the same can be said for all of the "criminals and traitors" who make up the remainder of Socrates' interlocutors and companions. Whatever its notoriety, no single factional group is recognizable within this collection of characters. Socrates' friends and interlocutors come from all of the different factions—and range from violent oligarchic revolutionaries like Critias to democrats, such as Chaerophon, who died attempting to restore the democracy in the civil war against Critias and the other members of the Thirty (Socrates' friend Chaerophon actually received the famous Delphic oracle about Socrates; see *Apology* 21a ff.). Even the most notorious of these men gained their notoriety in very different ways and from misdeeds of several different kinds.

Perhaps the most reasonable thing to do in the face of such evidence is to try to look a little more closely at how Socrates interacts with the "criminals and traitors" with whom we find him consorting in Plato's early dialogues. In doing this, we maintain, a very different picture emerges. Socrates, after all, is a man whose style is to *refute* those with whom he talks. Plato's Socrates can hardly be said to support, flatter, or encourage the (always later) crimes and misdeeds and evil plots of these "criminals and traitors." Invariably, instead, we find Socrates *deflating* the smug arrogance of these men, showing them that they do not know what they think they know, showing them (and those witnessing the conversations) that they do not have the wisdom they pretend to have, and—as is so explicitly the case with Euthyphro, whose foolish presumption has led him to do what all recognize as a ghastly impiety—showing them that without such knowledge and wisdom, their most excessive and unconventional plans are morally and rationally indefensible. Plato's Socrates is hardly a man who hatches plots with these "criminals and traitors." Instead, he seems to be a man whose philosophical interactions would tend to have a dampening effect on such men, if only they would pay better attention to the shortcomings Socrates is trying to point out. Finding Socrates "guilty by association" with such men, we contend, is to miss the *character* of Socrates' interactions with them, which we often see becoming tense or even hostile (see, for several examples, *Euthyphro* 11b-d [with Euthyphro]; *Charmides* 166b-c [with Critias]; *Meno* 94e [with Anytus]; *Republic* 1.343a [with Thrasymachus]; see also *Apology* 22e–24b). Alcibiades himself seems to have recognized this and allows that Socrates is the only man who ever made him feel shame, but he admits that his shamelessness returns as soon as he gets away from Socrates again (*Symposium* 216b). Moreover, at the times of their greatest infamies, the association with Socrates seems either to have ended long ago (as in the case of Alcibiades) or to have spoiled (as in the case of Critias—see *Apology* 32c-e; see also Xenophon, *Memorabilia* 1.2.29–38 and Diodorus Siculus 14.5.1–3).

6.3.5 Politics and the Trial of Socrates

But even if we are right about the nature of Socrates' associations with such bad men, it remains possible that the associations were none the less sufficient to arouse a mind-set of general prejudice against Socrates, and as we all know, prejudice can be deadly without being at all accurate. Scholarship on the trial of Socrates routinely assumed that it was just such prejudice, of a political nature, that was the true motivation behind the accusation—and the conviction—of Socrates. Recent scholarly attacks on what had been the established view, however, have raised serious questions.

Let us return, for a moment, to the ancient evidence. It is impossible to draw any decisive conclusions from the speech by Polycrates, but because it was a rhetorical display, there is no particular reason to suppose that the prejudices he mentioned (if, indeed, these are the same as those we find reported in Xenophon) were explicitly or implicitly featured in Socrates' trial. Similarly, just because Polycrates' specific accusations are later repeated by other authors in other speeches, it does not follow that these accusations had anything to do with the actual prosecution or conviction, for their appearance in the literature of the time is sufficient of itself—even without their being grounded in historical fact—to draw responses from Socrates' literary and philosophical defenders.

One very obvious problem with what had for many years been the received view of the trial can be seen in the nature of the actual charges against Socrates: Socrates is charged with *impiety*, and this charge, and the way it is specified in the indictment and in Meletus's representation of its meaning in Plato's *Apology*, seems plainly to identify a *religious* rather than a *political* motive. Defenders of the traditional view of the trial had evaded this problem by pointing to a peculiarity in Athens's legal system at that time. In late 403 or early 402 B.C., a reconciliation agreement was passed (in the aftermath of the restoration of the democracy, after the final removal of the Thirty from power) that called for a complete recodification of Athens's laws. According to the terms of this agreement, an amnesty was put into place, according to which no one except the surviving members of the Thirty themselves could be prosecuted for crimes alleged to have been committed during their brief hold on power, or before that; only crimes alleged to have been committed *after* the restoration of the democracy, under the laws as recodified in accordance with the reconciliation agreement, could be prosecuted.

It has been widely claimed that this general amnesty made it impossible to prosecute Socrates directly and explicitly on the basis of the political prejudice alleged to have been the true motivation for his trial, for all of the associations and activities that formed the basis of the alleged political prejudice against Socrates came from before the general amnesty. Instead, then, his prosecutors were said to have chosen the charge of impiety and to have prosecuted on that basis, but no one—including the jury—was actually fooled into thinking that this was the *real* issue at hand. But one very unfortunate consequence of this view is that it renders Plato's own account of the trial in the *Apology* highly suspect, for Plato's Socrates makes no explicit mention of any political bias against him and seems dedicated to addressing the religious issue instead. Moreover, the actual prosecutor we do meet in that work, Meletus, seems quite vehement—if not entirely clearheaded—in defending his religious animus against Socrates. Of course, this could be (and has been) taken as evidence either that Plato was not giving an honest account of the historical trial or that Socrates either evaded or at least did not bother to try to make an effective defense against what he had to know were the *real* charges and prejudices against him, namely, the political ones. Either way, Plato's *Apology* becomes largely irrelevant to the actual historical facts of the case—a most unhappy result from the point of view of the interpretive *Principle of Charity*, as discussed in the introduction to this book! Moreover, it is even more worrisome that the evidence on which this assessment is made is even more assailable and dubitable (as later, as coming from a rhetorical display) than Plato's work itself, which may not be historically compelling but which nevertheless remains the most proximate and most consistent evidence we have.

At any rate, this argument about the prosecutorial subterfuge, required by the amnesty of 403–402 B.C., has been revealed as simply mistaken. First of all, the argument ignores the fact that the amnesty continued to allow prosecutors (and defendants, for that matter) to recall all sorts of perceived infractions and misdeeds that occurred during and before the Thirty's reign as evidence in open court.[13] The amnesty ruled out only legal charges whose sole basis was crimes alleged to have occurred prior to the reconciliation. Had the prosecution sought to use the evidence of Socrates' supposed past political wrongs against him, they would only have had to claim, under the amnesty, that Socrates had committed some crime of the relevant sort *after* the passage of the reconciliation agreement; then they would have been free to use all of his supposed earlier misdeeds as evidence of a pattern of continuing political evils.

Of course, this would have required them to identify some *current* law, which they would have to be prepared to claim Socrates had broken. Given the testimony of a few convenient witnesses (see *Gorgias* 471e–472b [T6.7, above]) claiming the sort of thing we find averred by "the accuser" in Xenophon (T6.10), the following law, which was literally written in stone at the entrance to the Council building in Athens, would surely have sufficed.[14]

T6.14 Andocides, *On the Mysteries* 96–97 [trans. MacDowell[15]]:

> If anyone subverts the democracy at Athens, or holds any office when the democracy has been subverted, he shall be an enemy of the Athenians and shall be killed with impunity, and his property shall be confiscated and one-tenth of it shall belong to the Goddess; and he who kills or helps to plan the killing of such a man shall be pure and free from guilt . . . .

In other words, had Socrates' prosecutors supposed that they could make the case that Socrates had engaged in sedition against the democracy at Athens, they would not have needed to resort to such contortions as filing bogus religious charges against him. They could simply have tried him as a subverter of the democracy and then killed him. At any rate, there can be no serious question that had the prosecutors' motives been the political ones identified in traditional accounts of the trial, there was no legal impediment to their undertaking a more direct and explicit expression of these political motives. We are forced to conclude, therefore, that the trial was, in fact, grounded in religious concerns. We consider these concerns, and the more recent scholarly views that have taken them seriously, in the next chapter.

6.4 Socrates on Obedience to Law

6.4.1 A Conflict of Words and Deeds?

In the *Laches*, Socrates gently chides Laches, saying that he and Laches need to be sure to make their words and their deeds more consistent.

T6.15 *Laches* 193e:

SOCRATES: . . . I don't suppose, Laches, that according to your statement you and I are tuned to the Dorian mode, because our deeds are not harmonizing with our words.

But as many readers have noticed, Socrates seems to create just such a lack of harmony for himself when he talks about what a person ought never to do in the *Apology* and what a person ought never to do in the *Crito*.

T6.16 *Crito* 51b-c:

(Socrates speaking on behalf of the Laws, addressing himself) . . . in war and in courts and everywhere else, one must obey the commands of one's city and country, or persuade it as to the nature of justice.

T6.17 *Apology* 29c-d:

(Socrates speaking) If you said to me in this regard: "Socrates, we do not believe Anytus now; we will [let you go],[16] but only on condition that you spend no more time on this investigation and do not practice philosophy, and if you are caught doing so, you will die"; if, as I say, you were to [let me go] on those terms, I would say to you: "Gentlemen of Athens, I am grateful and I am your friend, but I will obey the god rather than you, and as long as I draw breath and am able, I shall not cease to practice philosophy . . . ."

On the one hand, in the *Crito*, Socrates appears to be saying that it is never just to disobey civil authority, "in war and in courts and everywhere"; on the other hand, in the *Apology* (in court) he seems entirely prepared to disobey the jury, if its members were to require him to stop philosophizing. The problem in these two texts is obvious and has become perhaps one of the most famous problems in Socratic scholarship, usually known as "the *Apology-Crito* problem."

6.4.2 Approaches to the Apology-Crito Problem

In this section, we review the interpretive options available to scholars and readers of Plato's dialogues, in the face of this famous problem, surveying in a general way the various solutions scholars have offered. Because there has been so much written on this problem, we are not able to go into any great detail on the variations in any of general approaches we survey, but we try at least to lay out the general logical structure of each of the options that have been offered, to the best of our knowledge. We conclude with our own proposed solution, which we encourage our readers to compare with the other proposed solutions and the relevant texts to judge its adequacy for themselves.

Let us begin by breaking down our options in a logical way. We start by noting that there are two main options here: We can accept that there is a genuine conflict in the texts, or we can not accept this. Each of these options contains other options: If we accept that there is a conflict, we can either decide that either Socrates or Plato (or both) was simply unaware of the conflict or that, if aware of it, did not have any way of solving it. In this view, Plato simply represents the problem, whether aware of it or not and gives us no way to get out of it. This result clearly offends what we have called the *Principle of Charity*; it may, however, be what the texts and the failures of proposed solutions drive us to. But as we said in the introduction, we should be very wary of accepting this sort of conclusion without giving all proposed solutions very serious consideration first, precisely because such a negative conclusion is so blatantly uncharitable.

But a similarly negative solution might be offered in a much more charitable way. We might accept that there is a genuine conflict here but suppose that Socrates or Plato (or both) was not only aware of the conflict but created this conflict for some specific reason, which—if only we can identify that reason—would be edifying for us to recognize. This option allows for proposing an indefinite number of possibilities: Perhaps Socrates or Plato (or both) wished to show that this is an intractable problem for all human existence, a tragically inescapable conflict of equal but opposed absolute moral duties; perhaps Socrates did not bother to style his conversations in a way that took consistency *between* conversations seriously; perhaps Plato did not write his dialogues in such a way as to expect his readers to compare them in the way we are doing here; or perhaps we should reconsider whether both *Apology* and *Crito* belong to Plato's early-period group, and in this conflict, Plato was announcing a *departure* from Socrates' philosophy, replacing it, on this issue at least, with his own; and so on. The placement of Plato's *Apology* and *Crito* in Plato's early-period group, however, is as well established as any of the dialogues in this group, so that an argument for taking one of these two dialogues out of the group is not really an option. The problem with all the other "constructive conflict" views is that they seem to fly in the face of all of the texts in which Socrates shows the highest regard for consistency and never once (unless it is in this unique conflict!) gives us any reason to think that there are specific inconsistencies in reasoning that we cannot overcome, if we lead "the examined life."

T6.18 *Gorgias* 482b-c (= **T2.37**; immediately follows **T2.50**):

SOCRATES: . . . I think it's better to have my lyre or a chorus that I might lead out of tune and dissonant, and have the vast majority of men disagree with me and contradict me, than to be out of harmony with myself, to contradict myself, though I'm only one person.

Now, maybe this passage can *also* be given some subtle reading, but at least on the face of it, Socrates does not here seem to be the sort of man who thinks there are tragically inescapable inconsistencies confronting human existence, nor does he seem to suppose that his personification of "Philosophy herself" recognizes any such inconsistencies. Accordingly, we are not inclined to any theory that either separates the dialogues or portrays Socrates or Plato as philosophers who are unconcerned with—or who feel tragically trapped by—what they actually do recognize as philosophical inconsistency.

This result, then, puts us back to the original position: We must either accept that there is a genuine conflict—which we must now suppose either Socrates or Plato (or both) were not aware of—or else we must deny that "the *Apology-Crito* problem" is a genuine conflict. But we cannot simply deny that it is a conflict and be done with it; we must have some reason for denying this. We must shoulder the burden of proof and show *why* it is not a genuine conflict. Most interpreters have taken this approach and have offered a wide variety of proposed solutions to the apparent problem.

An attempt to solve the problem in the more positive way can take several general forms: One could accept the apparent meaning of the *Apology* text and hold that Socrates would be quite ready to disobey legal authority in some cases (at least the case he seems to have in mind in the *Apology*) but then come up with some interpretation to "soften" the effect of the *Crito* text in such a way as to provide an understanding of what Socrates says there that does not conflict with his apparent willingness, in the *Apology*, to disobey legal authority. Or one could accept the apparent meaning of the *Crito* text and hold that Socrates would never find disobedience of legal authority morally acceptable but then come up with some interpretation to "soften" the effect of the *Apology* text in such a way as to show that he is not really willing to disobey legal authority, despite appearances to the contrary. Or one could attempt to work the problem from both sides, as it were, by "softening" the effects of both texts in such a way as to find some position they can both be understood as consistent with. Let us see what kinds of considerations have been brought to bear in trying to "soften" the two sides of this problem. Because most scholars have tended to attack the problem by reinterpreting the *Crito*, we begin with this passage.

6.4.3 Interpreting the Crito: *Persuading the Laws*

Let us look again at the troublesome *Crito* passage.
T6.16 *Crito* 51b-c (repeated):

> (Socrates speaking on behalf of the Laws, addressing himself) . . . in war and in courts and everywhere else, one must obey the commands of one's city and country, or persuade it as to the nature of justice.

A more subtle interpretation that avoids the obvious conflict requires that we attend first to the *two* options Socrates offers: We must obey the commands of legal authority *or* "persuade it as to the nature of justice." Several proposed solutions have fastened onto this part of Socrates' claim and have attempted to use an understanding of the "persuade" option to allow Socrates' hypothetical vow to disobey, in the *Apology*, to fall within acceptable "persuasion." If so, then Socrates would be shown to advocate a consistent position in the two dialogues after all, for he says that one must either obey or persuade, and in vowing disobedience in the *Apology*, he would only be inconsistent if such a vow counted as *neither* obedience *nor* persuasion.

Let us take a closer look at how this sort of argument might be made. Three main versions of "persuasion" have been considered by scholars, two of which would suffice to make Socrates' hypothetical vow in the *Apology* not inconsistent with the doctrine he announces in the *Crito*. The only form of persuasion that *does* create a conflict with the *Apology* is what we could call "successful prior persuasion." According to this conception of persuasion, in order to qualify as persuasion in the "obey or persuade" doctrine that Socrates announces in the *Crito*, one must *succeed* in persuading the law to change *prior* to acting in the way the law (currently) forbids. If the law commands one to do X and one thinks that one should not have to do X, then one must successfully persuade those who make the laws to rescind the law requiring X, after which, of course, it will be perfectly legal *not* to do X. Read this way, there is never really the possibility of disobedience, for it still allows no alternative to obedience—one must obey the law or else succeed in changing the law, so that one can obey the law after the change. In the meantime, however, we can assume that one obeys the law one finds offensive, until the appropriate change in the law has been effected.

But other possible understandings of what might count as legitimate persuasion, in Socrates' doctrine, have been offered, in which room is left open for acceptable *disobedience* to the law—a possibility, as we have seen, that the standard reading does not recognize. One such understanding was offered by A. D. Woozley,[17] who argued that Socrates should be seen as taking a position very like the ones taken by Ghandi or Martin Luther King, namely, that certain very restricted forms of disobedience to the laws were the best ways to persuade government to *change* unjust laws. Socrates, in this view, would disobey a court order to cease philosophizing as a kind of persuasive civil disobedience and would thus be consistent with the doctrine he announces in the *Crito* even if he were to disobey the court order.

This interpretation, however, seems to face the problem that civil disobedience, as a form of persuasion, requires that the disobedience is clearly conceived and represented as a form of protest against the relevant law, with an eye to changing it. In this way, it is different from what we might call "simple disobedience," in which one elects simply to disobey the law (for whatever reason), but not as part of a strategy to have the offending law changed or repealed. But nothing in the *Apology* passage suggests that Socrates would be disobeying the imagined court order as a form of *protest* against the court order (or for that matter, against some other law or legal command). He simply says that he will obey the god more than the jurors and would therefore disobey. Now, we can imagine, perhaps, that Socrates would *wish* that the court order be modified or rescinded, and we can easily imagine what his arguments for such modification or nullification would be. But what is missing in what Socrates says in the *Apology* is what is absolutely essential to civil disobedience as a form of persuasion: that the disobedience he vows would be his way of protesting the court order and would be a part of his effort to have that order (or some other legal command) changed or reversed. But Socrates does not say that he would seek to have the court order changed or reversed; he simply says that he would not obey it. As such, it clearly looks as if his vow, in the *Apology*, is not a vow to commit persuasive civil disobedience but is, rather, a vow to commit simple disobedience.

A different conception of persuasion, which allows for some disobedience to legal authority, is offered by Richard Kraut.[18] According to Kraut, the Greek word for "persuade" had what is called a "conative sense," according to which one actually "persuades" when one makes a sincere attempt to persuade and not just when one actually succeeds in convincing those one seeks to convince. One can be said to be "building" a house, for example, even if one never actually succeeds in finishing the house. One can be said to be "writing" a book, even if the book is never completed. Thus, "build" and "write" have conative senses. Similarly (in Greek and in English), one could claim that Socrates, in his first speech, was "persuading" the jury, even if, as it turns out, the jury was not, in the end, persuaded (now using the nonconative sense of the verb). By seeing the relevant form of the Greek word, in the troublesome passage in the *Crito*, as the *conative* sense of "persuade," Kraut allows that Socrates would not be in violation of his conception of legal duty if, as he hypothetically vows to do, he were to disobey the jury in the way he hypothetically vows to do in the *Apology*. And the reason this would be consistent with his conception of legal duty is that we find Socrates, in the *Apology*, "persuading" (in the conative sense) his jurors as to why obeying such a court order would be wrong. Because he would thereby have satisfied the "persuade" option in the "obey or persuade" doctrine, it would be consistent with that doctrine for Socrates to disobey.

Perhaps the reason that scholars have not widely accepted Kraut's subtle interpretation is that it does not seem to square with the way Socrates characterizes the nature of the relationship of the state to its citizens. Just before the troublesome passage we have been scrutinizing, Socrates portrays this relationship in highly revealing terms.

T6.19 *Crito* 50e–51b:

> (Socrates speaking on behalf of the Laws, addressing himself) . . . could you [Socrates], in the first place, deny that you are our offspring and slave,[19] both you and your forefathers? If that is so, do you think that we are on an equal footing as regards the right, and that whatever we do to you it is right for you to do to us? You were not on an equal footing with your father as regards the right, nor with your master if you had one, so as to retaliate for anything they did to you [. . .] Is your wisdom such as not to realize that your country is to be honored more than your mother, your father and all your ancestors, that it is more to be revered and more sacred, and that it counts for more among the gods and sensible men, that you must worship it, yield to it and placate its anger more than your father's?

The difficulty Kraut's interpretation must face is that Socrates compares the relationship of citizen to state to the relationships of child to parent and slave to master (taking the latter two sorts, apparently, to be comparable in the relevant respect). Kraut does make a case for showing that in Greek culture, adult children might still be expected to obey or (at least try to) persuade a parent who commanded them to do something.[20] But it seems much more difficult to think that a sincere attempt to persuade would be sufficient to make it permissible for very young children to disobey their parent, much less for slaves to disobey their master. At any rate, we have no evidence for supposing that Socrates or Crito had radical views about the conventions involving slavery, and these were sufficiently harsh, in ancient Athens, to make it inconceivable that Socrates or Crito would take as permissive a stance regarding slaves as Kraut's version of "obey or persuade" would seem to require. If not, then the comparison of citizens to children and slaves would appear to make sincere attempts at persuasion insufficient to relieve these "inferiors" of the obligation to obey their superiors. This, then, puts us back to the traditional understanding of "persuade" in Socrates' doctrine: To avoid obedience to some law, one must succeed in convincing the state to change the law, so that one can obey the law as changed. In other words, Socrates says that one should always obey the law—which is why one must (successfully) persuade the law to change if one does not wish to follow the dictates of the (present) law.

6.4.4 Interpreting the Crito: "Trumping" the Requirement to Obey

Several scholars have argued that in the *Crito*, Socrates is not claiming that obedience to the law is an *absolute* duty, that is, one that must never go unsatisfied, morally. We might suppose that moral duties form a kind of hierarchical structure, in which one can be presumed to have the relevant duty *unless* that duty is overridden by some *higher* duty. Scholars have come up with several arguments for why we should suppose that the duty to obey the law that Socrates announces in the troublesome passage in the *Crito* is of this sort and have pointed to evidence that they have supposed identifies *higher* duties.

One famous example of this sort of approach is given by Gerasimos Santas,[21] who encourages us to pay attention to the specific way in which Socrates phrases his hypothetical vow to disobey the jury, in the *Apology*.

T6.17 *Apology* 29c-d (repeated in part):

> (Socrates speaking) . . . if, as I say, you were to [let me go] on those terms, I would say to you: "Gentlemen of Athens, I am grateful and I am your friend, but I will obey the god rather than you, and as long as I draw breath and am able, I shall not cease to practice philosophy . . . ."

Socrates does not simply vow to disobey—he lets his jurors know that he would disobey only because he has the highest possible duty a human being can have, which in this case *requires* that he disobey: his mission on behalf of the god. In effect, then, the *Apology* passage explicitly specifies what duty "trumps" Socrates' duty to obey legal authority: He must always obey legal authority *unless* divine authority makes some opposing command. This exception does not come up in the *Crito* passage, because the kind of case Socrates and Crito have in mind there does not raise the issue of conflict between divine and human law. Accordingly, Socrates announces his doctrine of legal obedience in the *Crito* in a way that specifies no exceptions—for even though exceptions to the doctrine do exist, none are pertinent to the issue Crito and Socrates are considering in their discussion.

One question this view must answer, however, is how Socrates can be so certain that the divine command Socrates finds absolutely compelling does not, in fact, apply to the question of whether Socrates should (illegally) escape from jail. After all, if he would disobey a court order to stop philosophizing on religious grounds, why also should he not disobey a court order to stay in Athens and be executed, when obedience, surely, will bring about an even more certain end to his philosophical mission! But even if Socrates can produce evidence for distinguishing the two cases, the view that Socrates sees religious law as a higher authority than civil law is not well supported by the text of the *Crito*, where Socrates argues as if obedience to civil law *is* one's religious duty.

T6.19 *Crito* 50e–51b (repeated in part):

> Is your wisdom such as not to realize that your country is to be honored more than your mother, your father and all your ancestors, that it is more to be revered and more sacred, and that it counts for more among the gods and sensible men, that you must worship it, yield to it and placate its anger more than your father's?

Socrates makes his appeal in this passage just before announcing his doctrine of legal obedience in the name of divine authority. Thus, it is not as if Socrates does not have the role of divine authority in mind in making his declaration—and any potential for conflict that such authority might cause; rather, Socrates seems to think that divine authority lends unqualified support to the authority of civil law. If Socrates saw the two as potentially in conflict, why would he talk as if divine law *supported* civil law?

Another hierarchical approach is given by R. E. Allen,[22] who argues that we need to see Socrates' announcement of his doctrine in the *Crito* as conditioned upon the overriding point the specific issue in question is supposed to address, namely, Socrates' view that it is never morally acceptable to do injustice.

T6.20 *Crito* 49c (partially repeats **T2.28**):

> SOCRATES: One should never do wrong in return, nor injure any man, whatever injury one has suffered at his hands.

Socrates' argument, then, is that one should "obey or persuade" precisely because—and only because—this is the just thing to do. When he announces this doctrine in the *Crito*, however, he does not have in mind—nor is his argument with Crito considering—a case in which obeying the law might be an *unjust* thing to do. Such a case, however, is what we find, in Allen's view, in the *Apology* passage, for in this passage, Allen says, Socrates is considering a court order forbidding him to do what he has a god-given mission to do in Athens, namely, philosophize. Because it would be wrong for Socrates to abandon his philosophical mission, any court order requiring this would be tantamount to a legal command to do injustice. To cases such as this, however, Socrates cannot appeal to the overriding principle "never do injustice" in defense of *obedience* to such a legal command. Therefore, unless he conceives of one of these two duties—never do injustice and never disobey the law—as hierarchically arranged so that one takes precedence over the other, in cases where they conflict, then, Socrates is committed to an incoherent theory in the *Crito* itself. Allen suggests that we should not be so uncharitable as to assume that Socrates would miss such a point, and he is certain that Socrates would count the prohibition of injustice as the higher duty, which would trump the duty to obey the law in cases of conflict.

Allen may be right that if Socrates thought he had to choose between obeying the law and being just, he would take the latter to be the most compelling consideration. The problem is that Allen's arrangement of the two obligations in a hierarchy comes without any very specific support from our texts. Certainly, we never see Socrates even so much as hinting that the prohibition of injustice might have exceptions. But the problem is that wherever Socrates argues that it is wrong to disobey legal superiors, he shows no recognition of exceptions, either. Consider yet another passage—this time in the *Apology*—where Socrates seems to recognize a requirement of obedience to legal authority, just a few lines before making his hypothetical vow to disobey.

T6.21 *Apology* 28e–29b (partially overlaps with **T3.4** and **T7.20**):

It would have been a dreadful way to behave, gentlemen, if, at Potidaea, Amphipolis and Delium [famous battles in which Socrates took part], I had, at the risk of death, like anyone else, remained at my post where those you had elected to command had ordered me, and then, when the god ordered me, as I thought and believed, I had abandoned my post for fear of death or anything else. [...] It is perhaps on this point and in this respect, gentlemen, that I differ from the majority of men, and if I were to claim that I am wiser than anyone in anything, it would be in this, that, as I have no adequate knowledge of things in the underworld, so I do not think I have. I do know, however, that it is wicked and shameful to do wrong, to disobey one's superior, be he god or man. I shall never fear or avoid things of which I do not know, whether they may not be good rather than things that I know to be bad.

In this passage, only a few lines before he makes his vow to disobey the jury, Socrates seems unready to recognize exceptions to a moral duty to obey the commands of legal human authorities. Either sort of disobedience—to god or man—appears to qualify, in Socrates' eyes, as shameful.

Of course, it is open to us to speculate how Socrates *would* order such duties—the duty to obey legal authority, the duty to obey divine authority, and the duty not to do injustice—if they were to come into conflict. But the problem we face in this issue is that—even at the very times he is supposed to be considering such potential conflicts—he speaks as if he recognizes no such cases or possibilities. In each case, he articulates his commitment to the relevant obligation, as if it were exceptionless.

6.4.5 Interpreting the Apology: The Jury and the Law

We said earlier that in order to avoid the conflict, one might seek either to reinterpret the *Crito* passage, which is what we have been considering in the last two sections, or to reinterpret the *Apology* passage. Our own position on this famous problem takes the latter approach. All along, we have been referring to Socrates' "hypothetical" vow to disobey the jurors. We should begin by noticing that the *Apology* passage does not create conflict with the *Crito*, or for that matter with Socrates' expression of respect for legal authority at 29b (**T6.21**), unless there is some *actual* violation of law or legal authority that we can be sure that Socrates did or would commit. The situation at *Apology* 29c-d (**T6.17**) is, in fact, purely hypothetical: The jury does not *actually* make Socrates any such offer, nor does Socrates *actually* disobey any genuine court order. But no doubt we should take Socrates at his word and accept that he *would* disobey the order he imagines the jurors giving him, *if* they were to make such an order.

However, we should try to get clear on what sorts of conditions would be required for the jurors to make such an order. Several can be imagined: They might find Socrates innocent on the condition that he cease philosophizing; or they might find him guilty and make ceasing philosophizing his assigned punishment; or they might find him guilty and condemn him to death but then suspend the sentence on the condition that he cease philosophizing; or they might find him guilty and condemn him to death, but then issue a pardon on the condition that he cease philosophizing, and so on. We will not go into the details here,[23] but in brief, the problem with every such scenario is that there is simply no way, within Athenian law, for any of them to be legally valid *unless* Socrates himself offers ceasing philosophizing as a penalty or as a condition he would be willing to accept, in the case of a legal pardon. But this is something that Socrates makes very clear that he would *not* do, even if the alternative is death. As long as Socrates will not offer such a condition to the jury or to the Assembly, which was charged with considering pleas for pardons, there is simply no way for the jury to make the condition Socrates says he would disobey *legally*. But this means that the specific case raised in the troublesome *Apology* passage cannot represent a situation in which Socrates actually *would* disobey legal authority. Of course, the jury is a legal authority in some sense—it does have the authority to do some things; but since the jurors would not be acting legally if they made such a condition in Socrates' case, if he did disobey, as he says he would, he would not be in conflict with even an absolute duty to obey legal authority. To be a genuinely *legal* authority, the jurors would have to avoid making commands that went beyond their legal authority.

But this does not go far enough, and we have been criticized for not taking the next step and noticing that even if the jury could not make such a provision, surely other Athenian legal authorities *were* in a position to do so.[24] For example, what would Socrates do if the Athenian Assembly passed a law banning philosophizing? This question assumes two things: first, that it would be legally unproblematic for the Assembly to pass such a law, and second, that we are in a position to know what Socrates would do in the face of such a law. The first assumption raises important questions about the legal system that was in place in 399 B.C. We are convinced, however, that at least one thing stands in the way of this imaginary law's unproblematic application to Socrates' own case: Socrates makes the case for philosophizing on the basis of *piety*—he claims his philosophizing is a mission given him by the god. But we know that there was a prior law (prior, that is, to the imaginary one that Socrates would be confronted with, in this scenario) against impiety, for it was on the basis of a perceived violation of this law that Socrates was put on trial. If Socrates believes that piety requires him to philosophize and the law requires him to be pious, then the law requires him to philosophize. If some new law requires him to cease philosophizing, then Socrates would have every reason to suppose that the laws were issuing contradictory commands. As we put the point in an earlier book, "when two laws contradict one another, even the most steadfast adherent to civil authority cannot find a way to comply with both."[25] Notice, moreover, that what is at issue is not whether *others* accept that philosophizing is Socrates' pious duty but only whether *Socrates himself* accepts this. As long as he does accept it, the law against impiety and the imaginary law against philosophizing would conflict, from Socrates' point of view. In such a case, he could not avoid violating at least one of the conflicting laws, but such a violation could not be counted as evidence against even an absolute commitment to a duty to obey the law, such as the *Crito* seems to call for.

We said that there were two assumptions behind the objection to our stipulation about the jurors' lack of legal authority to make the condition Socrates imagines, in the *Apology* passage, and we have been questioning the first one. The second assumption is that we could *know* what Socrates would do in the face of such a law being passed. His commitment to philosophizing appears to be absolute and complete, as we have seen, but we have also seen no exceptions noted in his commitment to obey legal authority, and this alone should make us wary of jumping to any conclusions in cases that are—as this one now is—purely imaginary. It is worth noting, at least, that Socrates does say, in the *Crito*, that the citizen has a third option, in addition to those given in "obey or persuade."

T6.22 *Crito* 51c-d:

> (Socrates speaking on behalf of the Laws, addressing himself) We have given you birth, nurtured you, educated you, we have given you and all other citizens a share of all the good things we could. Even so, by giving every Athenian the opportunity, after he has reached manhood and observed the affairs of the city and us the laws, we proclaim that if we do not please him, he can take his possessions and go wherever he pleases. Not one of our laws raises any obstacle or forbids him, if he is not satisfied with us or the city, if one of you wants to go and live in a colony or wants to go anywhere else, and keep his property.

If Socrates really did think that he had come to an impasse in which an Athenian law outlawed philosophizing, can we really be so certain that he would stay on and philosophize in Athens anyway, flagrantly violating such a law? Might he try instead to find some way to satisfy his divine mission to philosophize elsewhere? He makes it sound as if his mission is in Athens, but perhaps before we decide that Socrates' very plain expression of commitment to legal obedience must have some flexibility for exceptions, we should at least consider whether the necessary flexibility might rather be found in where his mission might be carried out. At any rate, we think that it is very risky to feel any confidence in coming to conclusions about completely imaginary cases to which we require our texts to apply, and we do not propose to take this particular line of inquiry any further than this. Instead, we believe a more promising avenue is still open to us if we go back now to the *Crito*.

6.4.6 Interpreting the *Crito*: Citizen, Child, and Slave

We have found little reason for thinking that Socrates invites speculation about exceptions to his "obey or persuade" doctrine, and yet such exceptions are required by all of the interpretations we have considered thus far. We have also seen, however, that the texts do not—or at least do not directly—require us to look for such exceptions, for it turns out that the main text usually cited as giving an example of such an exception, Socrates' hypothetical vow to disobey his jurors if they told him to stop philosophizing (**T6.17**), does not refer to anything that could qualify as a disobedience of legal authority. Accordingly, we have shown that our texts do not—or at least do not directly—conflict, once we understand that the relevant conflict would require us to ignore or misunderstand Athenian law. If this is right, we might suppose that there is no further scholarly reason for counting "the *Apology-Crito* problem" as a problem any longer, for as we have stressed, removing the appearance of textual conflict is one of the main goals of scholarship, and we seem to have done that now. But it might seem that the interpretation we have advanced so far solves the original problem only by creating *another* conflict in the texts, this time, with the texts in which Socrates seems absolutely and exceptionlessly to require one never to do injustice. Surely, one might argue, Socrates does not think that the laws of Athens are morally perfect. After all, if he did think this, the "persuade" part of "obey or persuade" would be empty—there would never be any need to persuade the laws that they are making some unjust command if they never commanded injustice! Remember what we found Socrates saying in the very first quote we included in this chapter.

T6.1 *Apology* 31c–32a (repeated in part):

> Do not be angry with me for speaking the truth; no man will survive who genuinely opposes you or any other crowd and prevents the occurrence of many unjust and illegal happenings in the city.

Notice that Socrates talks here about "unjust *and* illegal happenings in the city," as if there were two distinct possibilities—including unjust things that happen to be legal (even if they should not be). But the interpretation we have developed so far recognizes no exceptions to the doctrine that one must obey legal authority: Only if one can persuade the authority to change the relevant command can one not obey the command. But this *does* amount to a doctrine of "obey or obey," since even the "persuade" option requires obedience. The problem is this: What if one tries to persuade legal authorities to change some unjust command and then fails? If disobedience is *never* acceptable, according to "obey or persuade," then is it not simply inevitable that there will be some cases in which a citizen is required to obey an unjust law or legal command? And if this is so, it would seem that Socrates' philosophy contains a conflict after all: According to "obey or persuade," one would have to obey an unjust law or legal command; and according to the absolute prohibition against doing injustice, one would have to *disobey* an unjust law or legal command. If we are going to count ourselves as solving the notorious "*Apology-Crito* problem," then, we must also find our way out of *this* apparent conflict.

Let us return to the *Crito*. Recall that just before he announces his "obey or persuade" doctrine, Socrates compares citizens to children and slaves:

T6.19 *Crito* 50e–51b (repeated):

(Socrates speaking on behalf of the Laws, addressing himself) . . . could you [Socrates], in the first place, deny that you are our offspring and slave, both you and your forefathers?

Let us take the comparison Socrates is urging on us seriously, for a moment, and ask what justice requires of children and slaves. It may perhaps help us understand Socrates' point if we remind ourselves that slaves were the personal property of their masters and regarded as possessions, like tools or farm animals or even like extended parts of their masters' bodies.[26] Bearing this in mind, consider what we would say about some case in which a slave is commanded by the master to do something that the slave perceives as unjust. Imagine that the slave actually protests the master's command but is rebuffed: The master remains unmoved and reiterates the command. Then imagine that the slave goes ahead and obeys the master's command. Who is to blame for the wrong that is done? If we think of slaves as farm animals, tools, or extensions of their masters' bodies, the problem of whom to blame for something a slave does, under the master's command, does not arise at all: Oxen or shovels or hands (say) are not capable of moral action, and hence they never merit moral praise or blame. Thus, when we do place blame for what is done with any of these things, we blame the ox's owner, the one who used the shovel in the wrong way, the one whose hand did the evil deed.

If we now make such cases parallel to those involving children, as above, we can see that Plato must have had only very young children in mind—at such an age where we do not see them as having any moral capacity apart from what they get from their parents. A father tells his four-year-old to throw a stone through a neighbor's window. The child senses that this is a bad thing and tries to convince the father of this. The father shrugs the child's arguments off and repeats the command, and the child then, reluctantly but dutifully, throws the stone and shatters the window. The neighbor is incensed; justifiably so. But who is to blame? The father did not throw the stone, but from the moral point of view, he might as well have done so, because the wrong and the responsibility for it are exactly the same as if he has actually thrown the stone himself; perhaps it is even worse than this, for by making his child his instrument, he may reasonably be thought to have compounded the wrong. The point for our issue, however, is this: No one would blame the child for obedience in such a case. As paradoxical as it may seem, we might even praise the child for obedience in the same breath that we condemn the father for requiring it in such a case.

Socrates' comparison of citizens to children and slaves only makes sense if he thinks that "obey or persuade," in all these cases, is *morally* required. But to take this view, Socrates must believe that a citizen who acts under the command of legal authority cannot be assigned the blame for the commanded act. Instead, just as it does with children and slaves, the blame must fall on the commanding authority or authorities. If so, it follows that the apparent conflict between Socrates' prohibition of injustice and his "obey or persuade" doctrine does not arise, for Socrates can consistently say that one who obeys *even an unjust command or law* will not commit injustice, any more than would a child or slave in obeying parent or master, respectively. In the case of commanded injustice where the one commanded is so completely subservient to commanding authority, the one commanded is relieved of responsibility; the wrong that is done is only and completely the responsibility of the commander. This does not mean that the one commanded is relieved of *all* responsibility. It would be consistent, for example, for Socrates to hold the citizen responsible for failing to attempt persuasion in cases in which the citizen perceives some legal command as unjust. His doctrine, after all, is "obey or persuade," and it is not implausible for Socrates to think that it is every citizen's duty to attempt always to persuade everyone all the time that the best course of action (politically and otherwise) is the just course of action. Thus, we do not need to think of him as someone who endorses "blind" or unquestioning obedience.

Even if we try to solve the problems we have confronted in this section in the way that we have suggested, a last challenge is still possible. As we noted in the Introduction, the *Principle of Charity* requires that, all other things being equal, interpretations should always seek to provide views that are interesting and plausible. It might now be argued that the view this interpretation attributes to Socrates is a view so morally flawed that he cannot reasonably be said to have held it. Such a critic might now say that it is hardly charitable to Socrates to make him out to endorse blind obedience to legal authority, including the commission of the most unspeakable atrocities. Few modern moralists would be willing to say that citizens have *no* responsibility for what they do under legal command; compliance with evil laws and legal authorities is itself morally culpable, we tend to believe.

But in trying to assess this criticism of the view we are attributing to Socrates, it is important to understand that the *Principle of Charity* requires, first, that those who think our interpretation is unacceptable owe us a *more plausible* account of what the relevant texts say about Socrates' view of who should have the final authority to make the kinds of laws and judgments that the state must make. Second, the *Principle of Charity* does not requires that we *always* choose the interpretation that best fits our own convictions. Again, this principle guides us, "all things being equal," between two competing interpretations. If the *Principle of Textual*

Fidelity clearly favors one of the competing interpretations, then that is the interpretation we should choose, even if it attributes to the author a view that we ourselves find implausible or even repugnant. Finally, we must also keep in mind that Socrates thinks that the citizen's obligation to obey the law applies only in those legal systems in which one has the opportunity to leave if one thinks that one will not persuade and remains convinced that the law in question is unjust. His view, then, simply does not apply to those who were ordered to kill innocent people during either Stalin's or Hitler's reign of terror, for example. Socrates' concern, obviously, is that a state without such authority will not survive as a state, and Socrates does, after all, temper the authority he gives to the state by insisting that it must be reasonably open to persuasion and must permit its citizens the right to leave if they cease to be satisfied with the state. If we are right, any citizen would be culpable for participating in legally commanded injustice were that citizen to refuse to leave even though recognizing that the state's command required a terrible injustice and that the appropriate legal authorities were simply not open to persuasion about what justice requires. Once we see that Socrates' view of obedience to the law is governed by these limitations, it does not seem to us, at least, so clearly implausible to grant to such a state the final authority to command obedience and to pass final judgments, in cases where the state and one of its citizens have conflicting views of what is right.

6.5 Socrates on Just Punishment

6.5.1 Several Problems Involving Punishment

As we said in Chapter 5, Socrates is what is called an "intellectualist," that is, one who believes that everyone does what they do because of what they *believe* to be good or beneficial for them. Because he also believes that it is never good or beneficial for anyone to do wrong, then all who do wrong do so involuntarily in some sense, for all wrongdoers act in a way that is actually contrary to what they really want. Accordingly, one would expect that there would be no room at all for punishment in Socratic philosophy, unless by "punishment" we really mean simply some form of instruction.

But in a number of places in Plato's early dialogues, Socrates seems to think that some punishments, whose educational merits are, at best, unclear, are entirely appropriate, for example, whipping, bondage, imprisonment, fines, and even death.

T6.23 *Crito* 51b (immediately follows **T6.19** and immediately precedes **T6.16**):

(Socrates speaking on behalf of the Laws, addressing himself) You must either persuade it [the city] or obey its orders, and endure in silence whatever it instructs you to endure, whether blows or bonds . . . .

T6.24 *Gorgias* 480c (part of a longer quote given as **T5.24**):

(Socrates speaking) And if his unjust behavior merits flogging, he should present himself to be whipped; if it merits imprisonment, to be imprisoned; if a fine, he should pay it; if exile, to be exiled; and if execution, to be executed.

Socrates characterizes many of these forms of punishment as evils—at least if they were to be inflicted upon him (see *Apology* 37b-e). Yet Socrates is also well known for claiming that one ought never to return harm for harm or evil for evil.

T6.20 *Crito* 49d-e (repeated) (see also *Republic* 1.335b-e):

SOCRATES: One should never do wrong in return, nor injure any man, whatever injury one has suffered at his hands.

If such penalties are evils, how can he advocate the use of such punishments? There appears, then, to be a tension between the intellectualism so evident in the *Apology,* for example, and the forms of punishment Socrates elsewhere endorses, and there also appears to be a tension between his claims that one should never harm another, his calling certain forms of punishment harms, and his endorsing such punishments nonetheless as (at least in some cases) just.

6.5.2 Socratic Intellectualism

In the middle part of the *Gorgias,* Socrates discusses with Polus whether the tyrant, who can do whatever he thinks is best, is truly powerful. As the argument unfolds, Socrates and Polus agree that we always pursue what we think is best for us and so never pursue what we think is bad for us. Because all desire is desire for what is good for us (*Gorgias* 468a-b), however, it follows that all wrongdoing is the product of a *cognitive failure.* As we showed in Chapter 5, this is why Socrates does not accept the possibility of *akrasia,* the doing of what one recognizes as something bad or harmful to oneself.

Wrongdoing, then, must be a product of false belief: When we do wrong, we do so by *believing* that what we do is good for us when, in fact, it is not. If we supposed that what we were doing was actually *bad* for us (as it is, according to Socrates, when it is wrong or evil), then we would not do it. But not everyone is a good judge of what they are doing, and not everyone realizes that all evil is bad for those who do it. There can be two different forms of misapprehension in wrongdoing, therefore: (1) One could do the wrong or evil, thinking that it was right or good, or (2) one could do the wrong or evil, falsely supposing that the wrong or evil would benefit the wrongdoer. In the first case, plainly the best corrective would be to show the wrongdoer that the action *really is* wrong or evil. Such individuals need the sort of moral education by which they can become better judges of right and wrong. Clearly, the best way to do this would be to lead the "examined life," as Socrates exhorts his jurors to do in the *Apology* (38a [**T2.20**]). In the second case, the best corrective would be to show the wrongdoer how and why it is that wrongdoing is injurious to the wrongdoer, just as Socrates does with Polus in the *Gorgias*. Thus, for both of the possible sorts of ignorance and error, which are the root causes of all evil, the best corrective would appear to be to subject the wrongdoer to Socratic examination, or something like it.

6.5.3 Punishment, Wrong, and Harm

Socrates' intellectualism, by itself, does not entail any specific theory of punishment. Intellectualism is compatible with the view that correction of the wrongdoer is not the only—or even the main—purpose of punishment. But a Socratic theory of punishment can be inferred from his conviction that it is always wrong to harm anyone, even in return for harms done to one (see **T6.20**). From this, it follows that it is not open to Socrates to accept any form of punishment that is harmful to the one punished. Protecting society from the wrongdoer, then, cannot be a sufficient excuse for harming the wrongdoer. But exactly which forms of punishment does this prohibition rule out?

To answer this question, we need to look more carefully at Socrates' conception of what constitutes harm. As we said in Chapter 4, Socrates was an eudaimonist—one who connects the conception of goodness with *eudaimonia* (happiness). In the same chapter, we also showed that Socrates believed that the only absolute good—the only good that is sufficient for happiness—is good activity. That which is conducive to vice and evil activity Socrates regards as evil and harmful precisely because it promotes wretchedness, the opposite of happiness. But the specific way in which Socrates conceives of these linkages implies that many of the things normally regarded as goods can, when employed by vice or ignorance, actually be evils or harms. The good looks of the confidence artist or the robust health of the thief are examples. It would be better *for them* to be ugly, poor, or physically disabled. Of course, it would be far better for them to aspire to virtue. But it would nonetheless not count as a harm if some suffering that frustrated and diminished their ability to carry out their wrongdoings befell them.

We are now in a position to see why what might well count as a wrong or harm for one person would not be a wrong or harm for another: Penalties such as imprisonment or banishment, which would take away one's freedom of movement or expression, for example, would be wrong and harmful to Socrates because his actions aim at what is good for himself and his fellow Athenians. This is why he says such punishments would be evil and harmful (to him) in the *Apology*. To one who perpetrates evils, however, the loss would be right and beneficial—not only for those who might otherwise become victims of the prevented evils but also for those who would otherwise have done the evil deeds. This, then, is how we can resolve the apparent tension between Socrates' sometimes calling such punishments harmful and sometimes saying that they are just, despite his claim that we should never do what is harmful. Imprisonment and banishment that we inflict upon the wicked are not only not wrongs; they are not harms to them.

6.5.4 Punishment and Faulty Beliefs

Our explanation of Socrates' view of punishment is, however, still incomplete. What we have said so far works only for punishments that serve as a kind of restraint, that prevent the wrongdoer from pursuing further evils. Socrates also endorses certain forms of punishment—for example, whipping—whose purpose is surely not simply to *restrain* the wrongdoer. How, then, could Socrates endorse such a variety of painful, alienating, disabling, and even fatal catastrophes as just punishments?

Socratic intellectualism allows for wrongs to be committed for a variety of reasons. In particular, an agent might fail to calculate correctly the consequences of some action, so that the resulting harm is unintended. In cases such as these, education is appropriate insofar as the harm results from some lack of understanding. Education, not punishment, also seems the appropriate means of correction where the agent falsely supposes that the wrongdoing is actually an example of doing what is right. This is the sort of case Socrates has in mind when in the cross-examination in the *Apology*, he ridicules the folly of Meletus's position. As Socrates says there, it is not the business of the law to bring people to court for such errors but, instead, to provide them with instruction and admonishment in private (*Apology* 26a).

But there is yet another cause of wrongdoing, in which the wrongdoer plainly does intend to wrong and harm some other or others, but this time the error is in thinking that by doing so, the wrongdoer expects some personal advantage. What would lead anyone to commit such an error?

Presumably, the error here, if we are to preserve Socrates' simple motivational theory and intellectualism, must lie in how such individuals would conceive of what benefit consists in, for plainly they do not think that benefit is only to be achieved through morally good actions. The error here, then, comes from either failing to see that moral virtue is a good or regarding other things as goods whose value outweighs moral virtue. But as we saw in Chapter 3, this is precisely the point Socrates is making in the *Euthydemus* (278e–281e) when he says that he regards none of the things so many other people take to be goods—health, wealth, pleasure, and honor—to have any intrinsic value of their own.

As we said in Chapter 4, Socrates is convinced that there is only one thing that is good in itself: virtue (see *Euthydemus* 281d-e). Only this invariably benefits its possessor; these other so-called goods benefit only those who are already good and actually harm the wicked. Because all desire is desire for benefit, it follows that all wrongdoers have benefit as their aim. In other words, wrongdoers who take wealth or honor or pleasure to be more important than moral goodness mistakenly suppose that ill-gotten wealth or honor or pleasure will benefit them.

If the connection wrongdoers make between wrongdoing and its perceived benefits for them were severed, they would no longer be attracted to wrongdoing. Given their own conception of benefit, then, if they were to become convinced that a given sort of wrongdoing would bring them just the opposite of what they were seeking, that sort of wrongdoing, at least, would no longer be attractive to them. As such, we can now see why whipping, imprisonment, banishment, and fines or property confiscations could count to Socrates as appropriate things to do to certain wrongdoers. Such penalties benefit the wrongdoer insofar as they change the cognitive connection the wrongdoer makes between wrongdoing and benefit. Such corrections are, admittedly, incomplete—surely, it would be better if the wrongdoer came to hold the right general view of what benefit consists in and the essential place virtue occupies within that conception. But it should now be clear that *precisely because* the wrongdoer undergoes a favorable shift in beliefs about what particular acts will produce benefit, the wrongdoer's improvement, produced by the pain of the whip, can be understood in the intellectualist way Socratic philosophy requires.

6.5.5 Punishment and Cure

To the extent that the wrongdoer no longer believes wrongdoing provides any personal benefit, the wrongdoer is clearly made better off, for to that extent there is no longer any motivation to engage in wrongful acts. But this cannot be the only reason Socrates thinks that the infliction of pain as a punishment is a good for the wrongdoer. To begin with, there is a straightforward sense in which such a person is not *cured*. In the *Gorgias*, Socrates seems to think that effective punishment does much more than merely increase the likelihood that the wrongdoer will find vicious activity unprofitable. At the end of his discussion with Polus, Socrates reviews why we value the crafts of moneymaking, medicine, and justice.

T6.25 *Gorgias* 478a-b (see also 479c-d):

> It's financial management, then, that gets rid of poverty, medicine that gets rid of disease, and justice that gets rid of injustice and indiscipline.

He then goes on to explain why punishment, rather than escape from punishment, makes the wrongdoer better off.

T6.26 *Gorgias* 478d (part of longer quote at **T4.21**):

> SOCRATES: Now, wasn't paying what's due getting rid of the worst thing there is, corruption?
>
> POLUS: It was.
>
> SOCRATES: Yes, because such justice makes people self-controlled, I take it, and more just. It proves to be a treatment against corruption.

As long as criminals continue to hold the wrong conception of the good, their reluctance to engage in vice is contingent upon the strength of the link between the punishment received and the belief that future vicious actions will result in punishment. We can easily imagine situations, for example, robbers who have been beaten severely for thievery but who have excellent reason on a particular occasion to think they will not get caught—in which it would only be rational, given a misguided conception of the good, for the previously punished criminal to revert to wrongdoing. One might argue, of course, that this would only show that the original punishment was not sufficiently severe and that had it been so, the criminal would never characterize any situation as one in which it would be beneficial to do wrong. But this is possible only if we think that punishment can instill an irrational fear of getting caught that is always sufficient to deter robbers. This may be a possibility in some accounts of human motivation, but not in Socrates'.

Until recently,[27] the only answer to this problem that had ever been offered relied upon acceptance of a claim made by a number of scholars that an important development in Plato's theory of human psychology occurs within the *Gorgias*.[28] In the discussion with Polus, we are told, Socrates acknowledges only one form of motivation: desire for benefit (and, presumably, the corresponding aversion to harm). But scholars have claimed that by the time we find Socrates speaking with Callicles, a distinct and independent form of motivation—one that is independent of the desire for benefit—is introduced, namely, desire for pleasure (and the corresponding aversion to pain). In this view, Plato is, in the *Gorgias*, working his way toward the *even more* complex psychology of the *Republic* and *Phaedrus*, which provide *three* distinct forms of motivation: the rational; the *thumotic*, or spirited; and the appetitive. In this view, Plato's Socrates abandons his denial of *akrasia* in the last part of the *Gorgias*. But by relying on this alleged change in the conception of motivation between the discussion with Polus and the one with Callicles, one might find a solution to the problem of punishment by supposing that Socrates would regard painful forms of punishment as effective precisely because they work on the wrongdoer's independent desire for pleasure. In this view, the work these forms of punishment performs is to "chasten" the wrongdoer's appetite for pleasure by bringing it under the control of the rational motivational element.

One serious disadvantage this view confronts is that it characterizes the *Gorgias* as advancing two distinct and incompatible theories of human motivation without any clear signal from Plato that there has been such a shift. This seems obviously to run afoul of the *Principle of Charity* as well as the *Principle of Textual Fidelity*, both of which tell us not to accept inconsistencies, if at all possible. But even if Plato did introduce a new theory of motivation in the discussion with Callicles, it does not help us to solve the problem of punishment. Socrates' endorsement of various punishments occurs within argumentative contexts in which the alleged new theory of motivation has not yet been introduced. Recall that the problematic passages with which we began this section (**T6.23** and **T6.24**) occur in the *Crito* and in the discussion with Polus, which comes *earlier* in the *Gorgias* than the discussion with Callicles, in which the "new theory" is allegedly introduced.

What such interpretations miss is that what the supposedly "new" theory "introduces" in the discussion with Callicles has actually been there all along. Socrates' view, we claim, is *not* (what we regard as the absurdity) that human beings have no motivational impulses other than the desire for benefit but that such impulses (which Socrates typically refers to as "appetites") can never lead one to act *against* what one thinks is best for one.[29] But even if scholars have seen a "development" in Plato's philosophy where there was none, they were not entirely wrong about how to explain Socrates' acceptance of painful forms of punishment. Let us now see why this is so.

6.5.6 *"Treating" Appetites*

Before we ask how punishment could *cure* the wrongdoer, we would do well first to ask why Socrates thinks that wrongdoing is always bad for the wrongdoer. If we are right, Socrates thinks that all vice manifests itself in the pursuit of the wrong sort of pleasures. As we have seen, people may have unruly appetites for pleasure and aversions to pain, but for these to lead to wrongdoing, according to Socrates' intellectualism, the wrongdoers must take such pleasures to be beneficial, thinking that by having them they will be better off.

Socrates' frequent comparisons between vice and disease suggest that he thinks that just as illness inflames the body and keeps it from functioning well, so vice infects the soul and keeps it from performing its function of ruling and taking care of things well (*Republic* 1.353e). For Socrates, vice consists, in part, in a false belief that certain sorts of pleasures ought to be pursued. Such a disastrous belief may be formed by listening to the advice of the wrong people. But if coming to acquire the worst sort of character were *only* a matter of taking the wrong people too seriously, Socrates would have no reason to say, as he does in the *Gorgias,* that vice, unless treated, becomes "protracted and cause[s] [one's] soul to fester incurably" (480b).

We can explain the notion of a belief becoming ingrained in this way, however, if we think that Socrates takes the satisfaction of certain appetites, in the *experience* of some pleasures, to have the power (1) to cause the agent to think that pleasures of that sort are good and (2) to hinder, or even to prevent, rational thinking about the agent's good. Because of (2), Socrates thinks of harmful pleasures as like intoxicants. If this is right, the danger of listening to Callicles is very real, for he may well persuade one to believe that a life of violent pleasures is good. And because of (1), as we would expect, it is even worse to act on Callicles' advice and to partake of the most violent pleasures.

Our appetites provide us with basic motivations required for our survival, and so they are not all bad. But our appetites do not at all distinguish between which of their satisfactions will genuinely benefit us and which will actually do us damage. All of us, Socrates thinks, have appetites for pleasures—including pleasures we should not pursue. The more one actually does pursue and experience *these* pleasures, the more one's appetites for such pleasures become accustomed to achieving their goals and the more these appetites will come to demand and expect satisfaction. In short, "feeding" such desires nourishes them and makes them stronger. On the contrary, however, if these appetites are controlled at all times, their power to interfere with our "better" judgment will be minimized. If they are allowed to grow out of control, however, the only solution is to do whatever will help us to shrink them again.

If punishment is actually to cure one who has become convinced that the most violent pleasures are beneficial, then the wrongdoer must first be freed from the intoxicating control that pleasure—and the engorged appetites that aim at pleasure—has. Socrates might well suppose that the infliction of pain for an act of wrongdoing has precisely that effect, as a kind of antidote. Thus, after suffering the pain of the whip, for example, the thief's appetites for the wrong sorts of pleasures are diminished, having been "chastened" by the sharp pain of the whipping, and the thief will be left better able to consider soberly whether stealing is the better course to take. Of course, here we must ask why Socrates would count this as a "cure," for surely the thief may still expect to profit from future thefts and that circumstances might be such that future punishments, regardless of how severe, are worth the gain.

If we recall Socrates' analogies between medicine and physical training, on the one hand, and legislation and criminal justice, on the other (see *Gorgias* 517e ff.), we can see that Socrates does not have to suppose that the "cure" of punishment must make the wrongdoer into someone who never could or would perform injustice again. To do this, punishment would have to make the wrongdoer virtuous. But Socrates has seen no evidence that even the most assiduous pursuit of philosophical inquiry, as he conceives it, can achieve that.

In our view, Socrates thinks that punishment "cures" the wrongdoer and "rids" the wrongdoer of injustice, not by replacing the wrong conception of the good with another conception, or even by replacing the wrong conception with the belief that it is wrong, but rather by loosening the grip harmful pleasure has on the soul, thereby creating an openness to question what the good is. If so, when Socrates says that punishment should "cure," he does not mean that the wrongdoer is somehow indemnified against all future wrongdoing. There is nothing about the experience of the pain of punishment that would prevent thieves from listening to and being persuaded by someone to think that they should engage in crime again. Moreover, even after punishment, wrongdoers will continue to have appetites for pleasures, the satisfaction of which would, once again, drive them back to unreflective lives of vice. But unless they suffer the pain of paying the penalty for their crimes, they will continue to think, mindlessly, that the pleasures for the sake of which they steal are the greatest benefits they can possess. If this is correct, by seeing how to solve the problem of punishment in Socratic philosophy, we learn something of the first importance about Socrates' conception of vice. Vice is not merely false belief about how to live; it is false belief about how to live that is itself not entirely open to reason. And at the root of this evil, we find our appetites, which seek pleasure and are indifferent to what is really good for us. Unless, therefore, we are diligent in controlling them, we run the risk that our ability to make rational judgments will be damaged or lost.

We can now see how Socrates could distinguish between those who have mistakenly *concluded* that a life of vicious pleasure seeking is good but who have not yet experienced such pleasures, and those who have experienced violent pleasures and, thus, mindlessly think they are good. The former may yet be improved by Socratic discussion, for even if their appetites have been quickened, they have not yet begun to wreak their havoc on these individuals' ability to reason. In discussion with Socrates, therefore, they may yet reach another, more judicious, conclusion on the basis of what seems most reasonable to them. Those who have already given themselves to the wrong pleasures, however, need punishment, for only the pain of punishment for a specific act of wrongdoing will free them from the control of their bloated appetites. It also follows from this account that not even Socrates is immune from being taken over by his appetites, should he, through some mistake or misfortune, happen to experience an especially intoxicating pleasure. Socrates is wiser than others in part because he realizes that such pleasures are to be avoided. But even this "human wisdom" gives him no special power to overcome pleasure's effect on the mind once the mind has experienced it. Only the kind of knowledge he lacks could give him full indemnity against such a disaster.

The souls of those who merely believe violent pleasure is good are in danger: Given this false belief about the good, it is likely that they *will* pursue violent pleasure, with the subsequent result that their appetites will be further inflamed, to the point that they will no longer be capable of reflecting soberly about the good. Nevertheless, until actually sampling the pleasure they value, such people are still capable of being ruled by reason and, hence, are not yet vicious. The souls of vicious people, by contrast, already suffer the harm of being incapable of reasoning about how best to live, a harm to which those with mere false beliefs about the good are, as yet, merely liable. Corporal punishment may help vicious people to see why they should not pursue violent pleasure. But because corporal punishment actually frees the soul from the distorting influences of the appetites, it removes the harm that constitutes vice and so can truly be said to cure the wrongdoer.

Finally, it does not follow from the fact that punishments aim at curing the one punished that they can always do so. Pleasures may vary in the effect they have on the souls of those who experience them. Moreover, if left untreated, the hold that pleasure has over a soul will tend to grow increasingly strong. If so, that grip may become so strong that no amount of punishment can release the soul. Such people are doomed mindlessly to remain convinced that the wrong sort of pleasure is good; no amount of pain can make them question their conviction. In effect, their appetites have so maimed their reason that they have become irremediably irrational.

We are now in a position to see why, in the great myth at the end of the *Gorgias*, Socrates states that punishment can be appropriate in either of two ways.

T6.27 *Gorgias* 525b-d:

It is appropriate for everyone who is subject to punishment rightly inflicted by another either to become better and profit from it, or else to be made an example for others, so that when they see him suffering whatever it is he suffers, they may be afraid and become better. Those who are benefited, who are made to pay their due by gods and men, are the ones whose errors are curable; even so, their benefit comes to them, both here and in Hades, by way of pain and suffering, for there is no other possible way to get rid of injustice. From among those who have committed the ultimate wrongs and who because of such crimes have become incurable come the ones who are made examples of. These persons themselves no longer derive any profit from their punishment, because they're incurable. Others, however, do profit from it when they see them undergoing for all time the most grievous, intensely painful and frightening sufferings for their errors, simply strung up there in the prison in Hades as examples.

There is tragedy here: For some, the only benefit of proper punishment must go to others, not to the wrongdoers themselves. Even the gods cannot correct what has been ruined by the most egregious wrongs.

Proper punishment for wrongdoers, then, falls far short of what we might conceive as an ideal. Those punished may be made better, but much of what made them go wrong to begin with may remain with them. In endorsing punitive "corrections," Socrates did not imagine that such corrections were ideal solutions to the problem of wrongdoing. But his dim view of even his own powers of correction, which aimed for higher goals, left him, realistically, with no clearly better option than those the state legally provided. His pessimism about the human capacity to be made good, however, was not worsened or confused by a contradictory position regarding the goals and methods of criminal corrections. Punishment was, for Socrates, not a problem for the coherence of his views but a necessary feature of the human condition. It was an instrument for the remediation of evils, which, though they could become ruinous, could never, in all likelihood, be wholly eliminated.

Notes

1. There is considerable scholarly disagreement as to whether these two texts are referring to the same time of office—and even to the same specific events during that time of office. For discussion and references to the various positions, see Brickhouse and Smith (1989), 176, n. 29, and 179, n. 32.

2. We use the plural, "factions," because we are persuaded by historians' arguments that identify several different factions in Athenian politics during Socrates'

time, and not just two: an oligarchic one and a democratic one. Strauss (1987), for example, counts "a minimum of six leading factions" in Athens, which would align and disalign on different issues. Scholars who have counted Socrates as an oligarchic sympathizer have not, to our knowledge, ever tried to tie Socrates to any of these actual factions. Without evidence for such a tie, however, we find the claim that Socrates was a significant figure in Athens's factional politics highly speculative, at best. Our argument in this section, at any rate, will show that the evidence generally cited for this speculation does not, in any case, support the speculation.

3. This is the principal thesis of I. F. Stone (1988). Although the book is beautifully written throughout, we believe it is confused about the relevant evidence. Although we do not detail these mistakes in what follows, we should point out here that Stone has not been alone in making the mistaken assessments he did. In many instances, he actually repeats (unknowingly) errors made by a number of more careful scholars before him.

4. It is easy to forget, however, how *exclusive* it was nonetheless: Of something over a quarter of a million people living in Athens during this period, perhaps only 10 percent were included in Athens's political life at any time. The remainder were citizen women (who were granted special protections and privileges but could not actually participate in government) and children, resident foreigners, and slaves of both sexes, all of whom were entirely excluded.

5. Socrates is referring to the fact that "near the end of his life, they [the Athenians] voted to convict Pericles of embezzlement and came close to condemning him to death, because they thought he was a wicked man, obviously" (*Gorgias* 516a).

6. The title of the council's presiding committee member.

7. See Bury (1962), 328.

8. Chroust (1957), esp. 69–100.

9. See Brickhouse and Smith (1994), 174, n. 85.

10. For a detailed but perhaps not entirely reliable account of Alcibiades' infamous career, see Plutarch's *Lives of the Noble Greeks and Romans, s.v. Alcibiades.*

11. Critias is characterized as the leader in Xenophon's account (see *Hellenica* 2.3–4; *Memorabilia* 1.2); in Aristotle's *Politics* (V.5.4.1305b26), it is Charicles who was the leader. That Critias was one of the Thirty Tyrants, in any case, is certain.

12. Mogens Herman Hansen, in a letter to N. D. Smith, February 2, 1987.

13. As Loening (1981) puts it: "It was permissible to cite the conduct of an individual under the oligarchy at scrutinies and other processes in the way of character evidence" (vii; repeated verbatim on 203). The same can be said for anything alleged to have occurred prior to 403 B.C.

14. See MacDowell (1978), 176.

15. Ibid., 174.

16. In the bracketed phrase here and immediately following, we modify the translation that appears in Cooper (1997), which has the text say "we acquit you." The Greek does not explicitly state that the jurors would release Socrates, in this hypothetical case, by legal acquittal. Accordingly, we prefer our version, which is as vague as the Greek.

17. Woozley (1979).

18. Kraut (1984).

19. The translation in Cooper (1997) translates the word here (*doulos*) as "servant," but the Greek word is plainly the word for "slave"—a "servant" might be a hired helper; the word here is for a human being who is *owned* by another.

20. Kraut (1984), 94–103.

21. Santas (1979).

22. Allen (1980).

23. Those interested in such details should see Brickhouse and Smith (1989), 142–147, and (1994), 144–145.

24. See, for example, Kraut (1984), 13–15, responding to our first argument on this issue.

25. Brickhouse and Smith (1989), 152.

26. For such comparisons, see: Aristotle, *Politics* 1.2.1252b12 (slave and ox); Aristotle, *Politics* 1.5.1254b24–26 (slaves like nonhuman animals); Aristotle, *Politics* 1.4.1253b29–32 (tools); Aristotle, *Politics* 1.6.1255b11–12 (parts of their masters' bodies).

27. Brickhouse and Smith (1997b).

28. See Cornford (1933), 306–307 and 317; Irwin (1977), 123–132, and (1979), note on 507b, 222; Kahn (1988), 89–90; Mackenzie (1981), 161–162.

29. In what follows, we modify the account we gave in Brickhouse and Smith (1997b), in accordance with a change in our views about Socratic motivation (see Chapter 5, n. 15).

Suggested Readings

On Socrates' Political Affiliations

As we noted in this chapter, the most recent, and by far the most widely read, argument that Socrates engaged in seditious partisan political agitation—and that this was the most significant motive for his being brought to trial—is advanced in Stone (1988). A far more plausible appraisal, which nonetheless concedes that Socrates might have been *perceived* in this way, is offered in Vlastos (1994b; revised from an article published in 1983). We offer several different arguments against this view in Brickhouse and Smith (1989) and (1994), and Vlastos also changed his mind about the motivation for the charges against Socrates, which Vlastos later understood as religiously motivated (see Vlastos [1991], ch. 6).

On Socrates and Obedience to the Law and the Apology-Crito Problem

We reviewed each of the major interpretations of the *Apology-Crito* problem. A. D. Woozley (1979) argues that Socrates would authorize disobedience to the laws only when such disobedience served as a kind of persuasion, as in civil disobedience. According to Kraut (1984), Socrates would allow that as long as one was willing to make a serious effort at persuading the laws why disobedience was right, one could disobey legal authority. Santas (1979) argues that only divine authority can override the citizen's duty to obey the law, whereas Allen (1980) argues that the duty to obey the law is always conditional on the prior duty always to do only what is just. Our argument in Brickhouse and Smith (1989) is that Socrates would not recognize any conflict between the duty to obey the law and his duty to philosophize, on the ground that he counted his duty to philosophize as falling under the legal requirement to act piously. In Brickhouse and Smith (1994), we argue that there could be no conflict between obedience to the law and the requirement that one always act justly, on the ground that Socrates would always conceive of obeying the law as an example of acting justly. In the case where the law itself commanded some injustice, the law (or those who passed it) would be guilty of the injustice, whereas the obedient citizen would act justly by obeying the law and thus be blameless for the injustice commanded by the unjust law.

Socrates on Punishment

The rejection of retaliation in the early dialogues is discussed in Vlastos (1991). The comprehensive attempt to treat Plato's philosophy of punishment in a systematic way is Mackenzie (1981). Brickhouse and Smith (1997b) review the relevant literature on this topic and attempt to show why Socrates' theory of motivation not only is compatible with his endorsement of corporal punishment but, in fact, requires it. The view we present in this chapter, however, modifies the account we gave in that article (see this chapter, note 29, and Chapter 5, note 15).

Socrates and Religion

7.1 Survey of the Problems
Assessing Socrates' Religion

We close this book with a chapter on what is to modern readers the most alien aspect of Socrates' philosophy—his religious views. Socrates, recall, died almost four hundred years before the birth of Jesus and nearly a millennium before the birth of Muhammad. Of course, Hinduism, Judaism, and Buddhism all existed in Socrates' time,[1] but for obvious reasons, he was completely ignorant of these religions. The religion that Socrates knew well—Greek paganism—was very unlike any of the major religions we know today. Polytheisms continue to exist, of course, though they are not common in the West, but Greek religion was unusual in other ways as well. On the one hand, religion pervaded almost every aspect of Greek life, both public and private; on the other, there were no sacred texts, no dogmas, no organized churches, and no priestly class whose positions within the religion privileged their religious beliefs or interpretations in any way, and hence, no canonical theology. Instead, Greek religion consisted in several groups of often conflicting and constantly changing practices or rituals, both civic and private,[2] as well as in various stories (which we now call Greek mythology) about ancestors, heroes, gods, and other divinities of various sorts (including a full complement of monsters, local spirits, and a bewildering variety of other minor divinities)—stories that continued to be invented, told, and embellished upon, throughout Greek history. Moreover, the relationships between these stories and the rituals practiced by the ancient Greeks are extremely difficult to pin down. Often, the stories seem to have been invented long after the rituals had come into the culture, perhaps to explain rituals whose original meanings or significance had long ago been lost, yet somehow the rituals had been continued. Most scholars now believe, accordingly, that the heart of Greek religion is to be found not in Greek mythology but rather in the rituals and religious practices themselves, which are often only loosely and somewhat problematically tied to that mythology. Moreover, because these rituals and practices had both public (civil or legal) and private (familial or personal) elements—which in many ways have significantly different characteristics and which often seem entirely unrelated to one another—it ends up being very difficult to make any general claims about the religion of Socrates' culture and thus very difficult for us to situate Socrates within that religion in any very precise way. Most of all, it is difficult for us to assimilate the religion in which we must situate Socrates to modern religious views.

Because Greek religion is so alien to the modern mind, the ways in which religion influenced Socrates' life and philosophy are also likely to be very difficult for us to assess and are, in any case, almost surely inapplicable to our own lives or philosophical concerns. But just as religion and philosophy overlap (and sometimes conflict) today, so they did in Socrates' culture and time, and this is why no account of Socratic philosophy could be complete without a careful look at the connections between Socrates' philosophy and his religion, especially at those points where we might find influences passing from one to the other.

Perhaps the most obvious and troubling connection of this sort is in the undisputed historical fact that Socrates was tried, convicted, and executed on a religious charge: impiety. The three specifications of this charge were that he did not believe in the gods the city believed in, that he invented new spiritual things, and that he corrupted the young.[3] As we said in the last chapter, until recently, most scholars believed that the religious charges did not really represent the real motives behind the prosecution, which, we used to be told, were primarily political. If this were right, we would not need to worry about the actual charges, what they might have meant, or whether they fit the actual case of Socrates, for the answer to all such questions would simply be that they provided a conveniently legal mask to conceal the real motives. But we argued in the last chapter that this "political" interpretation of the trial has now largely been abandoned by scholars, because the evidence has recently been shown not to support this interpretation. This, however, requires us to return to the religious nature of the charges and to take them seriously. But what did they mean, and what could have motivated them, and why were a majority of the jurors convinced that Socrates was guilty of them?

One could, of course, be prosecuted for some private religious outrage or sacrilege, but in fact absolutely every one of our ancient sources tells us that it was Socrates' philosophizing that led, in some way, to his legal troubles. For this reason, if we are to comprehend the events that brought his life to an end, we must look as closely as we can at what Socrates' religious views and practices were and at how these might have been represented in his philosophizing, in order to see what might have aroused his prosecutors to bring him to trial and his jurors to find him guilty. We review the claims made by several scholars in recent years, suggesting that Socrates was, in some sense, guilty of the religious charges against him, but we argue that these claims are unpersuasive. Instead, we argue in Section 7.2 that Socrates' life ended because of a certain "tragic irony" of the sort we described in Chapter 2: Despite having been one of the foremost (and most formidable) intellectual opponents of the Sophists, in his prosecutors' and jurors' eyes, he was identified with the very philosophers he so vigilantly opposed and was tried, convicted, and condemned to death for beliefs that he did not hold, for teachings that he never endorsed and always rejected. His was an odd example, then, of mistaken identity—the Athenians correctly saw that he was an intellectual, but they were entirely mistaken about what sort of intellectual he was.

Socrates' prosecutors charged him with disbelief in the gods recognized by the Athenians, whereas in his defense, Socrates retorts that the very activities that led to his being charged with such disbelief were, as a matter of fact, nothing less than a mission given him by the god of Delphi. Accordingly, far from being impious, Socrates characterizes his life as a model of piety! But many of those who have read Socrates' account of the origin of this religious mission he claims to have been given by the god have not been satisfied with it, because Socrates seems to have concluded that he was given a mission without actually ever receiving anything that looks like a command from the god. We take this problem up in Section 7.3.

Plato and Xenophon both agree that the second specification of the impiety charge against Socrates—that he invents new spiritual things— was motivated by Socrates' claim to having had "since childhood" (*Apology* 31d) what he calls a "divine sign," or "voice," or even more vaguely, a "divine something"[4] (the Greek here would be *daimonion ti*, which is why scholars now customarily call this "divine something" "Socrates' *daimonion*") that would oppose him when he was about to do something wrong (*Apology* 31d, 40a, 40c). The questions here are obvious, and we discuss them in Section 7.4: What was this thing, and did this very spooky and irrational-sounding phenomenon have any influence on Socrates as (otherwise, at least) a man of reason?

We end the book with a look at what Socrates thought about how life comes to an end, in death. On the one hand, in his defense speech, Socrates claims that it is "the most shameful ignorance" to think that one knows what death holds (*Apology* 29b), and yet elsewhere we find him making very confident claims about what the afterlife is like, claims that seem to lend some support for various ethical views he holds. We consider in Section 7.5 whether this represents a tension in his philosophy, and whether his views of the afterlife cohere with his own other religious positions and with those of his culture and time.

7.2 Was Socrates Guilty?

7.2.1 The Complete Goodness of the Gods

Plato's dialogues only rarely depict Socrates directly discussing theological matters, and though Xenophon's works are much more detailed in this area, we argue (in Chapter 1) that we are on safer ground if we stick to Plato as our best source. But in Plato, we do nonetheless find several mentions of the gods and of Socrates' beliefs about the gods, and from these, a number of important—and a few troubling—consequences can be shown to follow. Perhaps the one tenet of "Socratic religion" that seems the most secure is that the wisdom lacking in human beings may be found in divinity.

T7.1 *Apology* 23a-b (partially repeats **T2.18**):

> (Socrates speaking) What is probable, gentlemen, is that in fact the god is wise and that his oracular response meant that human wisdom is worth little or nothing.

Notice that it is *human* wisdom, the wisdom Socrates says he possesses (*Apology* 20d-e), that is worth "little or nothing." The wisdom that the god has, however, is something entirely different from this relatively worthless "human wisdom."

Further evidence for the vastly superior wisdom of divinity, in Socrates' view, comes from the way in which he understands the activity of his *daimonion*, about which we have more to say in Section 7.4. For now, however, it is worth noting that Socrates thinks that the source of this "something divine," as he often calls it,[5] has a kind of knowledge that is vastly superior to his own and—because Socrates is the "wisest of men," according to the Delphic oracle given to Chaerophon (*Apology* 20e–21a)— vastly superior to anything he has ever encountered in a human being.

T7.2 *Apology* 40a (part of longer quote at **T7.19**):

> (Socrates speaking) At all previous times my familiar prophetic power, my spiritual manifestation, frequently opposed me, even in small matters, when I was about to do something wrong . . . .

In this passage, Socrates admits that he "frequently" finds himself in the position of being "about to do something wrong," despite a lifetime of devotion to what he calls "the examined life" (at *Apology* 38a), despite

being a man who (in contrast to so many of his fellow Athenians) has always sought to care about wisdom, truth, and the best possible state of
his soul, by attaching the highest value to the most important things
and much lower value to inferior things, caring always most of all for
virtue (see *Apology* 29e–30a, 31b) and fighting for justice (see 32a), despite having lived a life dedicated to his service to the god (see *Apology*
22a, 23b, 28e–29a, 30e–31b, 33c). Socrates seems to do his best, in his defense to the jury, to leave them with the strongest possible impression
that he is a man who is as concerned as a man can be never to do anything wrong, and yet the frequent activity of his *daimonion* shows that,
nonetheless, he continues to find himself all too often on the verge of
doing some wrong he had not recognized as such (or he would not be
on the verge of doing it and in need of the *daimonion's* admonition).
Given Socrates' low opinion of human wisdom, perhaps his proneness
to error should come as no great surprise. But even if Socrates does not
say that his *daimonion* detects and warns Socrates *every time* he is about
to make such errors, at least it does this "frequently." Accordingly, the
source of this daimonic warning plainly knows vastly more than this
"wisest of men" about what is right and what is wrong, and it is vastly
superior to Socrates in recognizing what Socrates should and should
not do. Here again, then, we find that Socrates appears to be deeply
committed to the enormous intellectual superiority of divinity, relative
to human beings.

The superiority is not simply intellectual. Recall that in Chapter 5, we
discussed how it was that Socrates believed wisdom is wisdom of what is
good and evil and that anyone who knows what is good will desire it.
The wisdom of the gods is not different in kind. This, then, explains why
Socrates, in a rare direct and unconditional affirmation, proclaims that the
gods are not only our greatest benefactors but also our *only* benefactors.

T7.3 *Euthyphro* 15a:

> SOCRATES: But tell me, what benefit do the gods derive from the gifts
> they receive from us? What they give us is obvious to all. There is
> for us no good that we do not receive from them . . . .

Moreover, Socrates' gods are so concerned about human morality that
they take care of good people, both in life and in death.

T7.4 *Apology* 41c–d (= **T4.10**):

> (Socrates speaking) You too must be of good hope as regards death, gentle-
> men of the jury, and keep this one truth in mind, that a good man cannot be
> harmed either in life or in death, and that his affairs are not neglected by the
> gods.

7.2.2 Socrates and the Myths

To those of us raised in religions that affirm the omnibenevolence of God, Socrates' commitment to the complete goodness and benevolence of the gods does not seem at all strange. But in the context of ancient Greece, such beliefs appear not to have been the norm. Anyone with even the most superficial acquaintance with Greek mythology will be able to recall several popular myths in which the gods do *not* qualify as all and only good and do *not* act in ways characterized by benevolence toward human beings. Recall (from our discussion in Chapter 4) that Socrates equates evils with harms. Greek mythology is simply *full* of stories in which human beings are harmed by various gods, where the harms done show not even the slightest regard for human welfare, morality, or divine concern never to harm a good man, either in life or in death! Socrates' conception of fully moral gods, then, is not consistent with much of Greek mythology.

Could this, then, be what got Socrates into so much legal trouble? One passage from Plato's *Euthyphro* seems to suggest that this was precisely the issue behind the prosecution of Socrates.

T7.5 *Euthyphro* 5a:

> SOCRATES: Isn't this, then, why I am a defendant in this case, because I find it hard to accept things like that being said about the gods, and it is likely to be the reason why I shall be told I do wrong?[6]

In this passage, Socrates himself seems prepared to accept that he was prosecuted for his moralizing beliefs about the gods. Not surprisingly, then, several recent scholarly analyses of the trial have suggested that it was Socrates' unusual religious beliefs that led to the first two specifications of the charge of impiety:[7] that he "did not believe in the gods the state believes in" and that "he invented new spiritual things" (see *Apology* 24b). Certainly, this makes better sense than the view we reviewed in the last chapter, which held that the trial was motivated by political rather than primarily religious considerations. Moreover, it makes the case against Socrates seem to be a continuation of the sort of concern we find expressed in Aristophanes' *Clouds*, which portrays Socrates as an intellectual innovator whose views would essentially eliminate divine agency from the list of explanations it was reasonable to give about natural phenomena. Insofar as natural events bring harm to human beings and Socratic morality forbids ever harming another, the gods cannot be invoked as the causes of natural disasters, it would seem. At any rate, it might appear that Socrates' gods are simply incompatible with too many of the religious beliefs of his contemporaries.

The worry is put in a particularly forceful way by the late Gregory Vlastos:

> What would be left of her [Aphrodite] and of any of the other Olympians if they were required to observe the stringent norms of Socratic virtue which require every moral agent, human or divine, to act only to cause good to others, never evil, regardless of provocation? Required to meet these austere standards, the city's gods would have become unrecognizable. Their ethical transformation would be tantamount to the destruction of the old gods, the creation of new ones—which is precisely what Socrates takes to be the sum and substance of the accusation at his trial.[8]

7.2.3 Socrates' Own Detailed Account of Why He Was Brought to Trial

As tempting as this understanding of why Socrates was tried for impiety has been to scholars, we believe that it cannot be squared with the account that Plato's Socrates actually gives for the prejudices against him, from which he claims the charges directly arose. At 18a in the *Apology*, Socrates takes up the specific question of what it was that led to his prosecution, and his answer makes it clear that it is because he has been assimilated to the "atheistic" Sophists and nature-philosophers, which has nothing at all to do with moralizing the gods.

T7.6 *Apology* 18b-c:

> (Socrates speaking) There have been many who have accused me to you for many years now, and none of their accusations are true. These I fear much more than I fear Anytus and his friends, though they, too, are formidable. These earlier ones, however, are more so, gentlemen; they got hold of most of you from childhood, persuaded you and accused me quite falsely, saying that there is a man called Socrates, a wise man, a student of all things in the sky and below the earth, who makes the worse argument the stronger. Those who spread that rumor, gentlemen, are my dangerous accusers, for their hearers believe that those who study these things do not even believe in the gods.

Socrates could not be clearer about what he takes to be the problem here: He faces a long-standing prejudice that has characterized him as an *atheist*. This trial, he makes plain, is not about how or how much he may or may not have sought to moralize the Greeks' conceptions of the gods; it is, rather, about his alleged disbelief in gods altogether. But if this is right, what are we to make of **T7.5**? We think that what Socrates is suggesting to Euthyphro there is not that it was his refusal to believe in immoral gods that got him into trouble but the fact that people who heard of his rejection of immoral gods and fanciful stories from the poets drew the mistaken inference that Socrates did not believe in the gods at all. That is, because Socrates could not believe stories about the gods such as the ones that so captivate Euthyphro, people thought Socrates had to be an atheist. Thus, as he says in **T7.7**, it is the belief that he is an atheist that got him into trouble.

T7.7 *Apology* 19a-d (immediately precedes **T2.7**):

(Socrates speaking) Let us then take up the case from the beginning. What is the accusation from which arose the slander in which Meletus trusted when he wrote out the charge against me? What did they say when they slandered me? I must, as if they were my actual prosecutors, read the affidavit they would have sworn. It goes something like this: Socrates is guilty of wrongdoing in that he busies himself studying things in the sky and below the earth; he makes the worse into the stronger argument, and he teaches these same things to others. You have seen this yourself in the comedy of Aristophanes [the *Clouds*], a Socrates swinging about there, saying he was walking on air and talking a lot of other nonsense about things of which I know nothing at all. I do not speak in contempt of such knowledge, if someone is wise in these things—lest Meletus bring more cases against me—but, gentlemen, I have no part in it, and on this point I call upon the majority of you as witnesses. I think it right that all those of you who have heard me conversing, and many of you have, should tell each other if anyone of you has ever heard me discussing such subjects to any extent at all. From this you will learn that the other things said about me by the majority are of the same kind.
    Not one of them is true.

Socrates makes it very clear here exactly what he takes to be the dangerous slanders that have led to his being on trial. Notice that he says nothing about moralizing the gods or about any supposedly odd religious positions he may or may not have taken in his philosophizing. The issue, as he puts it at least, is that he has been characterized as a word-twisting Sophist and nature-philosopher.

Moreover, it is not just Socrates who characterizes the problem this way. Later, when Socrates interrogates Meletus, the actual author of the charge against him, Socrates gives his accuser a golden opportunity to endorse the exact understanding of the charges that some recent scholars have urged, but Socrates' actual accuser, at any rate, rejects this understanding out of hand and instead makes it very plain that he wishes the jury to find Socrates guilty *of being an atheist*.

T7.8 *Apology* 26b-c:

(Socrates speaking) Nonetheless tell us, Meletus, how you say that I corrupt the young; or is it obvious from your deposition that it is by teaching them not to believe in the gods in whom the city believes but in other new spiritual things? Is this not what you say I teach and so corrupt them?

(Meletus replies) That is most certainly what I do say.

Then by those very gods about whom we are talking, Meletus, make this clearer to me and to the jury: I cannot be sure whether you mean that I teach the belief that there are some gods—and therefore I myself believe that there are gods and am not altogether an atheist, nor am I guilty of that—not, however, the gods in whom the city believes, but others, and that this is the charge against me, that they are different. Or whether you mean that I do not believe in gods at all, and that this is what I teach to others.

This is what I mean, that you do not believe in gods at all.

Socrates and Meletus agree on at least one thing, then, and both "testify" against the modern view that it was Socrates' moralizing theology that got him into trouble. Socrates and his accuser both plainly and unambiguously state that the charge, instead, was that Socrates was an atheist. Of course, Socrates and Meletus completely disagree on the matter of Socrates' guilt: Socrates denies it, whereas Meletus affirms it.

Perhaps what has led so many modern commentators to take a wrong turn here is, in a way, a certain charitable view of the ancient Athenians. Surely, one might argue, Socrates' democratic countrymen did not make it their business to prosecute people on charges for which there is not a trace of credible evidence! And one might well find it quite difficult to see how or why anyone would ever suppose that Socrates was simply an atheist, whereas we can all agree that there is solid evidence that Socrates engaged in a certain degree of moralizing theology. By arguing that this was the concern that was really at work in the charge against Socrates, modern commentators might suppose they make better sense of the prosecution's case and why that case was successful against Socrates. This understanding of the charge, of course, also supports these commentators' own endorsements of the Athenian jurors' final verdict.[9]

Such commentators, however, simply miss the fact that Socrates actually *does* explain—in what we think is an entirely plausible way—how and why he ended up with the sort of reputation he was given in the slander that he was an atheist. According to Socrates, his public examinations of other people led to their being publicly humiliated, and for this, they hated him. But when asked to explain why they hated Socrates so much, they found the standard slanders against intellectuals a convenient way of explaining Socrates' motives without revealing their apparent confusion. Socrates begins, as we have seen, by articulating what he takes to be the most dangerous slanders against him, and he flatly denies these (see **T7.6** and **T7.7**). But he realizes that simple denial cannot, by itself, allay the prejudices that have dogged him for decades.[10] Thus, he imagines that his jurors immediately confront his denials by challenging him to explain how else he could have gained such a terrible—and, it turns out, fatally dangerous—reputation.

T7.9 *Apology* 20c-d:

> (Socrates speaking) One of you might perhaps interrupt me and say: "But Socrates, what is your occupation? From where have these slanders come? For surely if you did not busy yourself with something out of the common, all these rumors and talk would not have arisen unless you did something other than most people. Tell us what it is, that we may not speak inadvisedly about you."

Socrates confronts this challenge directly, and once again, if he thought moralizing the gods had contributed to his predicament, now would be the obvious time to raise the issue, the time for him to argue that his views did not make him guilty of the charges. Instead, Socrates tells the famous story of the Delphic oracle to Chaerophon, which led Socrates to his life of questioning others and exposing their ignorance. This frequently leaves his "victims" feeling humiliated, and all too many of them are ready after that to slander Socrates. But then what about the final specification of the charge, that Socrates "corrupts the young"? Socrates answers this question, too, as he concludes his account of the origins of the slanders he faces and how these relate to the charges he now faces.

T7.10 *Apology* 23c-d (repeats then continues **T2.23**; immediately follows **T2.19**):

> (Socrates speaking) Furthermore, the young men who follow me around of their own free will, those who have most leisure, the sons of the very rich, take pleasure in hearing people questioned; they themselves often imitate me and try to question others. I think they find an abundance of men who believe they have some knowledge but know little or nothing. The result is that those whom they question are angry, not with themselves but with me. They say: "That man Socrates is a pestilential fellow who corrupts the young." If one asks them what he does and what he teaches to corrupt them, they are silent, as they do not know, but, so as to appear not at a loss, they mention those accusations that are available against all philosophers, about "the things in the sky and things below the earth," about "not believing in the gods" and "making the worse the stronger argument."

What, then, about this business so many contemporary commentators think must have been the *real* motive behind the prosecution and behind the jurors' conviction of Socrates for impiety—that is, Socrates' allegedly impious moralizing of the gods? Socrates concludes this portion of his defense not only without mentioning this issue but by insisting that he has told the truth, the *whole* truth, and nothing but the truth, hiding nothing at all from his jurors' view, and he claims that no matter how much his jurors might investigate his claims—now or later—this is all they would find.

T7.11 *Apology* 24a-b:

> That, gentlemen of the jury, is the truth for you. I have hidden or disguised nothing. I know well enough that this very conduct makes me unpopular, and this is proof that what I say is true, that such is the slander against me, and that such are its causes. If you look into this either now or later, this is what you will find.

According to Socrates, he has been prosecuted as an atheist because he has acted in ways that have left many of his fellow Athenians feeling publicly humiliated, and for this, they hated him. As a result, they assume, uncritically, that the standard slanders must be true and that Socrates is an immoralist, a Sophist, and an atheist. Many younger Athenians, moreover, finding Socrates' examinations of others amusing to witness, have gone on to try their own hands at examining others and have themselves managed to humiliate even more of those who would prefer to pretend to be wise than to admit their own ignorance. And for this, Socrates has become known as a corrupter of youth. That is the whole story, according to Socrates, and there is nothing more to say about how he came to have such a bad reputation.

We find nothing about this story impossible or even implausible, so we are not at all inclined to side with other interpreters whose views have the consequence that Plato has Socrates simply lying to his jurors when he explains the troubles he faces in this way and proclaims very plainly to have "hidden or disguised nothing." If we recall the *Principle of Textual Fidelity*, we will see that this text directly contradicts scholars' claims that there is more to the story than Socrates tells here. And if we recall the *Principle of Interpretive Adequacy*, we will reject turning Plato's Socrates into a liar simply to preserve a favored interpretation. Like it or not, Socrates' explanation of his predicament leaves no room for interpretive speculation about the *real* motives behind the prosecution.

7.3 Socrates' "Mission"

7.3.1 Socrates and the Oracle

Socrates' defense, as we have seen, is at least in part based on his strange claim to have been given a religious mission to philosophize in Athens by the god of Delphi, Apollo. Socrates repeatedly claims to his jurors that his philosophizing is no less than a mission on the god's behalf, a "service" (*Apology* 22a, 23b, 30a) or "obedience" (*Apology* 29d) to the god. On the one hand, one can readily see how this claim could serve well in a defense against the charge of impiety—far from being impious, the very activities that got Socrates in all this trouble were undertaken as part of a religious mission, ordered by Apollo himself! There could be no reasonable doubt that Socrates believes in "the gods the city believes in" if his whole life is a devotion to the god of Delphi—to whom the Athenians regularly turned through oracles for advice in private and civic matters.

However, despite the importance of this link to the logical basis of the defense speech Plato gives to Socrates, several scholars have despaired of making any sense of the oracle story that would support Socrates' claim to have a mission in Athens.[11] The problem is that on the basis of the way Socrates relates the oracle story to his jurors, it does not seem at all clear exactly how Socrates managed to get a divine commandment to philosophize out of what happened between Chaerophon and the oracle. Chaerophon, recall, went to the oracle and asked if anyone was wiser than Socrates. The oracle gave the answer "No." This simple denial by itself, surely, cannot reasonably be understood as a command for Socrates to philosophize, especially when the oracle's answer was not even given to Socrates himself! But the same can be said of what Socrates gets later on, from his attempts to interpret the oracle. He goes around to those he supposes have some wisdom that he lacks and finds out either that they have no such wisdom—and are unaware of their lack—or that they have some minor wisdom (in the case of the craftsmen) but that this minor wisdom is outweighed by their far more significant ignorance of what Socrates calls "the most important things"—an ignorance, again, of which these people are also ignorant. In comparison to all these people, Socrates, who finds himself woefully deficient, discovers that his deficiency is, indeed, still less than all of those he questions.

But even in Socrates' reaching the conclusion that the god has shown him that he is the wisest of men only because others are doubly ignorant—not only ignorant in the way that he is but also ignorant of their ignorance, whereas he is only singly ignorant—it does not seem to modern readers at all obvious how this conclusion reveals that the oracle has given Socrates a *mission*. However, Socrates later expands significantly upon this version of the origin of his mission (which would attribute it exclusively to the oracle given to Chaerophon).

T7.12 *Apology* 33c (immediately follows **T2.13**):

To do this has, as I say, been enjoined on me by the god, by means of oracles and dreams, and in every other way that a divine manifestation has ever ordered a man to do anything.

This explanation of Socrates' mission is supplemental to the oracle to Chaerophon, since it also mentions dreams and oracles (in the plural), as well as "every other way" in which humans can receive divine commands. Nonetheless, it seems clear from the way Socrates tells the oracle story that he intends it to explain the origin of his mission. But it has not seemed evident to modern scholars exactly what feature of the story allows Socrates to draw this conclusion.

7.3.2 Stated and Unstated Explanations

Let us try to be clear about what is needed here. What exactly does it mean to insist that at least *some* explanation of Socrates' mission must be given within the oracle story itself? Does it mean that Socrates must explicitly state all of the premises and explanatory factors involved in the full explanation? Surely not—since many features of the explanation that Plato's Socrates gives, we might assume, would be so evident and uncontroversial to the intended audience that they would not need to be tediously enumerated and explicated. But exactly *who was* the intended audience of Plato's Socrates? If we read the *Apology* as if *we* were the intended audience, then much more needs spelling out (given the strangeness of the religious context of the story itself, from our point of view) than what is needed if we take the intended audience to be an Athenian jury in 399 B.C. or, for that matter, a general Athenian readership (or members of Plato's Academy) some few years after the historical trial. The question is this, then: To whom is the oracle story supposed to serve as an explanation of Socrates' mission, and what could they be reasonably expected to be prepared to supply to the explanation presumptively?

The view we prefer is that the oracle story alone would suffice as an explanation to ancient Greeks, about whom Socrates or Plato could make certain assumptions, which would not necessarily apply to later non-Greeks—including modern scholars and readers. Chaerophon asked if anyone is wiser than Socrates, and the answer he was given was simply "No." Unless we add something that will take us from here to something in the form of a command, it is obvious there can be no connection between the oracle and Socrates' mission. But would this logical gap have been a problem for the ancient Greeks, as it has been for so many modern interpreters? We doubt it. The Delphic oracle did not divulge information simply to show off Apollo's infallible discernment. An ancient Greek who is given shocking and on the face of it incredible information by the god would be bound by piety immediately to make every attempt to understand that information. As Socrates puts it early in the oracle story and long before he has managed to interpret the oracle, he felt compelled "to attach the greatest importance to the god's oracle," and he explains that it was because he recognized this compulsion that he "examined its meaning" despite the "sorrow and alarm, that I was getting unpopular" as a result of what he was doing in this search (*Apology* 21e). The very *fact* of the oracle, and its shocking content, was enough to make it clear to Socrates that the god had some "business" to be done. Similarly, once Socrates had come to understand what the oracle meant, he realized that what the god had revealed was that something was terribly amiss in Athens: All around Socrates were proud men who supposed that they knew all they needed to know about what Socrates calls "the most important things" (*Apology* 30a; see also 22d), when in fact (as the god had shown Socrates) they were culpably ignorant of such things. Socrates does not go on to assert as a premise in his explanation that the god does not reveal such things to people simply to edify them but instead to get them to do something about the problems the god has revealed. This would go without saying to an ancient Athenian, but since it is not explicitly said in the oracle story given by Plato's Socrates, as we noted above, some scholars have faulted the explanation that Socrates offers for his mission.

Our claim is simple. Considering the religious presuppositions of Socrates' or Plato's intended audiences eliminates the problem without much need for philosophical or interpretive subtlety: Socrates gets his mission from the oracle to Chaerophon out of his assumption that the god does not reveal shocking problems to mere mortals without also assigning to those mortals to whom the problems are revealed the task of doing whatever they can to fix the problems revealed to them. Socrates does not need to state this assumption to his jurors (or Plato, to his readers) for the simple reason that they could be expected to share it as uncontroversial and obvious.

7.4 Socrates' *Daimonion*

7.4.1 *"Socrates Invents New Divinities"*

Socrates' account of his mission, which he says is what led to the dangerous prejudices against him, however, does not help to explain the second of the three specifications of the charge of impiety, nor is it intended to do so. Recall that the single charge of impiety was formally explained in three specifications: (1) Socrates does not believe in the gods the city believes in; (2) Socrates invents new divinities; and (3) Socrates corrupts the youth.[12] In his account of the prejudices against him, Socrates has given an explanation of the first and third of these specifications: The first one amounts to an accusation of atheism—which, as we showed in T7.8, is corroborated by Meletus himself; the third specification derives partly from the (false) perception that he teaches his "atheism" to the young and partly from his young followers' attempts to imitate his examinations of the pretentious ignorant. But what is this business of "inventing new spiritual things"? The explanation of this specification of the charge, happily, is easy to come by.

T7.13 *Apology* 31d (part of longer quote at **T6.1**):

> (Socrates speaking) I have a divine or spiritual sign which Meletus has ridiculed in his deposition. This began when I was a child. It is a voice, and whenever it speaks it turns me away from something I am about to do, but it never encourages me to do anything.

Socrates' understanding that it is his claim to have this "divine or spiritual sign" that led to the charge that he "invents new spiritual things" is also supported by the character Euthyphro, in the dialogue named after him.

T7.14 *Euthyphro* 3a-b:

> EUTHYPHRO: [. . .] Tell me, what does he [Meletus] say you do to corrupt the young?
>
> SOCRATES: Strange things, to hear him tell it, for he says that I am a maker of gods, and on the ground that I create new gods while not believing in the old gods, he has indicted me for their sake, as he puts it.
>
> EUTHYPHRO: I understand, Socrates. This is because you say that the divine sign keeps coming to you. So he has written this indictment against you as one who makes innovations in religious matters, and he comes to court to slander you, knowing that such things are easily misrepresented to the crowd.

The very same explanation of the charge of "inventing new spiritual things" is also given by Xenophon (*Apology* 12).[13]

7.4.2 How Did Socrates' Daimonion *Influence Him?*

There is undoubtedly something quite spooky about Socrates claiming to have some "spiritual voice" that has come to him since he was a child. Nor does it help matters when later Socrates allows that this "voice" is not some rare aberration in an otherwise normal experience of life.

T7.2 *Apology* 40a (repeated; part of longer quote, given in **T7.19**):

> At all previous times my familiar prophetic power, my spiritual manifestation, frequently opposed me, even in small matters, when I was about to do something wrong . . . .

Such claims are enough to make modern interpreters, many of whom wish to characterize Socrates as the Father of Western Rationalism, squirm in their seats. The more adventurous of these interpreters, accordingly, have sought to explain away Socrates' strange experience by understanding it as nothing more than the experience of something like a "rational hunch" or "intuition" of the sort that often comes to those of us who spend so much time in thought and argument.[14] But Socrates is fully capable of describing *this* sort of experience without resorting to uncanny talk about signs and voices (see, for examples, *Lysis* 218c and *Phaedrus* 242d—**T7.18**, below), and all of the ancient sources show no hesitation in counting Socrates' "sign" as a religious phenomenon. Thus, however skeptical *we* might be about Socrates' understanding of the strange experience that he has, we must face the fact: As devoted to rational argument as he was, Socrates also supposed that he often received a "divine sign," which would "frequently" oppose him, even in small matters, when he was about to do something wrong.

Rather than simply close our eyes to this uncomfortable fact about Socrates, we would do better to try to assess the extent to which this "irrational" feature of his experience might influence (or simply subordinate) Socrates' justly famous commitment to rational thought and argument. A recent (and somewhat comforting) attempt to "restore" Socrates' rationality, in the face of this undeniably uncanny phenomenon, has been offered by Gregory Vlastos, who insists that Socrates would subject anything and everything—including most especially religious phenomena—to the rigorous standards of rational justification before giving any credence to it or, indeed, before even counting it as having any specific content for belief at all.

> So all he [Socrates] could claim to be getting from the *daimonion* at any given time is precisely what he calls the *daimonion* itself—a "divine sign," which allows, indeed, requires, *unlimited scope for the deployment of his critical reason* to extract whatever truth it can from these monitions. Thus, without any recourse to Ionian *physiologia*, Socrates has disarmed the irrationalist potential of the belief in supernatural gods communicating with human beings by supernatural signs. His theory both preserves the venerable view that mantic experience is divinely caused *and* nullifies that view's threat to the exclusive authority of reason to determine questions of truth or falsehood. . . . [T]here can be no conflict between Socrates's unconditional readiness to follow critical reason wherever it may lead and his equally unconditional commitment to obey commands issued to him by his supernatural god through supernatural signs. *These two commitments cannot conflict because only by the use of his own critical reason can Socrates determine the true meaning of any of these signs.* (Vlastos [1991], 170–171; emphasis in original)

Vlastos finds compelling reason for this interpretation from his understanding of what Socrates says about himself in the *Crito*.[15]
T7.15 *Crito* 45b:

SOCRATES: . . . [N]ot only now but at all times I am the kind of man who listens only to the reason[16] that on reflection seems best to me.

Of course, Socrates does not make this claim to secure the contrast Vlastos gets out of it, between reason and a "sign" from his *daimonion;* instead, Socrates proclaims his fidelity to reason to contrast his own trust in ratiocination over the commands or opinions of "the many," for whose views Socrates customarily shows no concern in any case. We should therefore ask how or if the passage from the *Crito* applies to Socrates' conception of his *daimonion*. Let us begin with Vlastos's claim that Socrates "requires unlimited scope for the deployment of his critical reason to extract whatever truth it can" from his "sign."

7.4.3 *Reason Versus the* Daimonion

It would be nice to know more precisely what the modality of Socrates' sign actually was. Socrates himself, in Plato's dialogues, says only that it is a "sign" or a "voice" (see **T7.13**). But the question is not exactly *what* Socrates experienced as his "sign"; the question is whether Socrates required "critical reason" to extract whatever truth Socrates got from his "sign." At least this much seems obvious, however: Socrates' *daimonion* does not supply Socrates with "propositions" or "arguments" but only with this: "[W]henever it speaks it turns me away from something I am about to do, but it never encourages me to do anything" (from **T7.13**). One who understands Socrates as wholly committed to the idea that only critical reason is persuasive might try here to supply some version of critical reason to allow Socrates even to derive the idea that it is *opposition* that he always gets from his *daimonion*. But one would attribute such a view to Socrates with no support from the text, for all we find him claiming in the text is that he has had this "sign" since childhood and that it has always only opposed him and never led him. We might be able to concoct some speculative history, in which Socrates at first has no understanding of what the "sign" meant and was only able to figure this out for himself by the use of "critical reason." But the very idea that the *daimonion* is something he has experienced since he was a child would seem to undercut the plausibility of such a speculative history, since (especially in ancient Greek culture) it seems unlikely that children would ever be counted as adequately skilled practitioners of critical reason. It seems more likely, therefore, that the message of opposition given by the "sign" is not, from Socrates' point of view, a matter of interpretation by critical reason but simply something so obvious that it is clear merely in the nature of the experience itself. Perhaps the "voice" Socrates hears simply says "No!" or "Stop!"

But one might argue that Socrates would still have to apply critical reason to determine from what the "voice" is telling him to desist. Thus, for example, Socrates recounts one episode with his *daimonion* in the *Euthydemus*.

T7.16 *Euthydemus* 272e–273a:

> SOCRATES: I was sitting by myself in the undressing room just where you saw me and was already thinking of leaving. But when I got up, my customary divine sign put in an appearance. So I sat down again, and in a moment the two of them, Euthydemus and Dionysodorus, came in, and some others with them . . . .

Even if we suppose that Socrates experiences his *daimonion* as unambiguously signaling opposition, how would he know exactly what it was opposing in this case—was it simply opposing his standing up? Or was it perhaps opposing his plan to leave? Or was there perhaps something else it was opposing, which Socrates was not even thinking about but which the *daimonion* wished to prevent Socrates from doing or suffering? There is not much information, then, in some unspecified and unexplained opposition from Socrates' *daimonion*. Plainly, the *daimonion* requires something more for Socrates to come to understand its opposition. Could this be critical reason?

In the episode Socrates recalls in the *Euthydemus* (**T7.16**), however, Socrates leaves the impression that he simply desists from his plan to leave, with no clue as to why his *daimonion* had opposed his plan, and waits until some others come in, greet him, and engage him in conversation. The reader is left with the impression that the *daimonion* opposed Socrates' leaving so that he could engage in the subsequent conversation, though this inference is never explicitly drawn. If so, then it was not Socrates' critical reason that revealed the *daimonion*'s intentions. Socrates simply sat down again and waited for something to happen that might explain his sign's sudden appearance.

In other episodes, moreover, the actual content of the *daimonic* opposition seems to be even clearer—and, hence, even *less* susceptible to free interpretation by Socrates' critical reason.

T7.17 *Phaedrus* 242b–c:

> SOCRATES: My friend, just as I was about to cross the river, the familiar divine sign came to me which, whenever it occurs, holds me back from something I am about to do. I thought I heard a

voice coming from this very spot, forbidding me to leave until I made atonement for some offense against the gods.

In this case, the voice not only opposes his plan to cross the river but also stipulates what Socrates must do before he does. The specific "offense against the gods" is not explicitly identified, but Socrates goes on to explain how he is able to identify what this offense was.

T7.18 *Phaedrus* 242c-d (continuing **T7.17**):

SOCRATES: In effect, you see, I am a seer, and though I am not particularly good at it, still—like people who are just barely able to read and write—I am good enough for my own purposes. I recognize my offense clearly now. In fact, the soul too, my friend, is itself a sort of seer; that's why, almost from the beginning of my speech, I was disturbed by a very uneasy feeling, as Ibycus puts it, that "for offending the gods I am honored by men." But now I understand exactly what my offense has been.

PHAEDRUS: Tell me, what is it?

SOCRATES: Phaedrus, that speech you carried with you here [one by Lysias, to which Socrates will refer again in a few lines]—it was horrible, as horrible as the speech you made me give.

PHAEDRUS: How could that be?

SOCRATES: It was foolish, and close to being impious. What could be more horrible than that?

PHAEDRUS: Nothing—if, of course, what you say is right.

SOCRATES: Well, then? Don't you believe that Love is the son of Aphrodite? Isn't he one of the gods?

PHAEDRUS: This is certainly what people say.

SOCRATES: Well, Lysias certainly doesn't and neither does your speech, which you charmed me through your potion into delivering myself. But if Love is a god or something divine— which he is—he can't be bad in any way; and yet our speeches just now spoke of him as if he were. That is their offense against Love.

Here, we certainly do find something like critical reason being used to discover the specific offense for which Socrates had to atone before he could cross the river. However, we find that critical reason is not employed by Socrates until he is induced to engage it by his "uneasy feeling" as he gave his offensive speech, followed by his sign's refusal to allow him to leave until he had atoned for the offense his soul had already sensed. Rather than finding itself in charge of this situation, Socrates' reason finds itself in the service of nonrational signals, whose content and significance is already largely determined. Reason, in this case, then, enjoys nothing like "unlimited scope" for its "deployment," as Vlastos has claimed. Socrates was not at liberty, surely, to deploy his critical reason in such a way as to conclude that he had *pleased* the gods and could now cross the river with their delighted blessings!

The *Phaedrus*, however, is not among the group of Plato's early dialogues, so we might regard the way in which this episode is presented with some suspicion. If we turn to what we find Plato's Socrates saying about his *daimonion* in the *Apology*, however, we will also find good reason to suppose that Socrates did view his *daimonion* with a degree of assurance and acceptance that was prior to and thus independent of the application of critical reason. Let us first return to what Socrates says about his *daimonion* when he tells his jurors about what he takes to be the significance of its *failing* to make an appearance.

T7.19 *Apology* 40a-b:

> (Socrates speaking) At all previous times my familiar prophetic power, my spiritual manifestation, frequently opposed me, even in small matters, when I was about to do something wrong, but now that, as you can see for yourselves, I was faced with what one might think, and what is generally thought to be, the worst of evils, my divine sign has not opposed me, either when I left home at dawn, or when I came into court, or at any time that I was about to say something during my speech. Yet in other talks it often held me back in the middle of my speaking, but now has opposed no word or deed of mine.

Plainly, the *daimonion* cannot explain *why* it is not making its appearance (at least without *making* an appearance to do so!), so Socrates must use his reason to understand why the *daimonion* has suddenly become so reticent in this situation. But the obvious inference is the one that Socrates makes—in this situation, he has done nothing wrong and has undertaken to say nothing from which the *daimonion* needed to restrain him.

Socrates' characterization of how frequently and in what situations the *daimonion* had made its appearance in the past, however, is very revealing: He says it would often come even in the middle of something he might be saying. What should we suppose was Socrates' reaction to the *daimonion*'s sudden opposition in such cases? Did he simply ignore it and continue with what he was saying, or did he immediately give in to the opposition of his sign? Every time we hear of Socrates' *daimonion*, we find him only and immediately obeying it, so we must suppose that this would also have been his reaction when it appeared during something he was saying. Shall we then suppose that Socrates was speaking carelessly or without any support from his critical reason at such times, or should we suppose that Socrates was, even at such times, being characteristically rational (only, in these cases, we must suppose, making some error of judgment of which he could not be aware—or about which he could have no more than some suspicion—until the appearance of his *daimonion*)? If we suppose that Socrates was saying something he *took* to be supported by reason, at least—as we are suggesting—then each of these cases would count as his *daimonion's* opposing his reasons. If so, then there can be no doubt that Socrates could and did allow his *daimonion* to overrule something he was about to say or do on the basis of what he thought were good reasons.

But if Socrates did allow his *daimonion* to overrule his reasons for having formed some intention, then how could he characterize himself to Crito, as he does at *Crito* 45b (**T7.15**), as "the kind of man who listens only to the reason that on reflection seems best to me"? It was on the basis of this passage, after all, that so many scholars have supposed that Socrates would never allow anything supernatural to "trump" critical reason. There are two things to say about this, however. First of all, despite all that scholars have made of this passage, Socrates is not contrasting his trust in reason with his trust in his *daimonion* in making this claim. In fact, his *daimonion* has absolutely nothing to do with what Socrates is saying here to Crito. Rather, in this passage, Socrates is characterizing his own trust in reason *as opposed to other people*. It is nonetheless true that he makes this contrast in such a way as to make it sound as though he would always follow reason over *any* other consideration, but since the *daimonion* is not explicitly under consideration here as a competitor to reason, we cannot draw any secure conclusions about it on the basis of Socrates' claim to Crito here.

Second, scholars have, we think, simply assumed that Socrates' attitude toward his *daimonion* would put its promptings in some category other than "the reason that on reflection seems best to me." Perhaps it is not entirely plausible to suppose that Socrates would count his *daimonion's* sudden appearances as the product of "reflection," since they always seem to come unexpectedly. But Socrates' apparently unhesitating and immediate obedience to the opposition of the *daimonion* seems to show that whenever it does appear on the scene, he immediately counts its appearance as a decisive reason to desist from what he was about to say or do. If so, whether or not we count this as a "reason that *on reflection* seems best" to Socrates, it seems at least to count as an absolutely compelling reason to desist from what he was about to say or do—and, hence, provides a better reason than whatever reasons he had to carry out what he originally intended to do. At any rate, precisely because Socrates shows us again and again that he will unhesitatingly allow his *daimonion*'s opposition to stop him in his tracks, he cannot consistently characterize himself as following only reflective reasoning if he means to exclude his *daimonion* from this category, as scholars have assumed. In giving his *daimonion* this priority, moreover, Socrates is just being consistent in his evaluation of his own wisdom compared to that of the divine. Socrates, recall, is the one who always disclaims knowledge and claims only the "human wisdom" of recognizing how woefully ignorant he really is. The *daimonion*, however, he recognizes as a "divine thing," and as such, it is only fitting that he would unhesitatingly give way to its opposition to something he had planned, for he can be sure at least that as something divine it derives from a more secure source than the faulty human reasoning this divine thing now opposes.

7.5 Socrates on Death and the Afterlife

7.5.1 What Were Socrates' Beliefs About the Afterlife?

In his defense speech, Socrates ridicules those who act shamefully out of what he regards as an indefensible fear of death.

T7.20 *Apology* 29a–b (partially overlaps with **T3.4** and **T6.21**):

> (Socrates speaking) To fear death, gentlemen, is no other than to think oneself wise when one is not, to think one knows what one does not know. No one knows whether death may not be the greatest of all blessings for a man, yet men fear it as if they knew that it is the greatest of evils. And surely it is the most blameworthy ignorance to believe that one knows what one does not know. It is perhaps on this point and in this respect, gentlemen, that I differ from the majority of men, and if I were to claim that I am wiser than anyone in anything, it would be in this, that, as I have no adequate knowledge of things in the underworld, so I do not think I have.

At the very end of the *Apology*, Socrates seeks to console those jurors who voted in his favor and who must therefore suppose that Socrates had been condemned to death wrongly. He explains to them why they should have "good hope" for him, even though no one knows what may follow death.

T7.21 *Apology* 40c–41a:

> (Socrates speaking) Let us reflect in this way, too, that there is good hope that death is a blessing, for it is one of two things: either the dead are nothing and have no perception of anything, or it is, as we are told, a change and a relocating for the soul from here to another place. If it is a complete lack of perception, like a dreamless sleep, then death would be a great advantage. For I think

that if one had to pick out that night during which a man slept soundly and did not dream, put it beside the other nights and days of his life, and then see how many days and nights had been better and more pleasant than that night, not only a private person but the great king would find them easier to count compared with the other days and nights. If death is like this I say it is an advantage, for all eternity would then seem to be no more than a single night. If, on the other hand, death is a change from here to another place, and what we are told is true and all who have died are there, what greater blessing could there be, gentlemen of the jury? If anyone arriving in Hades will have escaped from those who now call themselves judges here, and will find those true judges who are said to sit in judgment there, Minos and Rhadamanthus and Aeacus and Triptolemus and the other demi-gods who have been upright in their own life, would that be a poor kind of change? Again, what would one of you give to keep company with Orpheus and Musaeus, Hesiod and Homer? I am willing to die many times if that is true.

The gist of Socrates' argument seems to be this: Either death is the very end, in which case it will be like sleeping, which is nothing to fear, or else it is not the end, in which case the soul will go someplace else. Of course, all we have to go on is what the poets say about the afterlife, in which case—at least in the way Socrates reconstructs the account—Socrates again has nothing to fear. Either way, then, the jurors should not suppose that death will be a bad thing for Socrates.

Elsewhere, however, Socrates speaks in ways that leave no doubt that he accepts the second of the two possibilities that he presented to his jurors. In the *Gorgias*, for example, Socrates' belief in an afterlife where the dead will be judged fairly is stated plainly.

T7.22 *Gorgias* 523a–524a (excerpted):

SOCRATES: Give ear then—as they put it—to a very fine account. You'll think that it's a mere tale, I believe, although I think it's an account, for what I'm about to say I will tell you as true. As Homer tells it, after Zeus, Poseidon, and Pluto took over the sovereignty from their father, they divided it among themselves. Now there was a law concerning human beings during Cronus' time, one that gods even now continue to observe, that when a man who has lived a just and pious life comes to his end, he goes to the Isles of the Blessed, to make his abode in complete happiness, beyond the reach of evils, but when one who has lived in an unjust and godless way dies, he goes to the prison of payment and retribution, the one they call Tartarus. [...] Zeus said "... I have already appointed my sons as judges, two from Asia, Minos and Rhadamanthus, and one from Europe, Aeacus. After they've died, they'll serve as judges [...].

Rhadamanthus will judge the people from Asia and Aeacus those from Europe. I'll give seniority to Minos to render the final judgment if the other two are at all perplexed, so that the judgment concerning the passage of humankind may be as just as possible."

The problem is this: How can Socrates dare to have such well-defined beliefs about the afterlife if he is so ready to admit that no one knows what may come after death and that any confidence about this issue must be counted as "the most blameworthy ignorance"? Do his beliefs about the afterlife reveal Socrates himself to be guilty of "the most blameworthy ignorance"?

7.5.2 Regrouping the Dialogues?

Some scholars have found the apparent tension between Socrates' professed agnosticism about the afterlife, in the *Apology* (**T7.20**), and his willingness to affirm a belief in the afterlife, in the *Gorgias* (**T7.22**), to be flatly inconsistent and have therefore argued that we must remove Plato's *Gorgias* from the list of the early dialogues and place it, instead, in a distinct transitional group between the early and middle dialogues of Plato.[17] The advantage of such a move is obvious: By removing the *Gorgias* from the group of dialogues supposed to represent the philosophy of Socrates, we eliminate the tension between the apparently agnostic Socrates of the *Apology* and the apparently nonagnostic Socrates of the *Gorgias*. Plainly, one way to eliminate problems of apparent inconsistency in the texts is to remove one of the apparently inconsistent texts from the group accepted as appropriate for consideration![18]

But inasmuch as this solution gets us out of our present problem quite effortlessly, it also propels us into other problems, which seem to us to be even more intractable. For one thing, it is not just the *Gorgias* that provides evidence contrary to the *Apology* in this case, for in the *Crito*, too, we find Socrates alluding to judgment in the afterlife, as if his belief in this was not to be doubted.

T7.23 *Crito* 54b-c:

(Socrates speaking for the personified Laws of Athens) Be persuaded by those of us who brought you up, Socrates. Do not value either your children or your life or anything more than goodness, in order that when you arrive in Hades you may have all this as your defense before the rulers there. If you do this deed [escape from prison, as Crito has proposed to Socrates], you will not think it better or more just or more pious here, nor will any of your friends, nor will it be better for you when you arrive yonder. As it is, you depart, if you depart, after being wronged not by us, the laws, but by men; but

if you depart after shamefully returning wrong for wrong and injury for injury, after breaking your agreements and commitments with us, after injur-
ing those you should injure least—yourself, your friends, your country and
us—we shall be angry with you while you are still alive, and our brothers,
the laws of the underworld, will not receive you kindly . . . .

Must we now isolate the *Crito,* too, and refuse to see it as one of the dialogues we can safely consult in our search for the philosophy of
Socrates?[19]

Moreover, isolating the *Gorgias* (or the *Crito,* as well) raises other questions. By the time we get to the middle-period dialogues, we find Plato's
Socrates entirely committed to a very different conception of the afterlife
than we find him giving in the *Gorgias,* the *Crito,* and, indeed, to either of
the possibilities in the *Apology.* In the *Meno,* which most scholars regard
as transitional, we are given arguments that are supposed to give us some
reason for believing that all knowledge is recollection of what our souls
learned in some existence before our (current) lives. This account is extended in the *Phaedo* and several other later dialogues, where arguments
and myths are provided that are supposed to show that the soul survives
death and becomes reincarnated, sometimes into different life-forms (see,
for examples, *Phaedo* 81c–82b, *Republic* 10.614b–621d). Except that the subsequent lives are given in accordance with merits or faults in the preceding life (thus providing appropriate rewards or punishments for those
preceding lives), this conception of the transmigration of souls has nothing in common with what Socrates claims to believe in the *Gorgias,* with
what the Laws say about the afterlife in the *Crito,* or with what Socrates
recognizes as what the survival of death might be like, in the *Apology*—all
of which, we contend, represent a single view of the afterlife that plainly
contrasts with what we find in the *Meno* and in the middle dialogues. On
this ground, then, little is gained by counting the *Gorgias* among a later
group of dialogues or even as anticipations of them. We propose, accordingly, that it is better to try to explain how Socrates could believe what he
says he believes in the *Gorgias* and yet argue in the way he does in the
Apology.

7.5.3 *"No One Knows" and*
"I Believe" Are Consistent

In fact, we do not find this problem all that difficult to solve—and certainly we do not find it so intractable as to require us to abandon the evidence the *Gorgias* gives us about Socrates. In essence, our solution is to argue that there is, in fact, no contradiction to be resolved here. In the
Apology (**T7.20**), Socrates claims that no one knows what follows death,

and surely there would be a contradiction if we ever find him in some other passage claiming to know what happens after death. But he never does this; even in professing his beliefs in an afterlife, in the *Gorgias* (and *Crito*), he never claims to *know* that there is an afterlife. Thus, nothing he gives us anywhere else in the early dialogues shows us that he thinks that death could not turn out to be the complete extinction Socrates compares to sleep in the *Apology*.

But this does not completely solve the problem, for it is appropriate for us to wonder how Socrates would dare even to hold beliefs he was willing to profess to others if he had no solid reasons for them. Under the circumstances, it might seem that Socrates not only could not *know* what is in the afterlife; he could not even have anything he regarded as a good reason for any *belief* about it. We should ask, therefore: Does Socrates ever give anything that would count as a good reason for belief about the afterlife?

We think he does give such a reason, in both the *Apology* and the *Gorgias*. When he tells his jurors, in **T7.21**, that death is one of two things, notice that he presents the first alternative—that death is like an endless sleep—as pure speculation: He does not claim to have heard this from anyone else. However, he reminds us both at the beginning and the end of his account of the second alternative—according to which there is life after death—that this is the story of the afterlife that is, as he says, "what we are told."

Socrates, let us recall, is wholly unimpressed by the mere fact that some opinion is popular among the mass of people.

T7.24 *Crito* 44c-d (= **T2.26**):

SOCRATES: My good Crito, why should we care so much for what the majority think? The most reasonable people, to whom one should pay more attention, will believe that things were done as they were done.

CRITO: You see, Socrates, that one must also pay attention to the opinion of the majority. Your present situation makes clear that the majority can inflict not the least but pretty well the greatest evils if one is slandered among them.

SOCRATES: Would that the majority could inflict the greatest evils, for they would then be capable of the greatest good, and that would be fine, but now they cannot do either. They cannot make a man either wise or foolish, but they inflict things haphazardly.

We must not suppose, therefore, that Socrates counts a belief in the afterlife as in any way supported simply on the ground that this belief is generally accepted. But when he says that the belief in the afterlife is something "we are told," he includes himself and others among those who are told such stories. The question is, who *tells* such stories to them, and where do they get their ideas?

The answer to this question, we contend, is that it is the poets of Greece who tell such stories—in particular, those poets who have established the religious traditions to which Socrates refers in recounting his account of the afterlife. The poets, recall, are the second group Socrates says he went to when he searched out the meaning of the Delphic oracle to Chaerophon. When he questioned them, however, he found that they suffered from a shocking lack of knowledge.

T7.25 *Apology* 22b-c:

> (Socrates speaking) After the politicians, I went to the poets, the writers of tragedies and dithyrambs and the others, intending, in their case to catch myself being more ignorant than they. So I took up those poems with which they seemed to have taken most trouble and asked them what they meant, in order that I might at the same time learn something from them. I am ashamed to tell you the truth, gentlemen, but I must. Almost all the bystanders might have explained the poems better than their authors could. I soon realized that poets do not compose their poems with knowledge, but by some inborn talent and by inspiration, like seers and prophets who also say many fine things without any understanding of what they say.

When he questioned the politicians, he discovered that they had no knowledge, and as we saw in the last chapter, Socrates was not much impressed by anything he found the politicians doing or producing. He finds a comparable lack of knowledge among the poets, but their case is different in an important way from that of the politicians: In the case of the poets, Socrates finds he must still recognize that there is something extraordinary in what they produce. Indeed, this is why their ignorance is so striking, for it shows that it cannot be that they produce such extraordinary creations from knowledge. Socrates concludes that there must be another source for what the poets do—he claims that the poets "do not compose their poems with knowledge, but by some inborn talent, and by inspiration, like seers and prophets, who also say many fine things without any understanding of what they say." We find Socrates coming to the same conclusion about poets and other literary figures in Plato's *Ion*.

The sources of such inspiration, the Greeks all agree, are the gods. Socrates, moreover, has at least some evidence for accepting this traditional belief: It would appear to be the best explanation of how the poets (and the seers and prophets), whom Socrates finds to be ignoramuses themselves, could produce poems (or prophesies) that are so beautiful, so

accurate, and so important to humankind. Poetry, in particular, has an obvious kind of *power* that it exerts over those who hear it.
   T7.26 *Ion* 533e–534b:

> (Socrates speaking) You know, none of the epic poets, if they're good, are
> masters of their subject; they are inspired, possessed, and that is how they
> utter all those beautiful poems. The same goes for lyric poets if they're good:
> just as the Corybantes are not in their right minds when they dance, lyric po-
> ets, too, are not in their right minds when they make those beautiful lyrics,
> but as soon as they sail into harmony and rhythm they are possessed by Bac-
> chic frenzy. Just as Bacchus worshippers when they are possessed draw
> honey and milk from rivers, but not when they are in their right minds—the
> soul of a lyric poet does this, too, as they say themselves. For of course poets
> tell us that they gather songs at honey-flowing springs, from glades and gar-
> dens of the Muses, and that they bear songs to us as bees carry honey, flying
> like bees. And what they say is true. For a poet is an airy thing, winged and
> holy, and he is not able to make poetry until he becomes inspired and goes
> out of his mind and his intellect is no longer in him.

Socrates, recall, counts the gods as having a kind of wisdom that is far
beyond what human beings can achieve. When these gods speak to us,
using poets, seers, or prophets as their mediums, we must not understand the profundities we receive thereby as having been given their content by the human mediums through whom the gods have spoken. Even
so, precisely because it is the gods who have thus spoken to us, it would
be impious to doubt the significance or the accuracy of what we have
been told—if only we can understand it rightly.
   Earlier in this chapter, we argued against Gregory Vlastos's claim that
Socrates thought that nothing had any cognitive value unless it was produced through rational means. In the case of religious phenomena, Vlastos argued, one would still need to interpret them and that would necessarily require the operation of critical rationality. We argued earlier that
Vlastos's claim was too strong in regard to Socrates *daimonion,* which
seemed to exercise an influence over him that was independent of what
Vlastos would count as Socrates' critical reason. But we think that Vlastos
is right about religiously significant phenomena other than the
daimonion—and even with the *daimonion,* we allowed, only Socrates' reason could provide any detailed explanation of *why* the *daimonion* had sig-
naled its opposition.
   Inspired poetry and prophecy tell us "many fine things." But we cannot
easily understand what these things tell us. Thus, even when the mes-
sages we have achieved through such means seem very clear, we must
never suppose that we are in a position to claim to *know* that "what we are

told" is true. In the case of stories about the afterlife, we are told wondrous things about our souls migrating to another place, where at last we might encounter real judges, whose judgments are the products of wisdom rather than prejudice and unjustified opinion. Can we be certain that such stories are true? We cannot. There surely is *some* truth here, given where we can suppose these stories come from. But what exactly that truth might be we do not know. Might death simply be extinction after all, like an endless sleep? Yes, and here is why: The gist of the afterlife stories, at least in Socrates' account, is that the afterlife is nothing for a good person to fear. Indeed, it is something for the good person to look forward to. People fear death, Socrates seems to suppose, because they fear extinction. But when he reviews what this might be like, he finds that even this would be a "great advantage." Could the gods tell us this, by having our poets speak of wonderful experiences in the afterlife? Why not? If they perceive that these stories will best reassure us about death and it is such reassurance they wish to convey to us, there is no reason that they cannot formulate their reassurance in such a way.

7.5.4 Another Socratic Revision to Greek Religion?

We have argued that Socrates does believe in an afterlife, one that he portrays as giving his jurors reasons for "good hope" that death will turn out to be a "great advantage" or even a "blessing." One might still be troubled, however, by apparent differences between Socrates' very hopeful understanding of the traditional stories of the afterlife and that of the poets Socrates probably has in mind when he talks about what the poets tell us about the afterlife. Consider what we find reported by Homer in the *Odyssey*, when Circe tells Odysseus that he must make the famous trip to the underworld to consult with the dead prophet Teiresias.

T7.27 Homer, *Odyssey* Book 10, lines 490–495[20]:
(Circe speaking to Odysseus)

> There is another journey you must accomplish
> and reach the house of Hades and of revered Persephone,
> there to consult with the soul of Teiresias the Theban,
> the blind prophet, whose senses stay unshaken within him,
> to whom alone Persephone has granted intelligence
> even after death, but the rest of them are flittering shadows.

When Odysseus does make the trip to Hades, he encounters the ghost of Achilles, the greatest fighter of all of the Achaians, who makes the frightening picture even clearer. Achilles wonders how the living

Odysseus could "endure to come down here to Hades' place, where the senseless dead men dwell, mere imitations of perished mortals" (*Odyssey* 11, 475–476). And when Odysseus complains of his own troubles and proclaims Achilles "blessed" because of how well honored he was before his death and because he now enjoys "great authority over the dead" (*Odyssey* 11, 482–486), Achilles, who had been so proud in his superiority when alive, offers this chilly retort.

T7.28 Homer, *Odyssey* Book 11, lines 488–491:

> O shining Odysseus, never try to console me for dying.
> I would rather follow the plow as thrall to another
> man, one with no land allotted him and not much to live on,
> than be a king over all the perished dead.

Clearly, Homer's senseless ghosts, flittering in the darkness and longing for the lives they lost—no matter how troubled or ordinary they might have been—do not seem to match the far more hopeful account offered by Socrates in Plato's *Apology*.

As we said at the very beginning of this chapter, however, secure and unambiguous conclusions about the religious beliefs of the ancient Greeks are easily stated but are very difficult to defend. The problem is that the Greeks seemed to tell so many different stories in the domain of religion and myth and seemed to have remarkably little concern to make sure that all of the stories were consistent with one another.[21] Even if we focus just on Homer as the ultimate authority, we will find very different possibilities given about the afterlife. **T7.27** and **T7.28** paint a terribly grim picture of life after death, but in another passage in the same work, Homer tells of another place to which some go after death—to the Isles of the Blessed, where the dead spend eternity in perfect bliss.[22] Plainly, these two accounts are not the same, and nothing in Homer secures any clear inference as to how we might attain the better alternative—one that would not appear to exist when the darker version is offered in Books 10 and 11 of the *Odyssey*.[23]

Socrates, as we showed in Section 7.2, found that he could not accept all of the contradictory accounts of the gods and religion his culture affirmed. Instead, he focused on one long-standing theme in these stories, one that held the gods to be flawlessly moral. The same commitment resurfaces, we claim, in Socrates' reconfiguring the myths of the afterlife. Ignoring those stories that hold the afterlife to be a terrible continuation of existence, Socrates reaffirms his commitment to the morality of the gods by insisting that they would surely structure the afterlife in a way that would ensure that justice was served, for all of the dead. On the one hand, Socrates' account does not provide grounds for all to regard death hopefully, for he allows that the souls of the wicked will have to endure terrible punishments for the evil in their souls. On the other hand, Socrates is convinced that he is a good man, and so his account of the afterlife does provide "good hope" for those who, like him, have lived good lives. And this is all he proposed to offer to those jurors who had voted in his favor. One might perhaps infer a rather grimmer prospect for at least some of those who had voted against Socrates!

Two further points can be made. First, we should attend to the fact that it is not Socrates' expressed intention in his final speech in the *Apology* to provide his supporters on the jury with a careful survey of what he takes to be our state of evidence regarding death and the afterlife. He is, instead, seeking to give them some reason for solace that what has happened is not a bad thing for him. Even if he does believe in an afterlife, as we have argued that he does, he does not owe it to his jurors in this context to show why he favors this conclusion over the one, which some of them may suppose is more likely, that regards death as extinction. Our conclusion, after all, is that "what we are told" is some reason to believe that there is an afterlife, but it might still be that there is no afterlife and that death is extinction after all. Accordingly, Socrates allows that death could be "one of two things" when he seeks to console his jurors. He does remind them that "we are told" about an afterlife. But what they make of this is up to them. Second, and perhaps even more important, we are now in a position to see even more clearly why Socrates would regard it as "the most blameworthy ignorance" to fear death, as he says it is in **T7.20**. For if what Socrates tells us is true and death is either of the two things he counts as possibilities, *neither one* counts as something to be feared. Accordingly, to act in shameful ways out of a fear of death is truly "the most blameworthy ignorance."

In this chapter, we have considered Socrates' religious beliefs, and we have found them to be an interesting mixture of elements from traditional Greek religion and elements deriving from Socrates' own unique experiences and his understanding of these. Scholars are right to see, in Socrates, a strong tendency to moralize Greek religion. We have disputed their claim that this may have provided a motive for his prosecution, conviction, or execution. But we find its influence in all of Socrates' religious professions. But this is only what we should expect of a man dedicated to achieving a consistency in his own beliefs, one that supports the most moral life a human being might aspire to.

Notes

1. The oldest known Hindu document, the *Rig Veda*, dates sometime between 1400 and 1000 B.C. (see J. Smith [1995], 425). Siddhartha Gautama, who came to be known as Buddha, was born ca. 566 B.C. (ibid., 135). Judaism is said to have begun

as a historical religion with the creation of the Pentateuch sometime in the sixth century B.C., and most of the Hebrew Bible was written or edited in the period from 538 to 333 B.C. (ibid., 600).

2. Even the "official" civic festivals recognized in Athens each year gained and lost new members all the time, with new ones constantly being introduced and old ones coming to be disregarded and being subsequently dropped from the civil religious calendar.

3. This is the order of the specifications given in most of the ancient accounts. In Plato's *Apology* (24b-c), Socrates gives a different order: corrupting the young, not believing in the gods the city believes in, and inventing new spiritual things. But Socrates seems not to be attempting to recite the specifications in their exact order here but gives them in the order in which he will address them in this phase of his defense. At any rate, we do not find any particular significance in the order of the specifications and will maintain the order we are given in other sources only for the sake of their greater familiarity.

4. For "sign," see *Apology* 40c, 41d; *Euthydemus* 272e; *Republic* 6.496c; and *Phaedrus* 242b. For "voice," see *Apology* 31d; and *Phaedrus* 242c. For "something divine," see *Apology* 31c-d, 40a; *Euthyphro* 3b; and *Phaedrus* 242b.

5. His deliberate vagueness about the source and nature of the *daimonion* suggests that Socrates did not suppose he knew anything very clearly about the *daimonion*, other than that it had some divine source. In his argument with Meletus (at *Apology* 27b–28a) about the "new divinities" the indictment alleges he invented, Socrates intimates that he believes not only in gods but also quite possibly in "spirits," which are themselves either gods or the "children of the gods, bastard children of the gods by nymphs or some other mothers" (27d), and possibly divine heroes, as well (28a).

6. Here we deviate from the Grube translation in Cooper (1997), which turns Socrates' question into a direct affirmation and which, as we show, creates a conflict with the account of the motives for the prosecution that Socrates gives in the *Apology*. In the Greek text, it is unambiguously clear, however, that Socrates is asking a question.

7. See, for examples, Connor (1991), Steinberger (1997), and Vlastos (1991), chap. 6. A more cautious—and impressively detailed—review of the evidence is offered in McPherran (1996). McPherran concludes that even if Socrates' moralizing of the gods was not the basis for the prosecution, it was nonetheless a potentially dangerous issue for Socrates, which could have led at least some of the jurors to vote against him (see esp. 141–174). As our following argument shows, we think even this weaker conclusion is not warranted by our evidence.

8. Vlastos (1991), 166. See also Connor (1991), 56; Burnyeat (1997).

9. Burnyeat (1997), Connor (1991), and Vlastos (1991, ch. 6) all concur that Socrates was guilty of the charge, as they understand it. McPherran (1996, esp. 156–160) says that Socrates was guilty of the charge, conceived in this way but claims that Meletus simply bungles the case by opting for the interpretation of the charge as atheism (see T7.8, above), which allows Socrates safely to skirt the more dangerous issue of his religious moralizing innovations. Had Meletus chosen the more plausible conception of the charge, however, McPherran thinks that the jurors would have had even more reason to convict Socrates. We obviously agree with none of these assessments.

10. Notice that Socrates mentions Aristophanes' *Clouds* in **T7.7** as evidence for his claim that these prejudices have been around for some time. Aristophanes' *Clouds* was produced in 423 B.C., nearly a quarter of a century before Socrates' trial in 399 B.C. Obviously, Socrates already had a problematic reputation in Athens when Aristophanes wrote his play, or his selection of Socrates as the stereotypical intellectual would not have seemed apt. We may assume, then, that Socrates is right in claiming to have had a bad reputation for a *long* time before his trial.

11. See, for examples, Hackforth (1933), 101–104; Montuori (1981), 133–143; Stokes (1992).

12. See note 3 above.

13. Notice, again, how this differs from the account given by Vlastos and those who agreed with him (Vlastos [1991], 166. See also Connor [1991], 56; Burnyeat [1997]). The way Vlastos saw it, it was Socrates' moralizing innovations that were at issue: "Their [the gods'] ethical transformation would be tantamount to the destruction of the old gods, the creation of new ones—which is precisely what Socrates takes to be the sum and substance of the accusation at his trial" (Vlastos [1991], 166). Neither of our two most important proximate sources on Socrates (Plato and Xenophon) corroborate Vlastos's account that it was moralizing innovation that led to the charge that Socrates invented new divinities.

14. See, for example, Nussbaum (1985), 234–235.

15. See Vlastos (1991), 157; also Reeve (1989), 71–72.

16. Here we modify the Grube translation in Cooper (1997), which gives "argument" instead of "reason." The Greek word is *logos*, which can mean either "reason" or "argument" (among other possibilities), but Grube's translation, as we shall argue, would beg the question about what might count as a "reason" for Socrates. Vlastos's version—"the proposition which appears to me to be the best when I reason about it" (Vlastos [1991], 157) is even more tendentious. Reeve (1989, 72) cites this passage for his uncompromising claim that "Socrates is . . . explicit that the *only* thing that would convince him . . . is an argument." Understood in this way, this passage has the effect of saying that Socrates would never be convinced of anything—even that he should desist from some course of action—just by some "sign" from the *daimonion*. We do not accept this result.

17. See, for example, McPherran (1996), 266–270.

18. Indeed, it has become fashionable among some scholars to argue that *none* of Plato's texts can be compared for consistent points of view with any others. Each dialogue, it is held, is intended (by Plato) to be read and considered entirely on its own terms, isolated from any arguments or positions offered in any other dialogues, which Plato made no attempt to make consistent with one another. Plainly, we have not taken this interpretative approach seriously in this book, for we find little plausibility in the claim that Plato would show so little concern for consistency, and we also believe that such an approach would be more of a hindrance than a help in our attempt to understand either Socratic or Platonic philosophy. Accordingly, we confess puzzlement as to why any serious scholars would find such an approach attractive except to avoid the very challenges of scholarly interpretation.

19. McPherran seems prepared to flirt with this result (see 1996, 266, n. 61) but also offers an alternative to it by claiming that we do not have to understand

Socrates' reference to the afterlife here as reflecting his own beliefs (1996, 265–266). Socrates is speaking here for the personified Laws of Athens, McPherran points out, and so their reference here may reflect only what Socrates regarded as an opinion reflected in Athens's laws. We tend to doubt that this specific conception of the afterlife could be found as a legal doctrine in Athens's laws, in which case Socrates' alleged attribution of this conception to the Athenian laws (while remaining noncommittal himself) is tendentious, at best. Moreover, since even McPherran seems prepared to accept that everything *else* the Laws say (through Socrates) in their speech can safely be attributed to Socrates, his exclusion of this point is unsupportable.

20. This and the following are Lattimore's translations (1965).

21. For a very judicious discussion of the uncertainties and diversities in ancient Greek religion, see Parker (1996).

22. Homer, *Odyssey* 4, 561–568. Other positive possibilities are given or suggested in the Homeric *Hymn to Demeter*, lines 480–482, and in Pindar, *Olympian* 2, lines 63–73. For discussion of the possibilities for a blissful afterlife, see Burkert (1987), 13–15.

23. We infer this from the fact that Odysseus does not need to confront the possibility that Teiresias—the seer for whom he searches in the afterlife—might be in some other, happier place.

Suggested Readings

General

An impressive, comprehensive book on Socrates' religious views and their connections with his philosophy is McPherran (1996). A new book (Smith and Woodruff, forthcoming) includes articles on the topic by several of the most prominent scholars, as well as an extensive correspondence—never before published—on Socratic religion, among Thomas C. Brickhouse, Mark McPherran, Nicholas D. Smith, and Gregory Vlastos.

On the Relation Between Socrates'
Religious Views and the Trial

The idea that Socrates' disbelief in immoral myths may have had something to do with his trial and conviction was, to our knowledge, first argued in Tate (1933) and (1936). This view has been revived, however, in a most forceful and impressive form, in Vlastos (1991, ch. 6; revised from an article published in 1989). As we noted in this chapter, the same view can also be found expressed in Connor (1991), Burnyeat (1997), and Steinberger (1997), as well as in a more cautious version in McPherran (1996). McPherran's view is more like Tate's original, according to which Socrates' religious moralizing was one possible source of the jury's distrust of Socrates. We have argued against this view, both in Brickhouse and

Smith (1989, sec. 3.1.5) and (1994, sec. 6.2). A view for the most part consistent with ours can be found in Gocer (forthcoming).

On the Oracle Story and Socrates' Claim to Have a Religious Mission in Athens

Our own view of the role the oracle played in the origin of Socrates' mission can be found in Brickhouse and Smith (1989, sec. 2.5; revised from an article published in 1983). McPherran offers a persuasive account of the mission and how Socrates thinks others can take part in it, in McPherran (1996, secs. 2.2 and 4.2; revised from articles published in 1985 and 1986, respectively). The skeptical position—that the oracle story in the *Apology* fails to account adequately for Socrates' claim to have a mission—is argued by Hackforth (1933), Montuori (1981), and in remarkable detail in Stokes (1992). A novel way of understanding how Socrates derived his mission from the oracle is given in Doyle (forthcoming).

On Socrates' Daimonion and Its Relationship to Socrates' Dedication to the Life of Reason

This topic is central to the debate among Brickhouse, McPherran, Smith, and Vlastos, in Smith and Woodruff (forthcoming). As we said in this chapter, Vlastos has argued for the dependence of Socrates' trust in his *daimonion* on his trust in reason, in Vlastos (1991, ch. 6; revised from an article published in 1989). A view very like Vlastos's is presented in Reeve (1989). The priority of Socrates' trust in his *daimonion*, relative to his trust in his own powers of reasoning, is advanced in McPherran (1996, sec. 4.1; revised from an article published in 1991) and in Brickhouse and Smith (1989, sec. 5.5), and (1994, sec. 6.3).

On Socrates' Views About Death and the Afterlife

Our earlier account of the position Socrates articulates in the *Apology*, in Brickhouse and Smith (1989, sec. 5.6.1) was refuted by Rudebusch (1991). We follow Rudebusch's proposed amendment to our earlier argument in Brickhouse and Smith (1994, sec. 6.5). As we noted in this chapter, McPherran (1996) finds the account of the afterlife in the *Gorgias* inconsistent with what we find in the *Apology* and doubts that the evidence from the *Crito* tells us anything about Socrates' own views. The view for which we argue in this chapter is our reply to his arguments.

Glossary

Akrasia   The view that one can believe that something is EVIL but pursue it in spite of that belief. Socrates denies that *akrasia* is possible. (See SOCRATIC PARADOXES.)

Aporia   The state of confusion in which Socrates' interlocutors find themselves when elenctic (see *ELENCHOS*) arguments show that they do not know what they claimed they knew. Many of Plato's early dialogues are said to be "aporetic" because they end with Socrates' interlocutors in a state of *aporia*.

Aretē   see VIRTUE.

Constructivism   The view that the outcome of the *ELENCHOS* allows Socrates to draw substantive moral conclusions, including conclusions that bear on the nature of VIRTUE. As opposed to NONCONSTRUCTIVISM, which holds that the *ELENCHOS* only shows that the interlocutor lacks knowledge. (See 2.2.)

Craft   A body of knowledge that enables its possessor to do something or to produce a product (see *ERGON*) in a rational, orderly, and unerring manner. People who possess a craft can teach what they know to others and, thus, can give an account of how it is that they do or produce what they do. (See KNOWLEDGE.)

Daimonion   The divine voice that Socrates claims to have heard throughout his life (see *Apology* 31d). When he hears it, it always "turns him away" from something he is intending to do because what he is intending is wrong (see *Apology* 40a). Although Socrates is confident that he is being turned away from something wrong, the *daimonion* never provides him with the reasons *why* what he is being turned away from is wrong, or what is wrong about it. (See 7.4.)

Elenchos   The refutative form of argument with which Socrates is generally associated. The premises of the *elenchos* consist of answers the interlocutor gives to questions, and the conclusion is the contradiction of some claim the interlocutor had previously claimed to know. Commentators agree that the *elenchos* serves a negative purpose (see NONCONSTRUCTIVISM). Whether the *elenchos* plays more positive roles (see CONSTRUCTIVISM), including exhorting the interlocutor to pursue virtue, is controversial. (See 2.2.)

Ergon   That performance or product that is the unique goal of a CRAFT. Health in the body, for example, is the *ergon* of the craft of medicine. One craft can be distinguished from other crafts on the basis of the *ergon* it produces and with which it is uniquely associated.

Eudaimonia   The Greek word usually translated as "happiness." (The opposite of *eudaimonia* is *athliotēs*: "misery" or "wretchedness.") Socrates uses this term interchangeably with expressions that mean "doing well" and "living well." (See *Euthydemus* 278e ff., *Republic* I.354a.)

Eudaimonism   The view often attributed to Socrates that *EUDAIMONIA* is the ultimate goal of every human being and that anything else that is good is good because and only because it contributes to this goal. (See 4.1.4.)

Evils   In general, Socrates uses the term to refer to things that harm us because such things in some way detract from our *EUDAIMONIA* or contribute to our misery or wretchedness.

Goods   In general, Socrates uses the term to refer to things that benefit us because they contribute to *EUDAIMONIA*. A constitutive good is one that makes up either the whole or part of what is valued for its own sake. An instrumental good is one that is causally productive of what is valued for its own sake. An independent good is one whose value comes from being the very sort of thing it is. A dependent good is one whose value comes from being employed by some other good.

Happiness   See *EUDAIMONIA*, EUDAIMONISM.

Irony   If we think of irony as saying what is false in order to achieve some effect other than mere deception, there are several different ways in which Socrates is ironic. Socrates engages in "mocking irony" whenever he says what he does not believe in order to make a joke at the expense of someone else. Sometimes he engages in "tragic irony," saying what he means but also realizing that what he says has a deeper meaning that is not actually stated and that his interlocutor does not grasp. Socrates is occasionally accused by his interlocutors of being ironic when he disclaims knowledge about the topic under discussion. The accusation is that when Socrates denigrates his own cognitive powers, he is really making a dishonest attempt to get the upper hand in the argument. Whether or not Socrates engages in this third sort of irony is controversial. (See 2.1.2.)

Knowledge   Socrates uses "knowledge" in several senses. Sometimes he uses the term to refer to a particular cognitive state in which one has a certain high degree or special kind of evidence that something is the case. This, one might say, is "propositional knowledge." Sometimes Socrates uses "knowledge" in a more restricted sense to refer to the cognitive state that a craftsperson possesses (see CRAFT) that enables the craftsperson to perform the corresponding craft well. Socrates also uses "craft knowledge" as a synonym for the sort of WISDOM that is moral VIRTUE. Socrates distinguishes knowledge from belief on the ground that the former is stable (see *Protagoras* 351b-e and *Meno* 97c–98a) and can produce the correct account of how it is that what is known is the case. (See Chapter 3.)

Moral paradox   Because Socrates (a) accepts the PRUDENTIAL PARADOX and (b) believes that action in accordance with moral virtue is always good for the agent, he believes that anyone who believes something to be a good will pursue it. (See 5.3.3.)

Necessity thesis   The view, often attributed to Socrates, that no one can possess *EUDAIMONIA* without the possession of virtue. (See 4.4.)

Nonrational desires   Desires that are independent of, and that may oppose, what one takes to be good (see RATIONAL DESIRES). Many commentators claim that Socrates denies that there are nonrational desires (but see, e.g., *Laches* 191d-e; see also 5.3.5).

Obey or persuade   The obligation Socrates believes that each citizen has to his or her city when the citizen believes that city has commanded him or her to do something unjust. (See 6.3.)

Priority of Definition (PD)   The principle that holds that knowledge of the definition of some quality is a necessary condition of knowing anything at all about that quality or whether or which things manifest that quality. The claim that Socrates accepts such a principle is controversial. (See 3.2.)

Prudential paradox   The Socratic doctrine that no one ever acts contrary to what they take to be good. A consequence is that every evil pursuit is the result of the agent's ignorance that what the evildoer is pursuing is evil. (See 5.3.2.)

Rational desires   Desires for what one takes to be good.

Socratic paradoxes   Two doctrines to which Socrates is committed that seemingly violate common sense: (1) the view that no one can have any one of the moral virtues without the others (see UNITY OF THE VIRTUES), and (2) the view that AKRASIA never occurs (see AKRASIA, MORAL PARADOX, and PRUDENTIAL PARADOX). (See Chapter 5.)

Soul   An entity, different from the body or any part of the body, whose function it is to "manage and rule over" the body (see *Republic* I.353d). The soul is improved by VIRTUE and harmed by VICE. Socrates thinks that it is possible for the soul either to cease to exist when the body dies or to leave the body at death. Several passages suggest that he thinks the latter is more likely than the former.

Sovereignty of virtue thesis   The view attributed to Socrates by Gregory Vlastos, according to which virtue is the chief component of *EUDAIMONIA* and, as such, is both necessary and sufficient for *EUDAIMONIA*. Other, dependent goods, however, can make one better off with respect to happiness.

Sufficiency thesis   The view often attributed to Socrates that virtue produces *EUDAIMONIA* either by causing one to be happy or by being a constituent of happiness. (See 4.2.2.1–4.2.3.)

Technē   See CRAFT.

Unity of virtue   One of the SOCRATIC PARADOXES. The Socratic doctrine that anyone who has any one of the five commonly recognized virtues—piety, temperance, justice, courage, and wisdom—will have the other four virtues as well. Why Socrates holds this view is controversial. Some scholars maintain that Socrates holds the equivalence thesis, according to which each of the virtues is definitionally distinct and each is constituted by its own distinctive form of moral knowledge. Nonetheless, anyone who possesses any one the virtues possesses each of the others as well. Other scholars attribute to Socrates the identity thesis, according to which each of the five virtues is really one and the same thing, namely WISDOM. (See 5.2.)

Vice   That condition of the soul that causes one to do what is evil. Socrates seems to have thought that vice is nothing more than ignorance of what is good.

Virtue   A condition of a thing that makes it an excellent example of the kind of thing that it is. In antiquity there was widespread agreement that human virtue is a very important GOOD. However, there was widespread disagreement about what human virtue is. Scholars disagree about what Socrates believed human virtue consists in, though the most widely accepted view is that he thought human virtue is a form of KNOWLEDGE, specifically, moral WISDOM with respect to good and evil.

Weakness of will   See *AKRASIA*.

Wisdom   Socrates seems to distinguish several senses of the term. One form of wisdom is "human wisdom," the recognition that when one lacks moral VIRTUE one does not possess wisdom that "is greater than human" (*Apology* 23a-b). Socrates seems to think that a wisdom greater than human is the wisdom that constitutes VIRTUE, the wisdom that is identical with craft knowledge of morality.

References

Allen, R. E. 1980. *Socrates and Legal Obligation*. Minneapolis: University of Minnesota Press.

Arrowsmith, William. 1969. *Three Comedies by Aristophanes*. Ann Arbor: University of Michigan Press.

Benson, Hugh. 1987. "The Problem of the Elenchus Reconsidered," *Ancient Philosophy* 7, 67–85.

_____. 1990a. "Misunderstanding the 'What Is F-ness?' Question," *Archiv fur Geschichte der Philosophie* 72, 125–142.

_____. 1990b. "The Priority of Definition and the Socratic *Elenchos*," *Oxford Studies in Ancient Philosophy* 8, 19–65.

_____. 1995. "The Dissolution of the Problem of the *Elenchus*," *Oxford Studies in Ancient Philosophy* 13, 45–112.

Beversluis, John. 1974. "Socratic Definition," *American Philosophical Quarterly* 11, 331–336.

_____. 1987. "Does Socrates Commit the Socratic Fallacy?" *American Philosophical Quarterly* 24, 211–223.

_____. 1993. "Vlastos' Quest for the Historical Socrates," *Ancient Philosophy* 13, 293–312.

Bolton, Robert. 1993. "Aristotle's Account of the Socratic Elenchus," *Oxford Studies in Ancient Philosophy* 11, 121–152.

Brandwood, Leonard. 1992. "Stylometry and Chronology." In *The Cambridge Companion to Plato*, edited by Richard Kraut. Cambridge: Cambridge University Press, 90–121.

Brickhouse, Thomas C., and Nicholas D. Smith. 1984. "Vlastos on the Elenchus," *Oxford Studies in Ancient Philosophy* 2, 185–195.

_____. 1987. "Socrates on Goods, Virtue, and Happiness," *Oxford Studies in Ancient Philosophy* 5, 1–27.

_____. 1989. *Socrates on Trial*. Oxford and Princeton: Oxford and Princeton University Presses.

_____. 1993. Review of *Socrates: Ironist and Moral Philosopher*, by Gregory Vlastos, *Ancient Philosophy* 13, 395–410.

_____. 1994. *Plato's Socrates*. Oxford: Oxford University Press.

_____. 1997a. "Socrates and the Unity of the Virtues," *Journal of Ethics* 1, 311–324.

_____. 1997b. "The Problem of Punishment in Socratic Philosophy." In *Wisdom, Ignorance, and Virtue: New Essays in Socratic Studies*, edited by Mark L. McPherran. Edmonton: Academic (Supplement, *Apeiron* 30), 95–107.

Burkert, Walter. 1987. *Ancient Mystery Cults*. Cambridge: Harvard University Press.

Burnet, John. 1924. *Plato's "Euthyphro," "Apology of Socrates," and "Crito."* Oxford: Oxford University Press.

Burnyeat, M. F. 1997. "The Impiety of Socrates," *Ancient Philosophy* 17, 1–12.

Bury, J. B. 1962. *A History of Greece.* New York: Random House.

Chroust, Anton-Hermann. 1957. *Socrates, Man and Myth.* Notre Dame, Ind.: University of Notre Dame Press.

Clay, Diskin. 1994. "The Origins of the Socratic Dialogue." In *The Socratic Movement,* edited by Paul van der Waerdt. Ithaca and London: Cornell University Press, 23–47.

Connor, W. R. 1991. "The Other 399: Religion and the Trial of Socrates." In *Georgica, Greek Studies in Honor of George Cawkwell.* Bulletin Supplement 58 of the Institute of Classical Studies, 49–56.

Cooper, John M., ed. 1997. *Plato: Complete Works.* Indianapolis, Ind.: Hackett.

Cornford, F. M. 1933. "The Athenians' Philosophical Schools, I. The Philosophy of Socrates." In *Cambridge Ancient History,* vol. 6, 302–309. Cambridge: Cambridge University Press.

de Stryker, Emile, and S. R. Slings. 1994. *Plato's Apology of Socrates: A Literary and Philosophical Study with a Running Commentary.* Leiden, New York, and Koln: E. J. Brill.

Devereux, Daniel T. 1992. "The Unity of the Virtues in Plato's *Protagoras* and *Laches,*" *Philosophical Review* 101, 265–289.

————. 1995. "Socrates' Kantian Conception of Virtue," *Journal of the History of Philosophy* 33, 381–408.

Doyle, James. Forthcoming. "Socrates and the Oracle," *Ancient Philosophy.*

Edmunds, L. 1985. "Aristophanes' Socrates." In *Proceedings of the Boston Area Colloquium in Ancient Philosophy,* edited by John Cleary, vol. 1. Lanham, Md.: University Press of America, 209–230.

Ferejohn, Michael. 1982. "The Unity of Virtue and the Objects of Socratic Inquiry," *Journal of the History of Philosophy* 20, 1–21.

————. 1983–1984. "Socratic Virtue as the Parts of Itself," *Philosophy and Phenomenological Research* 43, 377–388.

Geach, Peter. 1966. "Plato's *Euthyphro:* An Analysis and Commentary," *Monist* 50, 369–382.

Gocer, A. Forthcoming. "A New Assessment of Socratic Philosophy of Religion." In *Reason and Religion in Socratic Philosophy,* edited by Nicholas D. Smith and Paul Woodruff. New York and Oxford: Oxford University Press (forthcoming).

Gosling, J.C.B., and C.C.W. Taylor. 1982. *The Greeks on Pleasure.* Oxford: Oxford University Press.

Gower, B., and Michael C. Stokes, eds. 1992. *Socratic Questions.* London and New York: Routledge.

Grote, George. 1865. *Plato and the Other Companions of Socrates.* 3 vols. London: Murray.

Gulley, Norman. 1968. *The Philosophy of Socrates.* London: Macmillan.

Guthrie, W.K.C. 1971a. *Socrates.* Cambridge: Cambridge University Press.

————. 1971b. *The Sophists.* Cambridge: Cambridge University Press.

Hackforth, R. M. 1933. *The Composition of Plato's "Apology."* Cambridge: Cambridge University Press.

Irwin, Terence. 1977. *Plato's Moral Theory.* Oxford: Oxford University Press.

————. 1979. *Plato's "Gorgias."* Oxford: Oxford University Press.

————. 1995. *Plato's Ethics.* Oxford: Oxford University Press.

Kahn, Charles. 1988. "On the Relative Date of the *Gorgias* and the *Protagoras*," *Oxford Studies in Ancient Philosophy* 6, 69–102.

_____. 1994. "Aeschines on Socratic Eros." In *The Socratic Movement*, edited by Paul van der Waerdt. Ithaca and London: Cornell University Press, 87–106.

Kerford, G. B. 1981. *The Sophistic Movement*. Cambridge: Cambridge University Press.

Kraut, Richard. 1983. "Comments on Gregory Vlastos, 'The Socratic Elenchus,'" *Oxford Studies in Ancient Philosophy* 1, 59–70.

_____. 1984. *Socrates and the State*. Princeton: Princeton University Press.

_____. 1992. *The Cambridge Companion to Plato*. Cambridge: Cambridge University Press.

Lacey, A. R. 1971. "Our Knowledge of Socrates." In *The Philosophy of Socrates*, edited by Gregory Vlastos. Garden City, N.Y.: Anchor Books; reprinted by University of Notre Dame Press, 1980.

Lattimore, Richmond. 1965. *The Odyssey of Homer*. New York: Harper and Row.

Lesher, James. 1987. "Socrates' Disavowal of Knowledge," *Journal of the History of Philosophy* 25, 275–288.

Loening, T. C. 1981. "The Reconciliation Agreement of 403/402 B.C. in Athens: Its Content and Applications." Ph.D. diss., Brown University.

MacDowell, Douglas M. 1978. *The Law in Classical Athens*. Ithaca: Cornell University Press.

Mackenzie, M. M. 1981. *Plato on Punishment*. Berkeley and Los Angeles: University of California Press.

May, Hope. 1997. "Socratic Ignorance and the Therapeutic Aim of the *Elenchos*." In *Wisdom, Ignorance, and Virtue: New Essays in Socratic Studies*, edited by Mark L. McPherran. Edmonton: Academic (Supplement, *Apeiron* 30), 37–50.

McPherran, Mark L. 1996. *The Religion of Socrates*. University Park: Pennsylvania State University Press.

_____, ed. 1997. *Wisdom, Ignorance, and Virtue: New Essays in Socratic Studies*. Edmonton: Academic (Supplement, *Apeiron* 30).

Montuori, Mario. 1981. *Socrates, Physiology of a Myth*. Trans. J.M.P. Langdale and M. Langdale. Amsterdam: J. C. Gieben.

Morrison, Donald. 1988. "On Professor Vlastos' Xenophon," *Ancient Philosophy* 7, 9–22.

Nails, Debra. 1993. "Problems with Vlastos' Platonic Developmentalism," *Ancient Philosophy* 13, 273–292.

Nehamas, Alexander. 1986. "Socratic Intellectualism." In *Proceedings of the Boston Area Colloquium in Ancient Philosophy*, edited by John Cleary, vol. 2, 275–316. Lanham, Md.: University Press of America.

Nussbaum, Martha. 1980. "Aristophanes and Socrates on Learning Practical Wisdom," *Yale Classical Studies* 26, 43–97.

_____. 1985. "Commentary on Edmunds." In *Proceedings of the Boston Area Colloquium in Ancient Philosophy*, edited by John Cleary, vol. 1, 231–240. Lanham, Md.: University Press of America.

O'Brien, M. J. 1967. *The Socratic Paradoxes and the Greek Mind*. Chapel Hill: University of North Carolina Press.

Parker, Robert. 1996. *Athenian Religion: A History.* Oxford: Oxford University Press.

Penner, T. 1973. "The Unity of Virtue," *Philosophical Review* 82, 35–68.

_____. 1992. "What Laches and Socrates Miss—and Whether Socrates Thinks Courage Is Merely a Part of Virtue," *Ancient Philosophy* 12, 1–27.

Polansky, Ronald. 1985. "Professor Vlastos' Analysis of Socratic Elenchus," *Oxford Studies in Ancient Philosophy* 3, 247–260.

Rappe, Sara L. 1995. "Socrates and Self-Knowledge," *Apeiron* 28, 1–24.

Reeve, C.D.C. 1989. *Socrates in the "Apology."* Indianapolis, Ind.: Hackett.

Roberts, J. W. 1984. *City of Sokrates.* London: Routledge.

Robinson, Richard. 1953. *Plato's Earlier Dialectic.* Oxford: Oxford University Press.

Rudebusch, George. 1991. "Death Is One of Two Things," *Ancient Philosophy* 11, 35–45.

_____. Forthcoming. *Socrates, Pleasure, and Value.* Oxford: Oxford University Press..

Santas, Gerasimos X. 1964. "The Socratic Paradox," *Philosophical Review* 73, 147–164.

_____. 1971. "Plato's *Protagoras* and the Explanations of Weakness of Will." In *The Philosophy of Socrates,* edited by Gregory Vlastos. Garden City, N.Y.: Doubleday, 264–298.

_____. 1979. *Socrates: Philosophy in Plato's Early Dialogues.* London: Routledge.

Smith, J., ed. 1995. *The HarperCollins Dictionary of Religion.* San Francisco: Harper-Collins.

Smith, Nicholas D., and Paul Woodruff, eds. Forthcoming. *Reason and Religion in Socratic Philosophy.* New York and Oxford: Oxford University Press.

Steinberger, Peter J. 1997. "Was Socrates Guilty as Charged?" *Ancient Philosophy* 17, 13–29.

Stokes, Michael C. 1992. "Socrates' Mission." In *Socratic Questions,* edited by B. Gower and Michael C. Stokes. London and New York: Routledge, 26–81.

Stone, I. F. 1988. *The Trial of Socrates.* New York: Little, Brown.

Strauss, Barry S. 1987. *Athens After the Peloponnesian War: Class, Faction, and Policy, 403–386 B.C.* Ithaca: Cornell University Press.

Tate, J. 1933. "Socrates and the Myths," *Classical Quarterly* 27, 74–80.

_____. 1936. "Plato, Socrates, and the Myths," *Classical Quarterly* 30, 142–145.

Taylor, A. E. 1953. *Socrates.* Garden City, N.Y.: Doubleday.

Taylor, C.C.W. 1992. *Plato's "Protagoras,"* 2d ed. Oxford: Oxford University Press.

van der Waerdt, Paul. 1994. *The Socratic Movement.* Ithaca and London: Cornell University Press.

Vlastos, Gregory. 1981. *Platonic Studies,* 2d ed. Princeton: Princeton University Press.

_____. 1991. *Socrates: Ironist and Moral Philosopher.* Cambridge and Ithaca: Cambridge and Cornell University Presses.

_____. 1994a. "Socrates on *Akrasia.*" In *Studies in Greek Philosophy,* edited by D. Graham, vol. 2. Princeton: Princeton University Press.

_____. 1994b. *Socratic Studies.* Cambridge: Cambridge University Press.

Vlastos, Gregory, ed. 1971. *The Philosophy of Socrates.* Garden City, N.Y.: Doubleday.

Weiss, Roslyn. 1989. "The Hedonic Calculus in the *Protagoras* and the *Phaedo*," *Journal of the History of Philosophy* 27, 511–529.

Woodruff, Paul. 1976. "Socrates on the Parts of Virtue," *Canadian Journal of Philosophy*, supplement to vol. 2, 101–116.

_____. 1987. "Expert Knowledge in the *Apology* and *Laches:* What a General Should Know." In *Proceedings of the Boston Area Colloquium in Ancient Philosophy*, edited by John Cleary, vol. 3, 79–115. Lanham, Md.: University Press of America.

_____. 1990. "Plato's Early Theory of Knowledge." In *Companions to Ancient Thought I: Epistemology*, edited by Stephen Everson. Cambridge: Cambridge University Press.

Woozley, A. D. 1979. *Law and Obedience: The Arguments of Plato's "Crito."* Chapel Hill: University of North Carolina Press.

Zeller, Eduard. 1885. *Socrates and the Socratic Schools*. Trans. O. J. Reichel. New York: Russell and Russell, 1962.

Zeyl, Donald. 1980. "Socrates and Hedonism: *Protagoras* 351b–358d," *Phronesis* 25, 250–269.

_____. 1982. "Socratic Virtue and Happiness," *Archiv fur Geschichte der Philosophie* 64, 225–238.

Names Index

Subject Index

Index of Greek Terms

Index of Passages

288